DEVELOPMENT OF DOCUMENTATION IN INDIA

CONCEPTS IN COMMUNICATION INFORMATICS & LIBRARIANSHIP (CICIL)

General Editor: S. P. AGRAWAL

CICIL-1	*Development of Library Services in India: Social Science Information* by **S.P. Agrawal**
CICIL-2	*Development of Documentation in India: Social Science Information* by **S.P. Agrawal**
CICIL-3	*Unesco and Social Sciences: Retrospect and Prospect* by **S.P. Agrawal** and **J.C. Aggarwal**
CICIL-4	*INDIANA: A Bibliography of Bibliographical Sources* by **M. K. Jain**
CICIL-5	*Dimensions of Library and Information Science: Papers contributed in honour of the 61st Birthday Celebrations of Prof. P.N. Kaula* Ed. **V. Venkatappaiah**
CICIL-6	*Book Numbers: Indian Methods* by **M. P. Satija** and **S. P. Agrawal**
CICIL-7	*National Policy for University Libraries in India: Problems and Perspectives* by **N.B. Inamdar** and **L. S. Ramaiah**
CICIL-8	*Media Utilisation for the Development of Women and Children* by **B. S. Thakur** and **Binod C. Agrawal**
CICIL-9	*Terrorism: An Annotated Bibliography* by **Susheela Bhan**
CICIL-10	*Transnational Library Relations: The Indo-Americans Experience* by **M.B. Konner**

Concepts in Communication
Informatics & Librarianship - 2

General Editor:
S.P. Agrawal

DEVELOPMENT OF DOCUMENTATION IN INDIA

Social Science Information

S. P. AGRAWAL

CONCEPT PUBLISHING COMPANY, NEW DELHI - 110059

ISBN 81-7022-239-7

First Published 1989

S.P. **Agrawal** (*b.* 1929-)

Published by
Ashok Kumar Mittal
Concept Publishing Company
A/15-16, Commercial Block, Mohan Garden
NEW DELHI - 110059 (India)

Lasertypeset by
Microtech Advance Printing Systems (P) Ltd.
H-13 Bali Nagar, NEW DELHI-110015

Printed in India at
New Gian Offset Printers
495, Shahzada Bagh
DELHI-110035

General Editor's Introduction

CICIL is a new series launched by the publishers covering communication, information technology and librarianship fields which are interrelated and which at the same time, in themselves include in their scope a very wide stretch of topics for investigation, research and study.

Communication is a quality of the sentiment. Homo sapiens high up in the evolutionary order, had fashioned many modes and mediums of expression. Of late, technology has armed man with dynamic and effecting communication. All this necessitates us to reflect on the role of librarian in the emerging scenario. Librarianship, the grand discipline with the art and science of management, in a sense lords over all the subjects. The present series will look at ideas, old and new, in all the allied areas.

The first title to come out in the series relates to Library and Information Services, the second is concerned with Documentation and the third with Unesco and Social Sciences. Also slated for release are special bibliographies.

The numbers in the series will come in handy to libraries, both general and special. They will also appeal to professionals, social scientists, technocrats, indeed to a wide spectrum of qualified populace in India and abroad.

S.P. AGRAWAL

Preface

The book has seven theme sections, encompassing 19 chapters, each touching a specific activity in the field of documentation and information.

Chapter 1 presents a broad view of the state-of-art of documentation and information services in India.

Chapter 2 explains the information needs of the researchers/social scientists so as to design a matching information system.

Chapter 3 stresses the need for a dialogue with the users to facilitate optimum utilization of materials.

Chapters 4-6 deal with primary resources, *i.e.*, the periodicals, dissertations and government documents and the machanism for their bibliographical control, information dissemination and retrieval.

Chapter 7 pleads for an efficient document supply system to serve even those who may be working far away from the documentation/information centres.

Chapters 8-10 take a look at the human resource development in the field of Library and Information Science and the role of distance education in it.

Chapter 11 discusses the status of institutional base much required for overall documentation both for the services and utilization of these services by Social Science community.

Chapters 12-14 touch on the "Resource Sharing" theme, which is a necessity of the day. This involves national information system, a national network of libraries and an inter-library resource centre which are discussed in these chapters.

Chapters 15-16 cover information technology which has transformed the industrial age into an information age.

Chapters 17-20 of the final section "Linkages" dwell on the role of national libraries, documentation centres and data archives as also Children Libraries, which succintly enrich the base of social issues and are thus bricks in foundation of Social Science Information and Documentation.

Chapter 21 enumerates some of the references which formed the bases of this publication.

My thanks are due to Smt. Meene Walia, Kumari Indra Kaul, Kumari Harinder Kaur Manchanda, and Kumari D. Nagjyotsna, who were co-authors for some of the chapters. But for the assistance of Shri Manoharlal, if would not have been possible to bring out this publication. His cooperation is gratefully acknowledged.

S.P. AGRAWAL

Contents

SECTION FIVE : INSTITUTIONAL BASE

SECTION SIX : RESOURCE SHARING

SECTION SEVEN : INFORMATION TECHNOLOGY

SECTION EIGHT : LINKAGES

SECTION ONE
MAPPING

ONE

Social Science Documentation and Information Services in India

Social science research in India got great impetus after independence as a result of the socio-economic development process. Many research institutions were set up; the most important has been the Indian Council of Social Science Research, established in 1969. Over the years, ICSSR in its responsive & promotional role (Appendix-I) has built up a wide-ranging programme based on research enterprises at the individual, institutional, regional and national levels. So far as the research libraries and documentation centres are concerned, their development has also been very significant. In comparison to 1,000 libraries, attached to scientific establishments, there are about 500 social science research libraries attached to universities, government departments, research institutes and commercial organisations. All of these do not undertake documentation activities but most of the specialised ones do.

LIBRARIES

Some of the important libraries with their specialised fields are: Anthropological Survey of India, Calcutta (Anthropology); International Institute for Population Studies, Bombay (Demography); Centre for Development Studies, Trivandrum; Institute of Applied Manpower Research, New Delhi; Institute of Economic Growth, Delhi; Madras Institute of Development Studies, Madras; National Council of Applied Economic Research, New Delhi; Research and Information System for the Non-Aligned and Other Developing Countries, New Delhi (Economic & Developmental Sciences); National Council of Educational Research and Training, New Delhi;

National Institute of Educational Planning and Administration, New Delhi (Education); Gandhian Institute of Studies, Varanasi (Gandhiana); Indian Council of Historical Research, New Delhi; National Archives of India, New Delhi; Nehru Memorial Museum and Library (History); Indian Council of World Affairs, New Delhi (International Relations); Shri Ram Centre for Industrial Relations and Human Resources, New Delhi (Labour); Indian Institutes of Management at Bombay, Ahmedabad, Bangalore and Calcutta; Motilal Nehru Institute of Research and Business Administration, Allahabad (Management); Indian Institute of Mass Communication, New Delhi (Mass Communication); Gokhale Institute of Politics and Economics, Pune; Institute of Defence Studies and Analysis, New Delhi (Political Science); National Institute of Mental Health, Ahmedabad (Psychology); Administrative Staff College of India, Hyderabad; Indian Institute of Public Administration, New Delhi; HCM State Institute of Public Administration, Jaipur (Public Administration); Centre for Studies in Social Sciences, Calcutta; Institute for Social Sciences, Bombay (Social Sciences); Centre for Social Studies, Surat; Centre for Women Development Studies (Sociology); Indian Statistical Institute, Calcutta (Statistics); School of Planning and Architecture, New Delhi (Town and Country Planning). (See also Appendix III of ch. 2).

ICSSR provides financial assistance to many of the above research institutes. Beside these all the university libraries (130); Indian Institutes of Technology Libraries (5); public libraries like Khuda Baksh Oriental Public Library, Patna, National Library, Calcutta, and government departmental libraries including of course Planning Commission Library have a sizable collection of social science research material.

DOCUMENTATION AND INFORMATION CENTRES

The centres primarily engaged in documentation activities are: Centre on Rural Documentation, Hyderabad (1958); National Social Science Documentation Centre (NASSDOC), New Delhi (1970); Small Enterprises National Documentation Centre (SENDOC), Hyderabad (1971); Centre for Development and Instructional Technology, New Delhi (1972); ICSSR Data Archives, New Delhi (1973); National Documentation Centre on Mass Communication, New

Delhi (1976); Research and Information System for Non-Aligned and Other Developing Countries, New Delhi (1984); and Information Centre for Development Policy Modelling, Pune (1984), sponsored by IDRC, Canada.

The University Grants Commission after setting up a Science Information Centre at Bangalore, has also set up Social Science Information Centre at SNDT University, Bombay, and one more is being developed at M.S. University, Baroda. Besides this, six ICSSR Regional Centres at Bombay, Calcutta, Chandigarh, Delhi, Hyderabad, and Shillong have documentation units to provide information services.

Particular mention needs to be made of NASSDOC, which has been most active in developing documentation activities and services at the national level.

NATIONAL SOCIAL SCIENCE DOCUMENTATION CENTRE

Activities

i. Building up a collection of reference materials and works on research methodology; collecting (a) unpublished doctoral theses approved by Indian universities and foreign theses on India, (b) research reports of the projects undertaken by ICSSR and other social science research institutions assisted by ICSSR, (c) working papers presented at ICSSR funded seminars and conferences, and (d) periodicals of research standard in social sciences.
ii. Providing bibliographical information about Indian publications in social science disciplines to international documentation agencies.
iii. Striving for bibliographic control over social science materials by bringing out various documents under Research Information Series. (About one hundred titles have so far been brought out. A list of these is available on request).
iv. Providing select bibliographies on request.
v. Providing duplicating and reprographic services.
vi. Providing document supply services to scholars from outside Delhi.

vii. Awarding study grants to scholars for working at libraries of their interest in India.

viii. Providing consultancy to social science institutions in setting up documentation and information centres.

ix. Providing facilities for staff participation in professional seminars and conferences through contributing papers and taking active part in their deliberations; deputing staff to attend short refresher courses.

x. Conducting professional training courses under Continuing Education Programme.

xi. Processing project proposals involving financial assistance to documentation and bibliographical projects for consideration by ICSSR Committee on Documentation Services and Research Information.

xii. Entering into agreement with national and international organisations for mutual exchange of publications. (At present 2000 institutions are on exchange list).

DOCUMENTATION SERVICES

Indexing Service

Most of the discipline oriented libraries and information centres bring out current awareness/documentation lists to keep their clientele informed about the latest literature.

Besides these, some other important indexing tools covering current and retrospective material are:

Current Indexes

Articles from Telugu Newspapers and Journals (ICSSR Southern Regional Centre, Hyderabad) Bi-Annual.

Documentation in Public Administration (Indian Institute of Public Administration). Quarterly. (Financially assisted by ICSSR).

Documentation in Social Sciences (ICSSR Southern Regional Centre, Hyderabad). Quarterly.

Documentation on Asia (Indian Council of World Affairs Library, New Delhi). Annual. (Financially assisted by ICSSR). (Presently suspended).

Guide to Indian Periodical Literature (Indian Documentation Service, Gurgaon). Quarterly.

Index India (Rajasthan University Library, Jaipur). Quarterly (Financially assisted by ICSSR).

NEHUNERC Documentation Bulletin (N.E. Hill University Library and ICSSR North-Eastern Regional Centre, Shillong). Bi-Monthly.

Samajik Vigyan Samachar (NASSDOC, New Delhi) Monthly.

Select Documentation in Higher Education (University Grants Commission, New Delhi). Quarterly.

Social Science Documentation List (ICSSR Western Regional Centre, Bombay).

Social Science News (NASSDOC, New Delhi). Monthly.

Suchika (ICSSR Northern Regional Centre, New Delhi). Monthly.

ICSSR provides financial assistance to the National Council of Educational Research and Training, New Delhi and the Indian Institute of Management, Ahmedabad, for inclusion of abstracts and reviews in their journals, *Indian Educational Review* and *Vikalpa* in the field of Education and Management respectively.

Retrospective Indexes

NASSDOC has been working on Retrospective Indexing Project covering 240 Indian journals in social sciences. *Indian Education Index* (1947-78) was the first to be printed in the series. Another volume (in the series), covering disciplines of Anthropology, Psychology, Sociology and Social Work entitled Index to Indian Periodicals: Sociology and Psychology (1886-1970) was printed in 1987. The indexing work regarding other disciplines is in progress.

Newspaper Indexes

Newspapers are an important source for social science research. The tools covering this activity are:

Current Indexes (General)

Data India (Press Institute of India, New Delhi). Weekly.
Documentation Indian National Affairs, Chandigarh. Quarterly.
Indian Press Index (Delhi Library Association). (Financially assisted by ICSSR). Monthly.
Samajik Vigyan Samachar (NASSDOC, New Delhi). Monthly
Times of India Index (Times of India Publication, Bombay). Quarterly. (Presently suspended).
Social Science News (NASSDOC, New Delhi). Monthly
Current Indexes (Discipline Oriented)
Bulletin on Film (National Documentation Centre on Mass Communication, New Delhi). Monthly.
Clipping Services Bulletin (Lalbhai Group on Rural Development, Ahmedabad). Bi-Monthly.
Current Press Cutting Titles (Indian Institute of Management, Bangalore). Bi-Monthly.

Retrospective Indexes

Kesari Shatabdi Suchi : It covers Marathi newspaper Kesari from 1881-1980. The first volume covering the period 1881-1920 has been published.

Abstracting service

International abstracting services in all the disciplines of social sciences are available in hard copy and on tapes but their coverage of Indian material is meagre. To overcome this lacuna, a number of abstracting services have been taken up in India. These are:

Doc - Plan (Planning Commission, New Delhi). Quarterly.
Doc - Sat (Central Statistical Organisation, New Delhi). Quarterly.
ICSSR Journals of Abstracts and Reviews (in the disciplines of Economics, Geography, Political Science, Sociology and Social

Anthropology). (Details - Appendix III).

ICSSR Research Abstracts. Quarterly

Indian Dissertation Abstracts (ICSSR, New Delhi). Quarterly.

Indian Psychological Abstracts (ICSSR, New Delhi). Quarterly.

Indian Education Abstracts (Deptt. of Education, New Delhi). Quarterly.

Management Abstracts. (All India Management Association, New Delhi). Quarterly.

NASSDOC proposed to start Central Abstracting service in social science literature.

BIBLIOGRAPHICAL ACTIVITIES

Bibliographical Control of Research (Completed and in progress)

Doctoral Research

Association of Indian Universities (AIU), New Delhi, brings out annually *Bibliography of Doctoral Dissertations : Social Sciences* and *Humanities*, with financial assistance of ICSSR. The bibliography covers doctoral theses approved by Indian Universities. The retrospective coverage is from 1857. The association also reports current theses in its monthly journal *University News*.

ICSSR publishes abstracts of doctoral theses in its journal *Indian Dissertation Abstracts* and lists unpublished dissertations received in NASSDOC and those published with its financial assistance in its Newsletter. NASSDOC regularly brings out updated lists of *Theses in NASSDOC: A Bibliography* under its Research Information Series.

Long back, ICSSR made an effort towards bibliographical control of doctoral research in progress and brought out a volume *Doctoral Students in Social Sciences 1969*, but the publication was discontinued. NASSDOC now aims to map on a regular basis doctoral and post doctoral-research in academic institutions, as well as research projects under-taken by social science organisations dotting the country. One volume entitled *Social Science Research Index* has already been brought out. AIU also lists doctoral research in progress in its *University News*.

Non-doctoral Research

ICSSR, in its *Annual Report* and *Newsletter*, lists research projects, completed/in progress, published/unpublished, assisted directly by it and/or by the ICSSR financed twenty research institutes in India. It also publishes a journal *ICSSR Research Abstracts* (Quarterly) giving abstracts of projects supported by it. The research conducted in government departments, released in the form of reports and surveys, is listed in *Catalogue of Government of India Civil Publications* and kept updated. The Madras Institute of Development Studies compiles annually *Census of Social Science Research in Southern States*, covering States of Andhra Pradesh, Karnataka, Kerala and Tamil Nadu. Various research institutes and university departments provide such information through compiled lists or newsletters and/or annual reports.

NASSDOC periodically brings out lists of research projects held at the Centre. The latest compilation is entitled *Research Project Reports in NASSDOC : An Annotated Bibliography*, covering titles acquired up to 1980. *Social Science Research Index* (also brought out by NASSDOC) covers research projects in progress.

Bibliographical Control of Published Literature

There is satisfactory bibliographical control of published literature. The tools are:

Books

1. *Indian National Bibliography* (Central Reference Library, Calcutta) Monthly. Aims to cover official and non-official documents published in English and regional languages in India.

2. *Accessions List : South Asia* (Library of Congress office, New Delhi). Monthly. Covers serial and non-serial documents published in India and other countries of the region acquired for Library of Congress and other research libraries in the USA, participating in

one or more country programmes.

3. *Catalogue of Government of India Civil Publications* (Office of the Controller of Publications, New Delhi), Bi-Monthly. Covers reports and surveys brought out by Ministries and Departments of Government of India.

4. Other publications of this nature are *Indian Publisher, Indian Books Index, Indian Book Industry, Indian Book Review Index and Indian Book Chronicle.*

5. For retrospective researches, some of the important sources are cummulative volumes of *INB, Indian Books in Print, Reference Catalogue of Indian Books in Print and National Bibliography of Indian Literature.*

Periodicals and Newspapers

Press in India (Office of the Registrar of Newspapers, New Delhi), Annual. Covers periodicals and newspapers published in English and regional languages of India. The publication provides extensive statistics of Indian periodicals which are very helpful to researchers. *Press and Advertisers* Yearbook is another important tool that provides detailed information about Indian newspapers. *Accessions List : South Asia* is also a useful tool for this purpose.

Discipline Oriented Bibliographies

A few selective bibliographies under the above category are :

i. *Annotated and Classified Bibliography of Indian Demography (ICSSR).*

ii. *Annotated Bibliography on the Economic History of India, A.D. 1500-A.D. 1947* (Gokhale Institute of Politics and Economics, Pune). 4 V. (Financially assisted by ICSSR).

iii. *Foreign Researches on Indian Political System and Processes : A Bibliography* by K.G, Tyagi. (Financially assisted by ICSSR).

iv. *Mahatma Gandhi Bibliography.* Bibliographies on Gandhiji in English, Hindi, Sanskrit, Urdu and Bengali have so far been published by ICSSR.

v. *Asian Social Science Bibliography* (Institute of Economic Growth, New Delhi). Annual. (Presently suspended).

vi. *Area Studies Bibliographies* (NASSDOC). Covers literature on Indian States. (In progress).

vii. *Language Bibliographies* (NASSDOC). Covers social science research material in English and regional languages of India. (In progress).

viii. *NASSDOC Research Information series.* NASSDOC has so far brought out nearing 100 bibliographical documents under the series. Some of the current awareness titles are: *Conference Alert; Acquisition Update; Bibliography on Tap; and Paging Periodicals : Preview of Contents.*

BIBLIOGRAPHICAL SERVICES

Many specialised libraries and information centres provide bibliographical services but they are generally restricted to their own institutional members or clientele. But NASSDOC, New Delhi, National Library, Calcutta and IASLIC, Calcutta, provide short bibliographies on the request of research scholars at national level. NASSDOC also brings out a discipline oriented collection of bibliographies, provided earlier to the scholars, in mimeographed form under the title *Bibliographic Reprints.*

STATE OF ART PUBLICATIONS

ICSSR brings out periodically survey reports on various disciplines in social sciences, indicating research completed, gaps identified and areas of further research. These reports are available in published form (Appendix-IV).

INFORMATION REPACKAGING

Most of our documentation centres are providing documentation services of traditional nature which do not serve the information needs of the policy makers in government and in regional and international organisations. They need information which could be readily used. Research Information System for Non-Aligned and other developing countries, recently set up at New Delhi has decided to bring out reviews, summary papers and analytical digests of various topics of current interest supported by data for reference by the policy makers of the developing countries. Due attention will also be paid to dissemination conclusions of and findings arrived at national and international conferences.

The Research and Reference Division of the Parliament Library periodically brings out *Digest of Central Acts and Digest of Legislative and Constitutional Cases* for ready reference.

The Centre for Studies in Decentralised Industries, Bombay, succinctly highlights development issues discussed in the latest publications in its quarterly *Documentation Bulletin*.

ICSSR has also been working in this direction. An analysis of recommendations made in the various research reports of specific disciplines, like education and urban development, is being made and will be presented in a capsule form in order to bring these to the notice of planners, executives and policy makers. ICSSR Newsletter covers policy implications of research studies financed by it. In the days to come, this type of activity will be required more and more.

DATA SERVICES

Complex societal processes in modern times have made policy makers and researchers increasingly dependent on appropriate data. A large volume of data is generated in the country but remains under-utilised due to various reasons.

The sociological Research Unit of the Indian Statistical Institute, Calcutta, with the financial assistance of the International social Science Council, undertook a programme (1968-1970) of surveying ongoing empirical research in India for establishing an inventory of empirical data. Till the setting up of ICSSR Data Archives in 1973, no sustained effort had been made to inventorise quantitative data and process it into organised collection to promote and augment research.

The three main data generating sources identified in the country are:

1. Data generated by the ICSSR funded projects.
2. Data generated at institutions, and university departments without the funds of ICSSR.
3. Data generated by governmental and semi-governmental agencies.

ICSSR Data Archives

The ICSSR Data Archives was set up to undertake the following activities:

1. To acquire, organise and maintain the social science data in machine-readable form and to make them available to interested social scientists for secondary analysis.
2. To support selected research institutions in different parts of the country to develop institution-based data archives.
3. To develop and maintain relevant computer software for social science data processing.
4. To organise training courses in application of computers in social science research.
5. To provide guidance and consultancy services for data processing.
6. To act as liaison between the official data producing agencies and social scientists in order to incorporate the research interests of social scientists in data gathering and tabulation plans of these agencies.
7. To compile and maintain an inventory of data produced by different research institutions and governmental agencies in order to provide referral services on the sources of data.
8. To compile and maintain the *National Register of Social Scientists in India*.

9. To establish collaborative relations with social science archives abroad.

Acquisition of Data

ICSSR is the biggest research funding body in the country, supporting so far about 1,300 research projects. The Data Archives accords first priority to the data generated by these researches. Eighty data sets in machine-readable form out of this category and 12 data sets from other institutions have so far been collected.

Inventory of Data

To provide referral service as to what kind of data is available where and in what form, the Data Archives is currently compiling an inventory of data generated by different research institutions in India since 1951. Relevant information from 26 research institutions on 488 studies about the nature and content of data, universe and geographical coverage, form and mode of storage, conditions and accessibility restrictions on the data, etc., have already been collected. Governmental and semi-governmental agencies are to be subsequently covered.

Guidance and Consultancy Services

The Data Archives provides guidance and consultancy services to social scientists involving their problems of data processing with the help of computer. This service is also provided by some other ICSSR aided research institutes.

Data Archives Network

Over the years some of the research institutions have accumulated a large volume of data and developed appropriate skills to handle the data processing and organisation with the help of computer technology. To involve these into data organisation programme at national level, a network of institution-based data archives in the country is being planned.

International Collaboration

The Data Archives is a member of International Federation of Data Organisations (IFDO) and is the Regional Secretariat of the International Association for Social Science Information Services and Technology (IASSIST). A plan for exchange of data and software with many archives is being worked out. Possibilities are being explored for undertaking joint projects of mutual interest with other IFDO member archives.

Besides ICSSR Data Archives, National Informatics Centre is assisting government departments in computerisation of their data since 1980 and has succeeded in developing 150 data bases. It has a powerful computer system cyber CDC 170/730 and a network of 20 terminals for its activities. A large number of governmental agencies like the National Sample Survey Organisation. Office of the registrar General (Population Census), Reserve Bank of India and other nationalised banks, Planning Commission and State Governments have also started using computer technology in data processing in a big way.

All these developments have put more responsibility on Data Archives as the custodians of national data and to see that its utilisation is optimum.

REPOSITORY SERVICES

As most of the material in social sciences does not become obsolete from the point of view of research, it becomes necessary to have a repository of less used documents. In 1975, ICSSR, in collaboration with Jawaharlal Nehru University, launched a project novel in this part of the world by setting up the Inter-Library Resources Centre (ILRC) at 35 Ferozshah Road, New Delhi. Under the scheme the libraries deposit with ILRC their non-current, infrequently used, but important for research serials (i.e. newspapers, journals, Govt. reports, etc.). This solves the space problem in the libraries and also makes available at one place a large volume of research material for scholars. Thirty libraries in Delhi have so far deposited with ILRC about 1,00,000 volumes of periodicals.

LOCATION SERVICES

This service consists of (i) locating a document, (ii) locating the address of library/research institution/organisation and (iii) locating bio-data of social scientist. The available tools serving the above purpose in India are as under:

i. *Union List of Social Science Periodicals*: NASSDOC brought out union lists covering States of Andhra Pradesh, Bombay, Delhi and Karnataka during 1971-72. The Union List for Delhi has been continuously updated. Lucknow University's Department of Library Science has also compiled a Union List for Lucknow Libraries with financial assistance of ICSSR.

ii. *Union Catalogue of Social Science Serials*: NASSDOC published the *Union Catalogue* in 32 volumes, giving location of 31, 125 serials in 535 libraries in 17 states of India. The project was completed in 1976. The updating of the catalogue has now been taken up. ICSSR North Western regional Centre. *Holding List of social Science Periodicals of Libraries in Chandigarh, 1963-1984.*

iii. *Union Catalogue of Newspapers.*

iv. *Directory of Libraries*: In 1985, Indian Library Association brought out the 4th edition of its *Indian Library Directory* (covering 1,595 libraries) and the Indian Association of Special Libraries and Information Centres compiled and 2nd edition of the *Directory of Special and Research Libraries in India* (covering about 500 libraries). Government of India Libraries association released *Directory of Government of India Libraries and Who's Who in 1983.*

v. *Directory of Social Science Research Institutions* and *Directory of Professional Organisations in India*: NASSDOC updated the two directories originally published in 1971. The information is available on cards for reference. ICSSR, in 1981, brought out a *Directory of Social Science Research Institutions and Organisations in India* in cyclostyled form as a part of its study on the financing of social science research in India. NASSDOC has now compiled an *inventory* of 700 social science institutions and organisations in India. The *inventory* is being kept updated.

vi. *National Register of Social Scientists in India*: ICSSR Data Archives has brought out the National Register which contains basic information on scholars who have contributed through teaching and/or research in social sciences. The Register gives information of about more than seven thousand scholars classified under broad disciplines. The whole-information is being computerised.

TRANSLATION SERVICE

There is not enough demand for translation services by social scientists. However, NASSDOC has the facilities to provide this service on demand.

BIBLIOGRAPHIC RECORDS AND STANDARDISATION

The art of finding facts from various sources - encyclopaedias, research reports, conferences, theses, indexes, etc., is simplified if a proper standardised bibliographic record is available. The important standards compiled by Indian Standards Institution (ISI) on this aspect are :

1. IS: 18-1970
   Guide for abbreviation of words in titles of periodicals using Roman alphabets.
2. GIS: 795-1976
   Guide for preparation of abstracts.
3. IS 2381-1978
   Recommendations for bibliographical references.
4. IS : 9400-1980
   Guide for the preparation of bibliographic description sheet for technical reports.

The Director (NASSDOC) is a member of the Documentation Committee of ISI.

INFORMATION TECHNOLOGY

Computers, particularly micro-computers as service media, have become a common sight in information centres of the advanced countries. These are extensively used for inhouse activities, networking, maintaining information data bases, providing online bibliographic and textual data, and operating document delivery services. But in the developing countries, leaving aside science fields, their use is not much. In India, some centres, namely the Centre for Development of Instructional Technology (CENDIT), Centre for Social Development ICSSR Data Archives, Information Centre for Development of Policy Modelling, National Council of Applied Economic Research, National Informatics Centre, and Research and Information System for Non-Aligned and Developing Countries, etc., have computer facilities for documentation services. With decreasing cost of micro-computers and increasing availability of suitable software this technology will gradually be more used for documentation activities.

NASSDOC has at present, Eagle PC-XT micro-computer with CPU of 256KB and storing capacity of 20 mega bytes, and one UPTRON PC-XT, with 640KB memory, dot matrix and letter quality printers on its premises and has further access to main-frame computer available at the Centre for Social Development, New Delhi. The micro-computer will enable it to exchange bibliographical data with ICSSID in machine-readable form and to have online interaction with its central data base when the whole programme gets into action.

NETWORKS

Networking among libraries is not common. It obtains, to a certain extent, in public libraries set up in various states, among different libraries in a university campus and libraries of commercial undertakings, like those of Bharat Heavy Electricals Ltd. located in various cities. Networking among science libraries has been accomplished under the National Information System in Science and Technology (NISSAT). But no such system exists for social sciences though a proposal for National Information System in Social Sciences (NISSS) has been under consideration. A Working Group of the Planning Commission on Modernisation of Libraries Services and Informatics for the seventh Five Year Plan, 1985-90 has strongly recommended this proposal. Plans are now afoot to set up a network of ICSSR Regional Centres, its financially assisted institutions (20), other institutions like Chambers of Commerce and Industries and national labour organisations including the trade unions under

NISSS.

There are however some organisations which are acting as input centres for Indian literature for international data bases. Some of these are:

NASSDOC provides data to the International Committee for Social Science Information and Documentation (ICSSID), for *International Bibliographies* in the field of Anthropology, Economics, Political science and Sociology. The programme may become more effective now that the Director (NASSDOC) has been elected member of ICSSID. Similarly the data is provided for *International Bulletin for Bibliography of Education* (Madrid) as also for International Geographical Bibliography (Paris) NASSDOC also updated inventory of Indian social science research institutions, periodicals, research projects completed and in progress for Unesco DARE DATA BANK.

The Centre for Development of Instructional Technology, New Delhi (CENDIT) and the Indian Council of Agricultural Research are input centres for DEVSIS and AGRIS Systems respectively. Collaboration with other global information systems may be developed in the near future.

NASSDOC has also taken up various associate programmes to promote networking.

DOCUMENT DELIVERY SERVICES

Some centres in India specialise in a particular form of literature, e.g. NASSDOC has a good collection of unpublished Ph.D. Theses and research reports, Nehru Memorial Museum and Library has back files of newspapers of the pre-independence period, oral records containing interviews with eminent persons and a large number of photographs relating to modern Indian history, SENDOC specialises in reports on small industries, Raza Library, Rampur, in oriental manuscripts and ILRC in back files of periodicals. The resources of these centres can be further strengthened to be developed as national document delivery centres. In the field of social sciences, NASSDOC, National Library, Calcutta and Indian

Agricultural Research Institute, New Delhi, are already providing document delivery services to scholars and institutions in India and abroad.

HUMAN RESOURCES DEVELOPMENT

There are about 50 library schools of the universities which are providing traditional library education. Andhra Pradesh Open University, Hyderabad, has started a course of Bachelor of Library and Information Science using non-traditional methods of teaching. NASSDOC organised classes for the students from the Northern region of India for APOU for 1985-86 Session. (The staff of the documentation Centre participated in the teaching work). Indira Gandhi National Open University has also stepped into the field. Besides these, there are two important centres, namely Documentation research and Training Centre, Bangalore, and Indian National Scientific Documentation Centre, New Delhi, which provide more orientation to documentation services, preferably through modern information techniques. NASSDOC is now preparing to undertake library courses leading to Associateship in Library and Information studies in Social Sciences. The emphasis in the course will be on developing skills for managing and dissemination of Social Science information. Concurrent with this, under Continuing Education programme for library and information science professionals, short-term courses on various topics of current interest have been undertaken.

A course on Management Information System (MIS) in Libraries and Documentation Centres (IL-18 May 1987) was followed by computer application to indexing in Social Sciences in November 1987 and January 1988.

The overview of the library education system shows that training in the use of modern information techniques is greatly lacking. It is still tilted towards rules and procedures rather than towards inculcating capabilities in information handling and management. In order to keep pace with the advanced countries in maintaining excellent standards of information services, this imbalance has to be corrected.

CONCLUSION

It will not be an exaggeration to say that social science research libraries in India have achieved a reasonable standard in information services. There are some gaps too, and the priority areas, although under consideration, requiring immediate attention are:

i. There is still no exhaustive bibliographical control of non-doctoral research, both completed and in progress;
ii. There is no bibliographical control of working papers/reports submitted at the conferences/seminars/workshops;
iii. There is insufficient analytical type of documentation activities;
iv. Social science information system network towards cooperative partaking of information resources at tremendous savings in costs has not been given shape to;
v. Data archival activities are still at the nascent stage;
vi. There appears no visible impact of modern information technology on information services management. Inhibiting factors include lack of suitable software, lack of trained manpower in system management and moreover lack of financial resources.

In spite of all these gaps, infrastructural framework of library and information services in social sciences exists in India and it only requires to be strengthened and coordinated. This would be possible only when the role of social science information as an important input resource for the socio-economic development is recognised and adequate financial resources are provided.

APPENDIX - I

Indian Council of Social Science Research

The development of social sciences is an important dimension of the contemporary intellectual movement seeking a better social order. The gap in this direction in India was keenly felt in the post independence period because of the demands of the developmental process which necessitated the setting up of the Indian Council of Social Science Research (ICSSR) as an autonomous organisation under the Government of India in April 1969.

ORGANISATION

The Council is composed of a Chairman, 18 social scientists, six representatives of the Government (all nominated by the Government of India) and a Member Secretary (appointed by the ICSSR with the prior approval of the Government of India).

Policy matters are decided by the following functional Committees of the Council :

1. Policy and Administration Committee.
2. Research Committee.
3. Research Institute Committee.
4. Committee on International Collaboration.
5. Committee on Documentation Services and Research Information.
6. Committee on Data Archives.
7. Committee on Training.

The Council Secretariat is organised broadly on the basis of the above mentioned functional Committees.

The Council has set up in collaboration with respective State Governments six regional centres as part of its programme of decentralising administration and broad basing social science research at Bombay, Calcutta, Chandigarh, Delhi, Hyderabad and Shillong.

PROGRAMMES AND ACTIVITIES

Fortunately from the very beginning because of efficient leadership, ICSSR was able to bring about a great deal of dynamism in the development of social sciences in India, especially in terms of motivating scholars to adopt innovative approaches to research into the areas of national relevance. Over the years ICSSR, in its responsive and promotional roles, has built up a wide-ranging programme-based research enterprises at the individual, institutional, regional and national levels. The sponsored research grew out of ICSSR's concern with the need for defining priorities in research on the basis of the following criteria : (a) adding significantly to existing knowledge or making major contributions to methodology; (b) understanding of social reality and improvement of quality of life; (c) solving the basic problems the nation is facing; (d) contributing to the study of issues leading to policy formulation; and (e) highlighting comparatively less researched areas. In its promotional role, it provided opportunities for individual scholars and teams to find maximum creative expression. In response to the developmental needs of the country, the Council initiated a variety of research programmes such as Alternatives in Development, Women Studies, Population Studies, Analysis of Census Data, etc.

In this endeavour, importance was given to developing methodologies of inter-disciplinary nature towards a new policy and perspective on social sciences. The linkages with medical and agricultural sciences are noteworthy in this regard. The supportive programme of assisting and bringing out publications of various kinds has helped to disseminate research results widely.

An important subject being constantly debated within the ICSSR system is the issue of utilisation of research. The relevant inputs towards a national debate on this issue are being documented in a series of publications planned by the Council.

Additionally, the Council is collaborating with many countries in undertaking joint research programmes which are mutually instructive. Its initiative in setting up an Association of Asian Social Science Research Councils (AASSREC) following a Unesco Conference on Teaching and Research in Social Sciences in Asia, 1973 at Simla has been a landmark.

ICSSR has thus already flourished into a full fledged organisation at the national horizon to sustain and promote social science research and provide an institutional base for social scientists to interact mutually, as well as to convey their views on topics of national importance to policy makers in the government through it. It has thus played a significant role in regard to policy formulation and implementation, educating public opinion and changing social and individual behaviour.

APPENDIX-II

Documentation Resources

Abstracts of Books, Reports and Articles. Parliament Library, New Delhi. Quarterly.

Acquisition update. NASSDOC, New Delhi. Monthly.

Agricultural Land Rural Development Abstracts. Institute for Social and Economic Change, Bangalore.

Annual Bibliography of Banking Literature. National Institute of Bank Management Library, Bombay.

Area Guides on China and Pakistan. Institute for Defence Studies and Analysis, New Delhi.

Artha Suchi. National Council of Applied Economic Research. New Delhi. Quarterly. (Computerised; covers developmental literature on India).

Bibliographic Reprints. NASSDOC, New Delhi. Quarterly .

Bibliographics on Tap NASSDOC, New Delhi. Irregular

Bulletin of Documentation in Urban and Regional Planning. Town and Country Planning Organisation, New Delhi. Quarterly.

Bulletin on Film. National Documentation Centre on Mass Communication, New Delhi. Monthly.

Conference Alert. NASSDOC, New Delhi. Quarterly.

CORD Abstracts. Centre on Rural Documentation, Hyderabad. Bi-Monthly.

CORD Index. Centre on Rural Documentation, Hyderabad. Monthly.

Chetna. National Medical Library, New Delhi. Quarterly. (Covers health literature; also includes information about health-science meetings, training-courses, new Indian journals, MEDLARS searches printouts, etc.).

Current Articles of Interest. Institute for Defence Studies and Analysis, New Delhi. Monthly.

Current Awareness Service. Indian Institute of Mass Communication, New Delhi. Monthly.

Current Awareness Service. National Documentation Centre on Mass Communication, New Delhi. Monthly.

Current Contents. Ministry of Labour, New Delhi. Bi-Monthly.

Current Literature on Science of Science. National Institute of Science Technology and Development Studies, New Delhi. Monthly.

Current Management Literature. Administrative Staff College of India, Hyderabad. Monthly.

Current Management Literature. Indian Institute of Management, Ahmedabad. Quarterly.

Current News Weekly. National Institute of Bank Management, Bombay.

Current Press Cuttings Titles. Indian Institute of Management Bangalore. Bi-Monthly.

Development and Welfare. Delhi School of Social Work, Delhi. Quarterly.
(Index of material from journals and books with emphasis on developed and developing countries).
(Financially assisted by ICSSR).

DOC - NIPCCD. National Institute of Public Cooperation and Child Development, New Delhi. Monthly.

DOCSTAT. Central Statistical Organisation, New Delhi. Quarterly.

Documentation Bulletin. Centre for Studies in Decentralised Industries, Bombay. Quarterly.

Documentation Bulletin. Vaikunthabhai Mehta Samarak Trust. Bombay. Quarterly.

Documentation on Foreign Trade. Indian Institute of Foreign Trade, New Delhi.

Documentation List. National Cooperative Development Corporation, New Delhi. Monthly. (Index to articles in the field of cooperation and related subjects).

Documentation List. Centre for Studies in Social Science, Calcutta.

Documentation List, Society, Education and Islam. Jamia Milia Islamia, Dr. Zakir Hussain Library, New Delhi. Annual.

Documentation in Public Administration. Indian Institute of Public Administration, New Delhi. Quarterly. (Financially assisted by ICSSR).

Documentation in Social Sciences. ICSSR, Southern Regional Centre, Hyderabad. Bi-Monthly.

Documentation in Urban and Regional Planning Bulletin. Town and Country Planning Organisation, New Delhi. Quarterly.

Forthcoming Training Programmes/Seminars/Workshops. Management Development Institute, Gurgaon. Occasional.

Fortnightly List of Articles on India. Servants of India Society and Gokhale Institute of Politics and Economics, Pune.

ICSSR Journal of Abstracts and Reviews : Economics. Indian Council of Social Science Research, New Delhi. Quarterly. (Covers abstracts of selected articles in Indian economics periodicals and reviews on selected books including government reports published in English in India).

ICSSR Journal of Abstracts and Reviews : Geography. Indian Council of Social Science Research, New Delhi. Half-yearly. (Publishes abstracts of research works as well as book reviews).

ICSSR Journal of Abstracts and Reviews : Political Science. Indian Council of Social Science Research, New Delhi. Half-yearly. (Covers abstracts of articles on political science published in Indian journals, book reviews and list in of reviews published political science journals).

ICSSR Journal of Abstracts and Reviews : Sociology and Social Anthropology. Indian Council of Social Science Research, New Delhi. Half-yearly. (Publishes selected reviews of publications in the broad fields indicated in the title of the journal as well as abstracts of research works).

ICSSR Research Abstracts Quarterly. Indian Council of Social Science Research, New Delhi. (Covers abstracts of research reports in social sciences).

Index of Periodicals Articles on Industrial Relations in India. Sri Ram Centre for Industrial Relations and Human Resources, New Delhi. Monthly. (Included in Indian Journal of Industrial Relations.

Index of Articles Relating to Agricultural Economics. Indian Society of Agricultural Economics, Bombay.

Index to Indian Legal Periodicals. Indian Law Institute, New Delhi. Half-yearly.

Index of Literature on Productivity and Management. National Productivity Council, New Delhi. Bi-Monthly.

Indian Books : Annotated. Indian Council of World Affairs, New Delhi. Quarterly.

Indian Diary of Events. NASSDOC, New Delhi. Quarterly.

Indian Dissertation Abstracts. Indian Council of Social Science Research, New Delhi. Quarterly. (Covers synopsis of doctoral theses in social sciences submitted to Indian universities).

Indian Psychological Abstracts. Indian Council of Social Science Research, New Delhi. Quarterly. (Covers abstracts of research works done in the discipline on Indian themes).

Library Bulletin. Centre for Studies in Social Sciences, Calcutta. Monthly.

Library Bulletin. International Institute for Population Studies, Bombay. Quarterly.

List of Additions. Indian Statistical Institute, New Delhi. Bi-Monthly.

List of Parliamentary Reports. Institute of Public Enterprises Library, Hyderabad.

List of Selected Articles from Telugu Newspapers and Journals. ICSSR Southern Regional Centre, Hyderabad. Half-yearly.

Management Abstracts. All-India Management Association, New Delhi. Quarterly.

Manpower Documentation. Institute of Applied Manpower Research, New Delhi. Quarterly.

Mandev Documentation. Management Development Institute, New Delhi. Fortnightly.

NASSDOC Dockets. NASSDOC, New Delhi. Monthly.

National Catalogue of University Level Text-Books. Raja Ram Mohan Roy National Educational Resource Centre, New Delhi. Quarterly.

NEHUNERC Documentation Bulletin. North-Eastern Hill University Library and ICSSR North-Eastern Regional Centre. Bi-Monthly.

NIHFW Accession List. National Institute of Health and Family Welfare, New Delhi. Quarterly.

New Additions in NRLC Library. National Research Laboratory and Conservation of Cultural Property, Lucknow. Half-yearly.

Paging Periodicals. NASSDOC, New Delhi. Bi-Monthly.

Quarterly Documentation List. Indian Council for Child Welfare, New Delhi.

Recent Additions. Indian Institute of Management Library, Bangalore. Monthly.

SPA Abstracts. School of Planning and Architecture, New Delhi. Monthly.

Samajik Vigyan Samachar. NASSDOC, New Delhi. Monthly. Hindi.

Selected Articles on Modern Indian History. Nehru Memorial

Museum and Library, New Delhi. Monthly.

Selected Documentation in Higher Education. University Grants Commission, New Delhi. Monthly.

Social Science Documentation List. ICSSR North-Western Regional Centre, Chandigarh. Half-yearly.

Social Science News. NASSDOC, New Delhi. Monthly.

Suchika. ICSSR Northern Regional Centre, New Delhi. Monthly.

Social Science Research India. NASSDOC, New Delhi. Irregular

Urban Documentation. National Institute of Urban Affairs, New Delhi. Quarterly.

APPENDIX-III

ICSSR Journals of Abstracts and Reviews

ICSSR Research Abstracts Quarterly

Abstracts of research reports in the social sciences setting out the objectives, methodology and major findings of the research are published in this journal. It was started in October 1971.

Subscription: Inland: Single Copy: Rs. 10, Annual: Rs. 50.

Indian Dissertation Abstracts

This journal publishes synopses of Ph.D. theses in the social sciences submitted to Indian universities. Each synopsis gives the name of the university awarding the degree, the year, and the name of the supervisor. It is a quarterly published under the joint auspices of ICSSR and the Association of Indian Universities. It was started in March 1973.

Subscription: Inland: Single copy: Rs. 10, Annual: Rs. 50.

Indian Psychological Abstracts

This journal publishes short abstracts of research works done in the discipline on Indian themes. It commenced publication as a bi-monthly in January 1972. It is now a quarterly.

Subscription: Inland: Rs. 20 per volume (for individuals), Rs. 30 per volume (for institutions); Foreign: $ 6 per volume (for individuals) and $ 8 per volume (for institutions).

ICSSR Journal of Abstracts and Reviews: Sociology and Social Anthropology

This journal publishes selected reviews of publications in the broad fields indicated in the title of the journal as well as abstracts of research works. It is a half-yearly journal which commenced publication from January-December 1972.

Subscription: Inland: Single copy: Rs. 20, Annual: Individuals: Rs. 30, Institutions: Rs. 50.

ICSSR Journal of Abstracts and Reviews : Economics

Abstracts of selected articles from Indian economic periodicals and reviews of selected books published in English in India are published in this journal, four times a year.

Subscription: Inland: Single copy: Rs. 8, Annual: Individuals: Rs. 25, Institutions: Rs. 30.

ICSSR Journal of Abstracts and Reviews : Geography

This journal publishes abstracts of research works as well as book reviews. It is a half-yearly publication.

Subscription: Inland: Single copy: Rs. 10, Annual: Individuals: Rs. 30, Institutions: Rs. 50.

ICSSR Journal of Abstracts and Reviews : Political Science

This journal publishes abstracts of articles on Political Science published in Indian journals, book reviews and a list of reviews published in Political Science journals. It is published Half-yearly.

Subscription: Inland: Single copy: Rs. 20, Annual: Individuals Rs. 30, Institutions: Rs. 50.

APPENDIX-IV

ICSSR Surveys of Research in Social Sciences

ECONOMIC AND SOCIAL HISTORY OF INDIA
(New Delhi : Ajanta, 1986)
283 + xviii pp.,

ACCOUNTING THEORY
(Bombay : Popular, 1976)
94 + viii pp.,

DEMOGRAPHY
(Bombay : Popular, 1975)
440 + x pp.,

ECONOMICS - VOL. 1 : METHODS AND TECHNIQUES
(New Delhi: Allied, 1977)
136 + xxxvi pp.,

ECONOMICS - VOL. II : MACRO ECONOMICS
(New Delhi : Allied, 1976)
424 + xiv pp.,

ECONOMICS - VOL. III ; AGRICULTURE I
(New Delhi : Allied, 1975)
264 + xii pp.,

ECONOMICS - VOL. IV ; AGRICULTURE II
(New Delhi : Allied, 1975)
345 + xii pp.,

ECONOMICS- VOL. V ; INDUSTRY
(New Delhi : Allied, 1 75)
362 + xiii pp.,

ECONOMICS - VOL. VI : INFRASTRUCTURE
(New Delhi : Allied, 1980)
292 + xii pp.,

ECONOMICS - Vol. VII : ECONOMETRICS
(New Delhi : Allied, 1978)
395 + iv pp.,

GEOGRAPHY
(Bombay : Popular, 1972)
398 + xxiv pp.,

GEOGRAPHY, 1969-72 (SECOND SERIES)
(New Delhi : Allied, 1979)
234 + xii pp.,

PHYSICAL GEOGRAPHY
(New Delhi : Concept, 1983)
332 + xvi pp.,

GEOGRAPHY 1972-75 (THIRD SERIES)
(New Delhi : Concept, 1984)
194 + x pp.,

MANAGEMENT - VOL. I
(New Delhi : Vikas, 1973)
502 + xii pp.,

MANAGEMENT - VOL. II
(New Delhi : Vikas, 1977)
684 + xii pp.,

POLITICAL SCIENCE - VOL. I: POLITICAL SYSTEM
(New Delhi : Allied, 1979)
278 + xvi pp.,

POLITICAL SCIENCE - VOL. II: POLITICAL PROCESS
(New Delhi : Allied, 1981)
232 + xvi pp.,

POLITICAL SCIENCE - VOL. III ; POLITICAL DYNAMICS
(New Delhi : Allied, 1981)
170 + xvi pp.,

POLITICAL SCIENCE
(New Delhi : Allied, 1986)
288 + xvi pp.,

PSYCHOLOGY
(Bombay : Popular, 1972)
454 + xxxiii pp.,

PSYCHOLOGY, 1971-76 - PART I
(Bombay : Popular, 1980)
371 + xxiv pp.,

PSYCHOLOGY, 1971-76 - PART II
(Bombay : Popular, 1981)
507 + xxiv pp.,

PUBLIC ADMINISTRATION - VOL. I
(New Delhi : Allied, 1973)
352 + xvi pp.,

PUBLIC ADMINISTRATION - VOL. II
(New Delhi : Allied, 1975)
556 + xix pp.,

PUBLIC ADMINISTRATION (2ND SERIES) 1970-1979
(New Delhi : Concept, 1986)
267 + x pp.,

SOCIOLOGY AND SOCIAL ANTHROPOLOGY - VOL. I
(Bombay : Popular, 1974)
479 + xxvii pp.,

SOCIOLOGY AND SOCIAL ANTHROPOLOGY - VOL. II
(Bombay : Popular, 1974)
599 + xxi pp.,

SOCIOLOGY AND SOCIAL ANTHROPOLOGY - VOL. III
(Bombay : Popular, 1976)
336+xvi pp.,

SOCIOLOGY AND SOCIAL ANTHROPOLOGY 1969-79 - VOL. I
(New Delhi : Satvahan, 1985)
264+xi pp.,

SOCIOLOGY AND SOCIAL ANTHROPOLOGY 1969-79 - VOL.II
(New Delhi : Satvahan, 1985)
343+xvi pp.,

SOCIOLOGY AND SOCIAL ANTHROPOLOGY, (1969-1979) - VOL. III
(New Delhi : Satvahan, 1986)
265+xv pp.

SECTION TWO

REQUIREMENTS

TWO

Information Needs of the Social Scientists in Indian Context

INTRODUCTION

James (1842-1910) in *Prefaces : The Aspern Papers*, says, "The historian, essentially wants more documents than he can really use; the dramatist only wants more liberties than he can really take." And this, by and large, may be taken to reflect the attitude of whole academic community. While building up resources will largely depend on requirement and its meaningful projection, the requirement itself may be bogged down by unhelpful resources, thus making it absolutely necessary to have an investigation in depth and about the real needs of the users.

We have been witnessing tremendous changes in the field of information services particularly during the past one decade. On the one hand, new bibliographical tools compiled in the traditional as well as non-traditional format like Universal Reference System, Political Science, Government and Public Policy Series, Social Science Citation Index, and Environment Abstracts have appeared, on the other, information services techniques supported by fast-changing technology have brought to the forefront Information Networks, Resource Sharing Centres, Bibliographic Cooperatives, Data Centres and Data Banks. The satellite media has offered access to data centres set up in any corner of the world. Computer supported data bases are gradually replacing print media data bases. According to *Annual Review of Information Science and Technology* (Vol. 18), about 1,350 data bases covering all disciplines are functioning on line. These include bibliographic, textual and numeric data bases. All these products and services have been designed and set up with the sole objective of providing efficient information services to the users in the context of their information needs.

SCOPE

The paper endeavours to discuss the information needs of the social scientists engaged in research in India in the context of the availability of the resources required by them. By resources, we here mean the information tools (primary and secondary) and information services required by the researchers during the course of their work.

NEED FOR INVESTIGATION

Any system designer before he initiates designing a new system works towards improving the existing one, studies the needs of his clients, work flow in operation, and resources available so that the system which is created works efficiently towards improving productivity and/or services. Information system is no exception to the above general principle. Such studies are helpful in understanding information collecting habits of the scholars providing guidance for literature collection, for compilation of secondary information tolls and introducing innovations in the information services. We in the developing countries need more of such studies in order to have optimum utilisation of minimum available resources.

STUDIES IN THE WEST

A large number of studies to assess the information needs of the scientists have been made in the West. Their number, according to Line's observation, ranges from 400 to 800 depending on how you reckon them. The number in social sciences, however, is rather small. Britain could review only 18 user studies in social sciences that were available in the late sixties. Most of these had been patterned on science user studies. The only comprehensive study so far undertaken in social sciences is "Investigation into Information Requirements of the Social Sciences" (INFROSS) at Bath University, during 1968-1970. The methodology used was the combination of circulation of questionnaire, interviews with researchers and practitioners and day-to-day observation of a small number of social scientists. A list of reports issued as a result of this study, and a few other studies, have been given in Appendix-I for reference.

STUDIES IN INDIA

In India no study at the comparable level of INFROSS has been made so far. Whatever little, and that also with limited scope, has been attempted is due to the result of personal initiatives of a few professionals. Mention could be made of a few such studies.

Girja Kumar and Jayaswal undertook a study entitled "Information needs of economists : A study of availability of cost escalation and utilisation of foreign journals in India." A similar study in the field of sociology had been earlier completed by them. Kaula and Singh had attempted to ascertain the characteristics of information material used by social scientists through analysing citations given in the five leading Indian journals in the social sciences. A study of information-seeking behaviour of doctoral candidates was made at Sri Venkateswara University Library, Venkataramaniah made a study of the information-seeking behaviour of Bangalore University teachers and researchers in humanities. More recently A.R. Sethi has completed a study and his finding will soon be available in print form. Some other studies, but more in the nature of "use studies" in the context of resources and services, attempted in the university departments, have been listed in Appendix-II.

The Indian Council of Social Science Research (ICSSR), an autonomous organisation under the Government of India, among its other research oriented objectives, has one of developing a research information infrastructure to support the research activities of the social science community. In this context, it has agreed to provide finances to Delhi University for a project "Social Scientists in India : Their information requirements and suggestions for developing relevant library and information services".

The Objectives of this study are:

1. To ascertain the information requirements of the different

categories of social scientists such as policy makers, planners, researchers, decision makers, etc.

2. To specify the library and information services essential to meet these requirements.
3. To make a sample survey of the existing library and information services for social scientists in the country, and
4. To give suggestions for developing an overall library and information infrastructure based on 1-3 above.

USE OF INFORMATION RESOURCES

Information resources required by the social scientists can be broadly categorised into primary and secondary, the later also including tertiary documents. The comparative utilisation of these resources in each of the category is discussed below.

Primary Resources

On the basis of an INFROSS Study, Line has identified many primary information channels used by the social scientists (Table 2.1).

TABLE 2.1: Use of different information channels

CHANNEL	Using often (%)
Physical Forms	
Periodicals	57
Book (monographs)	57
Books (conference procs.)	32
Research reports	28
Theses	11
Newspapers	16
Government publications	34
Microforms	3
Maps	10
Films (pictorial)	1
Other (pictorial)	2
Sound Recordings	4
Video-tape	1
Computer Printouts	21
Informal Channels	
Radio or TV	1
Conferences	8
Colleagues in own institution	26
Colleagues or experts elsewhere	26

Further the quantitative use of these channels varies from discipline to discipline. Periodicals have been found to be more used in psychology than in other disciplines. According to Kaula and Singh, the ratio of use between periodicals and books in psychology is 63.3 : 36.7. Economists make more use of monographs and statistical data brought out by government and international organisations. Political scientists prefer newspapers and political parties documents. According to INFROSS Study, theses and project reports are not a favourite research source for the social scientists. The utilisation percentage is 11 per cent and 28 per cent respectively. The analysis may be correct in the case of senior academicians but not so in the case of young social scientists. Personal experience shows that these are profusely used at the National Social Science Documentation Centre (NASSDOC), New Delhi, broadly for research methodology used in the parallel projects and for selecting relevant data. According to a study made at Venkateswara University, these are considered most useful for planning design of research and review of literature.

Secondary Resources

As in the case of use of primary resources, INFROSS Study collected data regarding utilisation of secondary resources as a tool for locating references for primary research material. Line has also analysed this data (see Table 2.2)

TABLE 2.2:Usefulness of methods of locating references for primary research interest

Method	Usefulness % of respondents/ very useful
Abstracts of indexes	32
Consulting expert	34
Discussion with colleagues internally	27
Discussion with persons elsewhere	23
Library catalogues	22
Searching own library shelves	18
Searching other library shelves	16
Consulting librarian	8
Specialist bibliographies	23
Bibliographies or references in books or journals	59
Book reviews	17

The data regarding utilisation of the secondary services is astounding. Only 32 per cent of the respondents used abstracts or indexes. Fiftynine per cent located references for further research in the primary material itself, i.e., books and journals. The most useful source, according to the researchers, had been personal consultation with fellow colleagues and experts. Conferences have also been found useful, not so much for the papers submitted as for facilitating exchange of ideas. The differences in the use of secondary tools, from discipline to discipline, have been identified as follows: Sociological Abstracts were used by only 16 per cent of the sociologists, Psychological Abstracts by 43 per cent of the psychologists, and Geographical Abstracts by 45 per cent of the geographers. Much less than full use of the secondary sources, however, should not discourage or depress the professionals. There can be different reasons for this.

The Unesco Ad-hoc Committee on Social Science Information (1977) felt that "insufficient awareness of available data and sources are often the major problems". With the advent of computer technology, more efficient on-line indexing and abstracting services are now being provided. According to Williams, on-line searches have increased from one million in 1975 to eight million in 1983. This figure covers searches for all disciplines. The observation made by Neufeld and Cornog shows that there is greatest increase in abstracting and indexing products in Social Sciences and Arts.

RESOURCES AVAILABLE IN INDIA

Primary Sources

Books : Books are the main source of primary information for the social scientists. According to a rough estimate, libraries of about 400 research institutes, besides university and government libraries, specialising in specific disciplines have been functioning in the country. Most of these have specialised collections of books which can be fruitfully exploited by the researchers. A disciplinewise selective list of research institutes/libraries is given in Appendix-III, for reference.

Periodicals

Periodical literature is the most sought for material after books. The specialised libraries mentioned in Appendix-III also maintain a good collection of current periodical literature for the users. Most of these subscribe to about 200 current periodical titles. In the retrieval of old material, Inter-Library Resource Centre (ILRC) set up in 1976 by ICSSR in collaboration with Jawaharlal Nehru University has been playing an important role. About 58 libraries at Delhi have provided, as deposit and/or gift, the back files of their periodicals to this Centre. In this way, it has collected about 100,000 serial volumes. Besides this, NASSDOC, as a policy, subscribes to all the social science periodicals of research value published in India.

Research Reports

These form an important segment of monographs consulted by the researchers. NASSDOC is the biggest collection centre for reports in the country. It receives copies of reports from the institutions and individual scholars in lieu of financial assistance provided by ICSSR, and also as a result of its extensive exchange of publications programme operative not only in the country but also abroad. It has at present a collection of 1,500 research reports. NASSDOC has brought out an annotated list of such reports received up to 1980, followed by a supplement, covering titles but unannotated received up to 1984. The information regarding ICSSR research supported programmes is regularly reported in the half-yearly ICSSR Newsletter and ICSSR Annual Report.

Theses

Each university library maintains a record of the theses approved by its university, but NASSDOC at present is the biggest theses collecting centre in the country. It receives copies of theses from scholars on a token payment of Rs. 400. The total collection at present is about 2,000. The classified acquisition list is regularly included in the ICSSR Newsletter. Besides this, it brought out a monograph. Theses in SSDC : A bibliography, in 1983.

Newspapers

Newspapers are an important source of research material for political scientists and economists, they being the primary source for official notifications or orders, policy matters, market information, import/export data, etc. Sometimes the most important research findings are first reported in newspapers. Some newspaper offices maintain back files of their papers and provide the old issues on payment. On account of their large size, few research libraries maintain complete back files of the papers. Microforms have now, however, made it possible to keep record of this rich resource within minimum available space. On a survey of holdings of newspapers in Delhi libraries, it has been observed that Jawaharlal Nehru University Library including its Centre for Russian Studies Library has a good collection of newspapers published in asian countries and Soviet Russia. Delhi University library and Nehru Memorial Museum and Library have collections of African and Indian newspapers respectively. Other notable libraries having useful collections are Central Secretariat Library, Institute for Defence Studies and Analysis Library (Press clippings), and Ministry of External Affairs Library, Parliament Library, etc. The general trend is towards discarding hard copy files in favour of microcopies. NASSDOC has an approved programme of getting microcopies of the back files of such newspapers, as are not available in libraries in Delhi.

Government Publications

Socio-economic surveys, national development programme/plans, progress reports of the ministries/departments, and statistical data documents form an important part of the Government publications. In Delhi, Central Secretariat Library, Parliament Library, Ministry of external Affairs Library, Ministry of Home Affairs Library, Planning Commission Library, etc., not only maintain good collection of Central and State Government publications but also of the publications of the foreign governments. Secretariat and departmental libraries in the States maintain publications released by their respective governments.

Manuscripts

Manuscripts are mostly consulted by the historians. India's cultural tradition goes back to the hoary past. The glimpses of our glorious heritage can still be had from the old manuscripts available in the country's archives. Some of the notable resource centres keeping record of such material are: National Library, Calcutta; National Archives Library, Delhi; Bhandarkar Oriental Research Institute Library, Pune; Khuda Bakhsh Oriental Public Library, Patna; Raza Library, Rampur; and Government Oriental Manuscript Library, Madras.

The Ministry of Human Resource Development, Government of India, is considering the setting up of a Central Microfilm Library and Documentation Centre to locate and preserve rare manuscripts in the country. It has also a programme of providing financial assistance to the institutions for converting old documents into microform.

Secondary Sources

The role of the secondary sources is to help introduce the right source of information to the user. There are different forms of it compiled at national and international levels. The emphasis in this paper is on Indian compilations because these cover the maximum volume of national material needed most by the researchers. (For a selected list of these, see Appendix-III to "Social Science Documentation and Information Services in India", Ch.1 : an overview.) This provides an idea of the different forms of resources available.

INFORMATION SERVICES

On the basis of different surveys, the following information services have been identified to be mostly in demand by the researchers:

i. Bibliographical Services
ii. Document Location Services
iii. Document Supply Services
iv. Statistical Data Services
v. Guidance Services in Research Methodology/Techniques
vi. Translation Services

Bibliographical Services

The researchers generally want short bibliographies on the topic of their interest. More often this demand is met by the institutions where they work. But many do not have the facility to provide this service. NASSDOC undertakes this service and receives on an average 600 requests annually from scholars and institutions all over India. The bibliographies compiled are listed in ICSSR *Newsletter* and cumulative listing is made in the document "Bibliography of Bibliographies Compiled in SSDC". The photocopies of these bibliographies are supplied on demand. Besides this, National Library, Calcutta, and Indian Association of Special Libraries and Information Centres, calcutta, provide this service on national level. The important bibliographies compiled by these institutions are reported in IASLIC *Newsletter*.

Document Location Services

It is a common experience of the researchers that great difficulty is faced in locating documents listed in the bibliographies. Union lists/catalogues lessen the ordeal to some extent. But no national union catalogue of books like the National Union Catalogue of the USA exists in India. NASSDOC took initiative, and has compiled the following Union Lists/Catalogues.

i. Union Catalogue of Social Science Serials/Periodicals available in India 32 Vols, 1970-1975.
ii. Union Catalogue of Newspapers available in Delhi Libraries, 1984.
iii. Union List of Social Science Periodicals Currently Received in Delhi Libraries, 1985.
iv. Union Catalogue of Books on Library and Informatics Publication in Delhi Libraries, 1986.

Some of the Other Catalogues of this Nature are

Union Catalogue of serials in Fifty Five Academic Libraries in the State of Rajasthan.

Union List of Serials in Humanities and Social Sciences in the Libraries in Mysore City.

NASSDOC has plans to bring out, in separate volumes, union catalogues of documents in libraries in Delhi, covering various social science disciplines.

Document Supply Services

Many of the scholars live in far off places where they do not have good library facilities. Such scholars would like to have the copies of the documents at the place of their work or residence. NASSDOC, depending upon its rich resource material available in the form of periodicals, research reports and theses, satisfies this demand up to 60 per cent. For the rest it has to depend upon other libraries in Delhi.

During 1986-87, about 8,53,452 and exposures from different documents were provided to the scholars and officers of the council. Similarly National Library, calcutta, not only provides documents or photocopies of the documents from its own resources but also arranges documents from foreign libraries.

Statistical Data Services

It has been observed that statistical data is used more by social scientists than by others. A large volume of data is being collected by the government departments, research institutions, university departments and individual scholars. But there are no centralised statistical data centres to store data generated at different places and make it available to other researchers. Partial attempts are being made in this direction by some organisations. ICSSR Data Archives unit maintains in machine-readable form the data generated during research programmes financed by ICSSR. It also invites other individuals and institutions to deposit data sets with it. It maintains inventory of data sets available at various research centres, and lists them regularly in the ICSSR Newsletter. The Small Industries Extension Training Institute, Hyderabad, holds large data in the field of small industries and provides it to entrepreneurs and researchers. The Small Industries Development Organisation, Delhi, also provides data service in the same field. According to the status report (1983) of the National Informatics Centre, Delhi, it has set up 150 statistical data bases for Central and State Government Departments. The Sixth Five Year Plan envisaged the setting up of a Central Statistical Data Centre to store data generated at departmental levels, it has yet to come to take off stage however.

Guidance Services in Research Methodology/Techniques

Most of the young researchers are not fully acquainted with the research techniques. They appreciate training in research methodology. ICSSR conducts training programmes in this field at the various institutions. A survey of such programmes undertaken at the Sri Venkateswara showed that researchers gained much from the programmes, through discussions with the experts and further had the opportunity to use institution libraries where the course was organised. The ICSSR Data Archives Unit provides assistance to researchers in handling their data processing problems especially with the help of computers. Eight other institutions also provide such facilities on behalf of ICSSR.

Translation Services

Translation services are not much sought by the social scientists in our country. Most of the foreign reading material, whether monographs or periodicals, is received from English-speaking countries. According to a survey of the "Union List of Social Science Periodicals currently received in Delhi Libraries", only few titles are received in languages other than English. NASSDOC which provides translation services in social sciences through the cooperation of other agencies gets few requests for this work. A systematic arrangement, however, is needed for this service so that those who require may get immediate attention.

ISSUES FOR CONSIDERATION

i. Much water has flown down the Ganges since the INFROSS study. That study also cannot provide guidelines to us as there is a great divergence in the level of standards of information services in the West and in our country. The ICSSR financed project regarding study of information needs of the social scientists mentioned earlier needs to be completed at the earliest.
ii. A National Institute of User Education on the lines of the

Centre for Research on User Studies at the University of Sheffield be set up to compile and under take user education programmes, keeping in view the different categories of users and their educational/cultural background.

iii. A Central Statistical Data Centre as envisaged in the Sixth Five Year Plan should beset up at the earliest. Besides collecting and storing data, it should coordinate the activities of other data centres, set up at various places.

iv. The Central Microfilm Library and Documentation Centre for looking after old manuscripts as proposed by the Ministry of Culture should be given proper shape.

v. Existing information tools like Indian National Bibliography and Catalogue of Government of India Civil Publications be improved upon in the context of their coverage and publication schedule.

vi. Supply procedures of government documents should be streamlined.

vii. Bibliographical and document supply services should be broad-based in the country.

viii. Automation of Library services should be a priority. Information centres should imbibe computer culture without losing more time. The National Informatics Centre will have to play a major role in this.

APPENDIX-I

Studies on Information Needs of Social Scientists in the West

Adams, R., Meeting the information needs of social scientists. *Information Scientist*, 9(4), Dec., 1975, p. 141-148.

Bath University

- 1968: Investigation into Information Requirements of the Social Scientists (INFROSS): Report on the preliminary stage, September 1967 – March 1968.
- 1971: INFROSS research report No. 2: Information requirements of social scientists in government departments. (A questionnaire survey).
- 1971: INFROSS research report No. 3: Information requirement of college of education lecturers and school teachers. (A questionnaire survey).
- 1971: INFROSS research report No. 4: The information needs of social workers. (A questionnaire survey).
- 1971: INFROSS research report No. 5: The research procedures of social scientists (as a means of establishing their need for and use of information).
- 1972: Experimental information service in the social sciences 1969-1971 : Final report.

Brittain, J.M., (ed.) The social sciences : The supply of and demand for documentation and data, a report to UNESCO. London : Resseddale, 1982.

Dews, J.D. and Pout, H.T., The use of information sources by teachers and research workers in the field of business studies. Manchester: Manchester Business School, 1970.

McBride, R.B., Foreign language serial use by social science faculty : a survey. *Serials Librarian*, 5(4): Summer 1981, p. 25-32.

Varughese, S., The use of periodicals literature by staff in a welfare service department. *Australian Special Libraries News* 13(1):

March 1980: p.21-27.

White, B., Information provision in town and country planning: a research report. London : Library Association, 1969. (OSTI Report No. 5059).

Wilson, T. and Streatfield, D.R., Information needs in local authority social services departments : an interim report on Project INISS. *Journal of Documentation* 33: 1977: p.277-293.

Wilson, T.D., Streatfield, D.R. and Mullings, C., Information needs in local authority social services departments : a second report on Project INISS. *Journal of Documentation* 35: 120-136:1979.

APPENDIX-II

Studies on Information Needs of Social Scientists in India

Baruah, Ms. Meera Bala. Readers' use of the university library in the North-Eastern region with special reference to the universities of Assam and Meghalaya. Ph.D. Thesis. Punjab University. 1984.

Bavakutty, M.A. Critical study of the organisation and utilisation of libraries in higher educational institutions in Kerala. Ph.D. Thesis. Kerala University. 1983.

Kaula, P.N. and Singh, S.N. Characteristics of information material. *Herald of Library Science*, 19(4); 1980: p.288-297.

Khare, Manoj Bala. Citation analysis of Ph.D. Thesis in social sciences presented by research scholars to Jiwaji University, Gawalior, during 1975-1980. Term Paper (MLIS). Ujjain University. 1981.

Lakshminarasamna, K.V. Information requirements of the linguists : a study of CILL, Mysore, term Paper (MLIS). Mysore University. 1982.

Nagajyotsana, D. Use of sociology periodicals in R.T.L. : A citation analysis study. Term Paper (MLIS). Delhi University. 1984.

Sangam, S.L. A citation analysis of doctoral dissertations in social sciences. Ph.D. Thesis. Gulbarga University. 1985.

Somashekar, Karnavar. The Information needs of Anthropologists : A case study of Anthropological Survey of India, Mysore. Term Paper (MLIS). Mysore University. 1980.

Sood, Asha. Study of Information needs of economists and A proposed plan for a National Information System for Economics. Term Paper (M. Phil). Delhi University. 1981.

Subrahmanyam, T. Study of information seeking behaviour of doctoral candidates in social sciences. *Herald of Library Science* 22(3-4): 1983: p. 200-204.

APPENDIX-III

Disciplinewise Selective List of Social Science Research Institutions in India

Anthropology

- Anthropological Survey of India. Calcutta.
- Madhya Pradesh Tribal Research and Development Institute, Bhopal.
- Tribal Cultural Research and Training Institute, Hyderabad.

Archaeology

- Archaeological Survey of India, New Delhi.
- National Archives of India, New Delhi.

Demography

- International Institute for Population Studies, Bombay.

Economics

- Centre for Development Studies, Trivandrum.
- Centre for Studies in Decentralised Industries, Bombay.
- Institute of Applied Manpower Research, New Delhi.
- Institute of Economic Growth, Delhi.
- National Council of Applied Economic Research, New Delhi.
- National Institute of Rural Development, Hyderabad.
- National Labour Institute, New Delhi.
- Sardar Patel Institute of Economic and Social Research, Ahmedabad.
- Shri Ram Centre for Industrial Relations and Human Resources, New Delhi.

- Small Industry Extension Training Institute, Hyderabad.
- Vaikunth Mehta National Institute of Cooperative Management, Pune.
- Xavier Labour Relations Institute, Jamshedpur.

Education

- Directorate of Adult Education, Delhi.
- National Council of Educational Research and Training, New Delhi.
- National Institute of Educational Planning and Administration, New Delhi.
- Raja Ram Mohan Roy National Educational Resources Centre, New Delhi.

Geography

- National Geographical Society of India, Varanasi.

History/Indology

- Asiatic Society of Bengal, Calcutta.
- Asiatic Society of Bombay.
- Bhandarkar Oriental Research Institute, Pune.
- Heras Institute of Indian History and Culture, Bombay.
- Indian Council of Historical Research, New Delhi.
- Nehru Memorial Museum and Library, New Delhi.

Law

- Indian Law Institute, New Delhi.

Linguistics

- Central Institute of Indian Languages, Mysore.
- Government Central Pedagogical Institute, Allahabad.

Management

- Indian Institute of Management, Ahmedabad.

- Indian Institute of Management, Bangalore.
- Indian Institute of Management, Calcutta.
- Motilal Nehru Institute of Research and Business Administration, Allahabad.

Mass Communication

- Indian Institute of Mass Communication, New Delhi.

Political Science

- Gokhale Institute of Politics and Economics, Pune.
- Gokhale Institute of Public Affairs, Bangalore.
- Institute of Constitutional and Parliamentary Studies, New Delhi.
- Institute for Defence Studies and Analysis New Delhi.

Psychology

- B.M. Institute of Mental Health, Ahmedabad.
- National Institute of Mental Health and Neuro Sciences, Bangalore.

Public Administration

- Administrative Staff College of India, Hyderabad.
- Administrative Training Institute, Mysore.
- Indian Institute of Public Administration, New Delhi,
- H.C.M. State Institute of Public Administration, Jaipur.

Social Sciences (Comprehensive)

- A.N. Sinha Institute of Social Studies, Patna.
- Indian Institute of Advances Study, in Indian School of Social Sciences, Trivandrum.
- National Social Science Documentation Centre, New Delhi.
- Tata Institute of Social Sciences, Bombay.

Sociology

- Institute for Social and Economic Change, Bangalore.

- Vidya Bhavan Rural Institute, Udaipur.
- Xavier Institute of Social Services, Ranchi.

Statistics

- Indian Statistical Institute, Calcutta.
- Indian Statistical Institute, New Delhi.

Town and Country Planning

- School of Planning and Architecture, New Delhi.

THREE

User Education for Information Seeking

INTRODUCTION

"Everyone talks about the weather, but no one seems to do anything about it", quipped Mark Twain once. Users, common or not so common, seem to have a dig at the state of libraries in India these days. Well, in user education we have a way to do something about it. And it is doubly beneficial because thereby users get to know various approaches to information, and library gets a better image projected of its utility as a social institution.

Viewed in this context, user education is clearly a pressing need of the day and this fact is increasingly being recognised in almost all parts of the world. An enormous growth of inter-disciplinary subjects, information explosion, changing concept of library and librarianship, etc., are some of the factors which have made the library system a complex organism, and greatly underscored the need for user education. Based on various case studies with different kinds of users and different types of libraries, user education has become a prerequisite for dependable know-how in many countries. The selection of this subject for discussion by the Indian association of Special Libraries and Information Centres (IASLIC) for its annual conference held at Waltair in December 1981, by Indian Library Association for its Seminar in February 1984 and as a sponsored project by NASSDOC as far back as 1980, clearly reveals that in India too, the need for user education is gaining importance. The nature and level of users may vary but user education in one form or the other is essential for the effective and efficient use of a library and its services.

SCOPE

User education aims to provide advice and instruction about the use of the library to the user, actual or potential, individually or collectively, in a formal or informal manner. Every product, for attaining popularity, requires some marketing techniques. While the physical outlay of the library and its services, display of most popular material and other such techniques can attract users temporarily, user education is still necessary as it acquaints the user with the information processing techniques used and the information services available in the library. It acquaints users with some basic elements of the library and librarianship.

User education programmes, according to Stevenson,[1] are generally of two types:

Orientation Programme

Introducing the user to techniques of library usage and services in general and to the organisation and arrangement of a particular library.

Bibliographic Instruction

Instructing about the use of library tools like abstracts, indexes, bibliographies, reports, patents, theses, etc.

NEED

User education, if designed and conducted properly, can be very profitable in various ways.

Promotion of Information Use

User education leads to the satisfaction of the librarians by increasing the use of the available information services. Studies reveal that in the absence of such an instruction, libraries may not be utilised at all or remain under-utilised. Mr. Ruth Alston,[2] a librarian of the Cambridge University, has observed, "The stock of Indian Libraries was significantly under-used because of user ignorance, and many thought that the information profession has not, on the whole, succeeded in projecting a good image of its capabilities."

The stress, now a days, is shifting from the conservation and storage of information to the transfer of information. The transfer of information being a complex process, user education becomes necessary for its optimum utilisation. It enables the user to identify and formulate his needs and to match them with the library resources. User, if properly educated, can also make an evaluation of the resources and services available and help in the re-designing of these services according to their needs or make an adjustment between the two.

Close Relationship between Librarians and Users

Through user education, librarians and users come in direct contact, enabling the librarian to understand the latter's needs better. The librarian in that case by understanding the actual requirements of the user can design and provide the information services, oriented towards user needs, and the user, by getting his required information without wasting his time, can utilise it to better purpose.

Bridging of Gap between Users and Information

User education brings the users and information closer to each other, ultimately reducing the role of an intermediary, i.e., the librarian. The time saved by the librarian as an intermediary can be utilised in search and provision of more information, thus increasing the pace of research.

Implementation of Laws of Library Science

User education puts in practice four out of the five laws of library science enunciated by S.R. Ranganathan. By introducing users to the information available, user education satisfies the first Law of Library Science, i.e., (1) Books are for use. By bridging the gap between the user and the information, it satisfies the Second and Third Laws, which are (2) Every reader his book; and (3) Every book its reader and by reducing the role of an intermediary, it satisfies the Fourth Law, i.e., (4) Save the time of the reader.

Appreciation for Librarians

Librarians can earn more appreciation from the user for the work done, if the user knows the technicalities and complexities involved in the process of information transfer.

METHODOLOGY

User education can be given in a formal or informal manner. Informal education can be covered in part by the public relations and the staff behaviour pattern of of the library. Oral communication is one of the best methods of user education. If the library staff has good relations with the users, they can informally acquaint the users with the resources and the information available in the library and the techniques for using them on a casual meeting or at the reference desk. If the user is inquiring about a source of information, then the librarian can inform him about other relevant sources also. Informal education does not require a fixed number of users, a fixed time or place and a laid down syllabus with the teacher. It is now greatly felt that the people learn and retain more in an informal set-up rather than the formal one. But it does not by any means lessen the need of a formal education programme for the users, with a fixed time, place and syllabus.

The course content and the teaching methods of the user education programme depend on the nature and level of users. User education should therefore be designed to suit the user's needs and not the librarian's. Various teaching methods have been employed for user education programmes. Lectures, seminars, tutorials, demonstrations, guided tours, etc., are some methods adopted for group instruction; films, video tapes, slides, audio-visual aids and library guides are some of the methods used both for individual and group instruction; and exercise books, programmed instruction, project reports, etc., are a few employed for individual instruction.

PROGRAMME EVALUATION

Some evaluation techniques for redesigning of user education programmes in the light of the user's changing needs have been devised and practised by a few librarians in their institutions. Janet R. Hanson[3] has made investigations into the following two models used for the evaluation of the library user education programme at the Learning Resources Centre (LRC) of the Dorset Institute of Higher Education. These models have already been applied to the SCONUL Tape-Slide Evaluation Project[4] and the Travelling Workshop Experiment (TWE) Project.[5]

Objectives Based Model

It aims to judge the success of the course and to find out the extent to which the objectives have been achieved after the course is over. It is a product oriented and not process oriented model.

Illuminative Model

This attempts to illuminate all aspects of the course from everybody's point of view, i.e., students, academic staff and the librarian. It is considered as more practicable as it is adoptable to different situations.

INTERNATIONAL SCENE

AT the UNISIST Seminar held in Rome in 1976, it was recommended that the national policy on user education should be formulated as an integral part of the national information policy and in correlation with the national education policy. UNESCO, under the auspices of UNISIST, brought out a guide for teachers, prepared by Evans, Rhodes and Keenen in 1971. Ten years later, it published guidelines prepared by T.D. Wilson, for developing and implementing a national plan for training and education in information use. In pursuance of these recommendations made by UNISIST and UNESCO, and based on various user studies and surveys, user education programmes have already been designed and administered in a number of countries.

In countries like the USA and the UK, most of these instruction programmes are administered by a centralised agency through co-operative ventures in order to avoid duplication. The project LOEX (Library Orientation Instruction Exchange) at the Centre of Educational Resources, Eastern Michigan University (USA) is a pioneer in this field. It is operated with an object to facilitate communication among libraries with instructional programmes, and to assist libraries interested in organising such programmes. Following LOEX, Travelling Workshops Experiment (TWE) at the New Castle-upon-Tyne Polytechnic and the establishment of Library Instruction Materials Bank (LIMB) at the Loughborough University of Technology, and the Centre for Research on User Studies (CRUS) at the University of Sheffield are the significant steps in this direction.

NATIONAL SCENE

In India too, user education programmes at a few libraries engaged in scientific research have been conducted. The Indian National Scientific Documentation Centre (INSDOC), Delhi, and the Documentation, Research and Training Centre (DRTC), Bangalore, have conducted some workshops and seminars on user education. The Indian Agricultural Research Institute (IARI) is conducting a course on "Library use, reference, compilation, scientific paper writing and proof correction". Still much remains to be done more so because the problem in India is a little different from that in other countries. The inculcation of reading habit and development of library sense amongst the users is the basic requirement for achieving our objectives of user education in India. It calls for the incorporation of user education in the prescribed syllabus at the school land college levels, and a national level programme of training and education in library and information use. Once the need for user education is accepted, different methods of teaching including of course those enumerated in METHODOLOGY would require to be examined.

User surveys and studies have also been conducted in various libraries in India. But nothing concrete has come out. Urgent attention of the authorities concerned is required for a well-organised user education programme in all types of libraries - academic, public or special - for the effective utilisation of resources and information services, with a provision for regular evaluation and redesigning of the programme according to the changing needs of the users.

CONCLUSION

In conclusion, we can say that it is high time we took some firm steps in this direction, resulting in a national level policy and programme in the instruction of library and information use, and the establishment of an agency at the national level to help and guide the libraries throughout India, to organise and conduct user education programmes.

REFERENCES

1. Stevenson, Malcolm. Education of users of libraries and information services. *Journal of Documentation* 33 (1) : 1977: 53-78.
2. Alston, Ruth. Hunger for the poor? Some observations on information provision in India. *Journal of Information Science* 6: 1983: 115-22.
3. Hanson, Janet R. The evaluation of library user education with reference to the programme at Dorset Institute of Higher Education (DIHE). *Journal of Librarianship* 16 (1): January, 1984: 1-18.
4. Hills, P.J. and others. *Evaluation of tape-slide guides for library instruction*. 1978. British Library.
5. Clark, D. and others. *The travelling Workshops Experiment in Library user education*. 1981. British Library.

SECTION THREE

RESOURCES ORGANISATION AND UTILIZATION

FOUR

Indian Social Science Periodicals

INTRODUCTION

As foundation of scholarship, periodical literature occupies an important place in social sciences. Journals seek to disseminate knowledge and enable researchers to publish their work, to become familiar with the work of others and to benefit from scholarly discussions and dialogues. In fact without journals, it is difficult to ensure the growth of any research discipline. As a discipline grows, the volume of research grows and the need for more journals to publish the research findings, becomes increasingly felt. Thus the number of research journals in a discipline is one indicator of its status and growth. In India, publication of social science journals increased correspondingly with the growth in research institutions/organisations. Before 1947 when the research activity was confined only to university departments and a few research institutions/associations, the number of learned journals in social sciences was also small. Tables 4.1, 4.2, 4.3 show the growth rate of social science journals decade-wise, the number of journals discipline-wise, and geographical area covered respectively.

CONTENTS

Most of the contributors to social science press are academics and their editors are professionals who have a good background and training in social sciences. A study made in 1964 of 10 journals shows that almost 80 per cent of the articles were found to be informative, about 15 per cent analytical with theoretical significance, while only

5 per cent had articles on policy formulation. According to the same study, the contributors to the social sciences were largely academics, very few bureaucrats and still fewer active social and political workers. Of a total of 315 contributors, 294 were academicians, 19 bureaucrats and only two social and political workers. These journals were mostly owned by learned societies, universities, educational institutions, etc.

TABLE 4.1:Period of starting of new Journals*

	Period	No. of Journals
1.	Up to 1900	3
2.	1901 to 1910	1
3.	1911 to 1920	3
4.	1921 to 1930	5
5.	1931 to 1940	6
6.	1941 to 1950	6
7.	1951 to 1960	46
8.	1961 to 1970	71
9.	1971 to 1980	102
10.	1981	12
11.	1982	9
12.	1983	1
	Total	265

*Analysis based on data collected for Unesco DARE System during 1982.

TABLE 4.2:Subject-wise distribution of Journals*

	Discipline	No. of Journals
1.	Accounting	1
2.	Administration	1
3.	Adult Education	2
4.	Africa	5
5.	Agricultural Economics	1
6.	Agriculture	2
7.	America	2
8.	Andhra Pradesh	1
9.	Anthropology	6
10.	Applied Psychology	1
11.	Archaeology	1
12.	Asia	7
13.	Australia	1
14.	Behavioural Sciences	2

15.	China (People's Republic)	1
16.	Clinical Psychology	1
17.	Comparative Law	2
18.	Constitutional Law	2
19.	Consumer	2
20.	Cooperatives	6
21.	Criminology	2
22.	Culture	2
23.	Democracy	2
24.	Demography	2
25.	Development	4
26.	Economic Development	11
27.	Economics	19
28.	Education	20
29.	Educational Psychology	2
30.	Energy	1
31.	Europe	1
32.	Family	2
33.	Folklore	1
34.	Futurology	2
35.	Gandhiana	1
36.	Geography	6
37.	Health	1
38.	Higher Education	3
39.	History	4
40.	Humanities	2
41.	India	6
42.	Indian Ocean	1
43.	Indology	1
44.	Industrial Relations	1
45.	Industry	3
46.	Information System	5
47.	International Affairs	8
48.	International Law	1
49.	Islam	2
50.	Japan	1
51.	Korea	1
52.	Labour	3
53.	Law	7
54.	Linguistics	4
55.	Local Government	4
56.	Maharashtra	2
57.	Management	7
58.	Manpower	2
59.	Mass Communication	2
60.	Mental Retardation	1
61.	Mongolia	1
62.	Orissa	1
63.	Parliamentary System	4
64.	Philosophy	4
65.	Political Science	8
66.	Politics	1
67.	Productivity	2

68.	Psychology	11
69.	Public administration	8
70.	Public Enterprises	1
71.	Public Opinion	1
72.	Punjab	1
73.	Rural Development	10
74.	Rural Industry	1
75.	Rural Planning	1
76.	Science	2
77.	Science Policy	1
78.	Social Anthropology	1
79.	Social Change	1
80.	Social Science	18
81.	Social Services	2
82.	Social Welfare	2
83.	Social Work	1
84.	Society	1
85.	Sociology	14
86.	Statistics	2
87.	Teaching	4
88.	Technology	1
89.	Tourism	2
90.	Urban Planning	1
91.	Women	1
	Total	305

* Analysis based on data collected for Unesco DARE System during 1982. Multidisciplinary journals have been counted in all the disciplines.

USERS

Academic libraries are the largest clientele of the learned journals. Serious reading in India is limited to research scholars, professionals, academicians, policy-makers and administrators. An average reader seldom uses these journals for information and enlightenment. He finds himself comfortable in the company of general type of periodicals, presenting information in a simple way.

Thus it will be seen that there are only a small number of users and even these do not fully utilise the documentary materials appearing in these journals. This is mainly due to lack of bibliographical control over the periodical material. International abstracting and indexing journals do include Indian journals but their coverage is very small. However, of late documentation activity in this direction is expanding. ICSSR has also taken up the project of indexing of about 240 Indian social science periodicals since the first volume of each title to the year 1970. *Indian Education Index* covering 26 leading Indian journals has so far been published, while information regarding journals in the field of Anthropology, Psychology and Sociology is available on the cards and the published volume will be released soon. The work on the remaining fields is in progress. When completed, a rich treasure of information will be available to the research community.

TABLE 4.3:Geographical area covered*

	Geographical Area	No. of Journals
1.	International	117
2.	Africa	7
3.	Asia	14
4.	Australia	1
5.	China	1
6.	Developing Nations	1
7.	Europe	1
8.	India	131
9.	North America	1
	Total	274

* Analysis based on data collected for Unesco DARE System during 1982. Journals dealing with more than one area have been counted under all areas.

The academic standard of Indian journals compares well with the foreign journals particularly in the field of Economics and Industrial Relations. But, inexplicably, while costly foreign journals are being subscribed to by most of the academic libraries, subscription to Indian journals is very poor. Even some highly specialised Indian journals are not received by some university libraries.

This sorry state of affairs can be due only to lack of up-to-date directories of Indian periodicals and injudicious subscription policy as a result of non-coordination in resource sharing and formulation of subscription policy. Compilation of Union lists/catalogues greatly helps in improving this unhealthy situation. ICSSR has brought out Union catalogue of Social Science periodicals/serials in libraries in India (32 volumes) and has periodically brought out union lists of periodicals currently received in libraries.

PUBLICATION HEALTH OF JOURNALS

Due to lack of periodicals directories, it is difficult to know the exact number of existing publications. The high death rate of periodicals is also astonishing and negates efforts to arrive at an accurate figure. Besides the birth rate of new periodicals is on the low side, thanks to the prohibitive cost of paper and printing. As if this was not enough, marketing hurdles block circulation prospects and advertisers who are nourishing resources, keep miles away. Academic journals are frequently shy of courting advertisements thinking rightly or wrongly that academics should keep themselves scrupulously out of non-academic or commercial pursuits. Price escalation to the extent of 100 per cent keeps away the medium-size libraries from subscribing to the journals, although, as Girja Kumar and Jayaswal have maintained, "The periodicals published in India are reasonably priced and their price graph does not tend to rise too steeply for variety of reasons. Considerable proportion of Indian periodical publications are brought out by governmental agencies, besides academic and research institutions. Periodicals brought out by agencies with commercial motivation are equally cautious in this respect. Considerable proportion of their subscription list is confined to Indian clientele who cannot afford too violent variations in prices. It is also a captive audience. Unfortunately, there is no ready-made data available of the price graph of Indian social science periodicals during the previous decade for comparative purpose". The publication is increasingly becoming a highly skilled professional job with almost unlimited resources to draw upon. If these assets are lacking, a periodical will find the going rough, if not impossible, with the result that its survival will soon be at stake. Government and private institutional financial assistance is a must for the survival of the academic journals and keeping higher professional standards.

STATISTICAL ANALYSIS*

There are at present 15,995 periodicals in circulation in the

---

* Based on Press in India 1980 Pt. II

country and information regarding their nature of contents was available in respect of 14,248 periodicals. These journals have been classified into 21 subject categories based on their contents.

The largest number of periodicals (5,862) came under the category of News and Current Affairs followed by Commerce and Industry (1,596), Social Welfare (426) and so on. Periodicity-wise, weeklies among the News and Current Affairs periodicals were the largest in number while monthlies were the largest in other social science periodicals (see Table 4.4).

In the social science fields journals were being published in English, Hindi, Assamee, Bengali, Gujarati, Kannada, Malayalam, Marathi and Punjabi (see table 4.5).

News and Current Affairs journals with a combined circulation of 9,423,000 were at the top followed by Finance and Economics (775,000), Commerce and Industry (585,000) and so on (see Table 4.6).

Language-wise break-up of circulation in each category is given in Table 4.7.

Tables 4.8 and 4.9 show periodicity-wise and language-wise respectively the number of periodicals for which data were available.
Information was available about the contents of 532 of the 558 periodicals published by the Central and State Governments. More than 100 (112) came under the category of News and Current Affairs. Sixty-eight journals were dealing with Social Welfare. Those under Agriculture and Animal Husbandry numbered 52. There were 42 journals in the field of Commerce and Industry.

Government publications were brought out in all but two of the 21 categories. There was no Film journal or a Sports magazine. All the periodicals in the category of Radio and Music, Art and Women were owned by the Central Government. On the other hand, the only periodical belonging to Religion and Philosophy was published by a State Government. Table 4.10 shows the position about Social Science journals brought out by Government bodies.

TABLE 4.4:Number of periodicals according to contents, 1979 (Periodicity-wise)*

Category	Weeklies	Fortnightlies	Monthlies	Quarterlies	Other periodiocities	Annuals	Total
News and Current Affairs	3919	1147	660	72	45	19	5862
Commerce and Industry	70	56	314	95	41	20	596
Social Welfare	43	51	229	80	23	-	426
Labour	33	55	220	22	9	-	339
Education	9	33	127	77	43	8	297
Law and Public Administration	24	50	174	39	11	4	302
Children	9	20	138	13	8	4	192
Transport and Communication	4	6	71	11	3	4	99
Insurance, Banking and Co-operation	18	11	54	25	7	1	119
Finance and Economics	10	12	42	19	17	3	103
Women	9	8	52	7	6	3	85

* Based on *Press in India-1980 Pt. II.*

TABLE 4.5:Number of Periodicals according to contents, 1979 (Language-wise)*

Category	English	Hindi	Assamese	Bengali	Gujarati	Kannada	Kashmiri	Malayalam	Marathi	Oriya	Punjabi
News and Current Affairs	590	2732	19	408	101	89	-	74	184	30	148
Commerce and Industry	420	41	-	5	6	3	-	3	6	-	-
Social Welfare	89	118	1	16	64	5	-	1	29	3	3
Labour	100	69	-	10	9	2	-	3	10	3	4
Education	103	37	2	13	18	10	-	3	15	1	-
Law and Public Administration	227	16	-	3	3	1	-	1	10	1	1
Children	12	44	1	32	11	3	-	12	10	5	3
Transport and Communication	59	10	-	4	1	1	-	1	2	2	1
Insurance, Banking and Co-operation	47	15	-	1	3	4	-	-	14	1	1
Finance and Economics	81	10	-	-	1	1	-	-	1	-	-
Women	22	21	-	3	13	-	-	5	6	-	1
	1750	3113	23	495	230	119		103	287	46	162
								Total			6328

TABLE 4.6:Circulation of Periodicals according to contents, 1979 (Periodiocity-wise)*

(in Thousands)

Category	Weeklies	Fortnightlies	Monthlies	Quarterlies	Other	Annuals	Total
News and Current Affairs	7012	1390	878	73	19	51	9423
Commerce and Industry	114	49	280	58	29	55	585
Social Welfare	41	46	347	28	13	-	475
Labour	19	55	258	76	3	-	411
Education	17	19	158	81	49	6	330
Law and Public Administration	43	53	261	40	2	-	399
Children	121	563	1708	3	2	13	2410
Transport and Communication	8	3	186	18	-	-	215
Insurance, Banking and Co-operation	28	8	123	147	10	-	316
Finance and Economics	51	21	74	8	6	-	160

* Based on *Press in India-1980 Pt.II.*

TABLE 4.7: Circulation of Periodicals according to contents, 1979 (Language-wise)*

Category	English	Hindi	Assamese	Bengali	Gujarati	Kannada	Malayalam	Marathi	Oriya	Punjabi	Sanskrit
News and Current Affairs	1887	3537	64	587	266	242	215	277	18	306	-
Commerce and Industry	441	53	-	16	6	1	1	7	-	-	-
Social Welfare	125	184	-	10	56	10	10	15	2	7	-
Labour	131	59	-	17	6	-	-	6	6	-	-
Education	64	88	-	11	20	10	4	10	-	-	-
Law and Public Administration	303	13	-	-	4	2	1	25	1	-	-
Children	192	870	4	296	122	102	298	123	42	5	-
Transport and Communication	103	21	-	7	-	-	-	64	-	-	-
Finance and Economics	132	6	-	-	13	-	-	-	-	-	-
Women	318	22	-	2	141	-	194	22	-	-	-
Insurance, Banking and Co-operation	222	12	-	1	8	2	-	24	-	5	-

TABLE 4.7 (contd.)

Category	Sindhi	Tamil	Telugu	Urdu	Bi-Lingual	Multi-Lingual	Others	Total
News and Current Affairs	44	507	249	808	333	43	35	9123
Commerce and Industry	-	1	-	1	49	9	-	585
Social Welfare	-	10	10	6	22	7	1	435
Labour	-	26	1	1	103	1	-	354
Education	-	4	12	4	91	11	1	330
Law and Public Administration	-	14	20	1	15	-	-	399
Children	-	134	173	16	20	8	5	2430
Transport and Communication	-	2	13	-	2	3	-	215
Finance and Economics	-	3	-	-	6	-	-	160
Women	-	36	13	26	1	-	-	775
Insurance, Banking and Co-operation	-	12	4	2	8	16	-	316

* Based on *Press in India-1980 Pt.II.*

TABLE 4.8: Number of Periodicals according to contents for which Circulation was available 1979 (Periodicitywise)

Category	Weeklies	Fortnightlies	Monthlies	Quarterlies	Other periodicities	Annuals	Total
News and Current Affairs	1715	452	267	36	15	11	2496
Commerce and Industry	35	26	154	38	24	6	283
Social Welfare	21	24	107	37	13	—	202
Labour	13	25	94	8	2	—	142
Education	4	9	68	42	14	4	141
Law and Public Administration	12	33	97	24	4	—	170
Children	6	11	79	3	2	3	104
Transport and Communication	3	4	37	6	1	—	51
Insurance, Banking and Co-operation	13	5	37	15	4	—	74
Finance and Economics	7	4	21	10	8	—	50
Women	5	5	22	3	1	1	37

* Based on *Press in India-1980 Pt.II.*

TABLE 4.9: Number of Periodicals according to contents for which circulation was available 1979*(Languagewise)

Category	English	Hindi	Assamese	Bengali	Gujarati	Kannada	Kashmiri	Malayalam	Marathi	Oriya
News and Current Affairs	248	1057	11	234	59	43	—	34	89	14
Commerce and Industry	207	18	—	3	4	2	—	2	3	—
Social Welfare	52	44	—	9	35	2	—	1	12	1
Labour	49	22	—	8	5	—	—	1	5	1
Education	50	17	—	7	10	4	—	1	7	—
Law and Public Administration	128	11	—	—	4	1	—	1	5	1
Children	8	17	1	18	6	3	—	7	7	2
Transport and Communication	32	7	—	2	—	—	—	2	—	—
Insurance,Banking and Co-operation	26	10	—	1	2	2	—	—	10	—
Finance and Economics	40	3	—	—	1	—	—	—	1	—
Women	7	6	—	2	8	—	—	2	3	—

Category	Punjabi	Sanskrit	Sindhi	Tamil	Telugu	Urdu	Bi-Lingual	Multi-Lingual	Others	Total
News and Current Affairs	69	1	10	40	57	305	182	25	18	2496
Commerce and Industry	—	—	—	1	—	1	34	8	—	283
Social Welfare	1	—	—	6	4	5	21	8	1	202
Labour	—	—	—	—	2	2	38	2	—	142
Education	—	—	—	4	4	4	25	7	1	141
Law and Public Administration	—	—	—	3	4	1	10	1	—	170
Children	2	—	—	9	7	7	4	3	3	104
Transport and Communication	—	—	—	1	2	—	3	2	—	51
Insurance, Banking and Co-operation	1	—	—	9	1	—	8	4	—	74
Finance and Economics	—	—	—	1	—	—	4	—	—	50
Women	—	—	—	2	1	5	1	—	—	37

* Based on *Press in India-1980 Pt.II.*

TABLE 4.10: Contentwise number of Government Publications, 1979*

Category	Central Government	State Government	Total
News and Current Affairs	48	64	112
Social Welfare	21	47	68
Commerce and Industry	32	10	42
Education	11	26	37
Transport and Communication	32	2	34
Law and Public Administration	10	11	21
Finance and Economics	2	7	9
Insurance, Banking & Cooperation	—	2	2
Women	2	—	2
Children	1	1	2
Religion and Philosophy	—	1	1

* Based on *Press In India-1980 Pt. II.*

FIVE

Social Science Dissertations in India

SCOPE

The paper excludes dissertations submitted in partial fulfilment of the requirements for a higher degree in conjunction with a written examination. Social Science subjects include Commerce, Economics, Education, Geography, History, Law, Management, Political Science, Psychology, Public Administration and Sociology. The bibliographical tools encompassing all disciplines including social sciences and broader areas including India have been covered. The dissertations on India submitted to foreign universities have also been taken care of. The terms "Dissertation" and "Theses" have been used interchangeably.

Introduction

It is generally agreed that the developed world has made tremendous progress in science and technology which has enabled it to adopt ways and means for achieving higher standards of living, while the under-developed world is struggling for the same. How has the developed world succeeded in bettermeans of prosperity? It is through higher standards in research. Research is done in universities, laboratories, research institutes, and in agriculture industry. The research findings appear in the form of dissertations, research reports and research articles.

Dissertations

There is generally not much divergence of opinion about the

definition of the term "Dissertation/Theses" as is evident from the two definitions given below:

> A substantial paper that is submitted to the faculty of a university by a candidate for an advanced degree that is typically based on independent research and that if acceptable usually gives evidence of the candidate's mastery both of his own subject and scholarly method. (Webster's Third New International Dictionary).

> A statement of investigation of research presenting the author's finding and conclusions reached and submitted by the author in support of his candidature for a higher degree, professional qualification or other award (Peter Auger, 1980).

Dissertations and theses submitted to various universities and institutions of advanced learning constitute invaluable information sources to research workers. They find in these the data and results already arrived at and relevant to their research work. These reports show the scholar's grasp of a given subject and the research methodology involved. Sometimes these are published in amended form or appear in the form of articles which are consulted and cited by the scholars, in the literature.

Bibliographical Control of Dissertations

A large number of doctoral degrees are awarded annually by universities and research institutions deemed as universities all over the world. An idea about their number can be had from the bibliographical tools listing them. A comprehensive dissertation index 1861-1972 by University Microfilms gives information of over 417,000 dissertations approved by universities in the USA and Canada in all the disciplines, *As lib Index to Theses,* 1982 issue, lists above 8,402 items. In India, the association of Indian Universities took initiative towards bibliographical control of dissertations produced in India as early as in 1935 by bringing out a list covering the period from 1930-1934. There was no differentiation of subjects, in the list were published at intervals of two-there years for a period of approximately a quarter century. The consolidated lists covering the period, 1857-1970, and 1971-1975 were brought out in 1974 and

1979 respectively. These lists have been kept up-to-date by annual supplements. A decadewise growth of doctorates awarded by Indian universities up to 1980 is given in Table 5.1. It not only shows the number of doctorates awarded but also the growth of research work on various disciplines in social sciences. The total number of dissertations listed comes to about 8,795.

TABLE 5.1: Development of Social Sciences in India*

Subject-and year-wise distribution of Dissertations in Social Science accepted by Indian Universities 1857-1980.

Subject	Up to 1920	1921 to 1930	1931 to 1940	1941 to 1950	1951 to 1960	1961 to 1970	1971 to 1980	Total
Commerce	—	—	2	7	35	78	184	306
Economics	3	4	17	71	293	647	1253	2289
Education	—	—	—	10	79	233	854	1176
Geography**	—	—	—	—	—	—	360	360
History**	—	—	—	—	—	—	1012	1012
Law	7	3	1	3	11	42	141	208
Management	—	—	—	2	15	65	226	308
Political Science	—	3	5	13	83	285	598	990
Psychology	—	1	2	3	36	169	451	662
Public Administration	—	—	1	12	34	103	252	402
Sociology	—	1	5	39	98	282	656	1082
Total	10	12	33	160	684	1904	5987	8795

* Year of award of Degree is not available for the following number of Scholars of Lucknow University :

Economics - 1 Political Science - 3 Sociology - 1

** Information available for the period 1971-80.

Source: Bibliography of doctoral dissertations: Social Sciences and Humanities, (Assoc. of Indian Universities, New Delhi): 1857/1970-1979/1980.

(Includes cumulative and annual supplements)

Efforts at individual and institutional levels are thus made in all the countries to have bibliographic control of this important grey material. In India university libraries are prominent in compiling the lists of theses retained by them. In addition to these, the Association of Indian Universities, as explained before, has been doing useful work in the field. Aslib in the U.K. and University Microfilms in the U.S.A. are working towards this end. The reference tools containing material of this nature generally appear in the form of (i) classified lists of titles with and without annotations, aided by suitable indexes and/or (ii) abstracts of theses arranged under broad subject readings with suitable indexes. These lists may further appear periodically or published ad-hoc covering retrospectively a fixed period. The subject coverage may range from one subject to a group of subjects and even comprising all disciplines of knowledge. The bibliographical information provided by each entry includes: the scholar's name; the tile; the institution's name awarding the degree; year of degree awarded and in its absence year of submission of the thesis; the name of the guide and abstract (only in case of abstracting publications). Some of these reference lists are given in the Appendix.

Availability of Theses

Unlike other published monographic materials, it is not easy to obtain dissertations/theses through the usual commercial publishing channel. Further, a limited number of copies usually in typed form are submitted to the universities. The holding institutions are, therefore, reluctant to provide these on inter-library loan. These can be consulted only in the library premises, which thus restricts their use. It becomes even more difficult for the researchers to make use of these if available at different centres. Special efforts are, therefore, required to be made to know about their existence and procurement if so desired.

In 1954, the Standing Conference of National and University Libraries Gt. Britain) proposed a fourfold standard of availability for theses as published in *Aslib Index to Theses*:

a. At least one copy of every thesis should be deposited in the University Library.
b. Subject to the author's consent every thesis should be available for inter-library loan.
c. Subject to author's consent, every thesis should be available for photo-copying.
d. Authors of theses should be asked at the time of deposit to

give their consent in writing to (b) and (c) and this consent should be inserted in the deposited copy of theses.

As a consequence of these efforts, British Library Lending Division (BLLD) has since 1970 been trying to increase the utilisation of British doctoral theses by microfilming the theses of those universities which have agreed to participate in an experiment to build up a central collection. The availability of theses is known from *BLLD Announcement Bulletin*. Photocopies and microfilm copies are available for loan or retention. About 40,000 British doctoral theses in all disciplines are available at present under the scheme.

In the United States more than 370 cooperating institutions provide abstract of dissertations retained by them to University Microfilms Inc. The abstracts are reported as already mentioned in *Dissertation Abstracts International*. The dissertations are available for purchase either in Microfilm or in Xerographic text from the publisher.

The National Social Science Documentation Centre in India has devised a Scheme to create a document base of dissertations. Under the scheme, the doctoral scholars are invited to deposit a copy of their theses along with its abstract at this Centre against a token payment of Rs. 400. The Centre has so far been able to collect about 2,500 theses, which will gradually go on increasing. To make room for incoming research material, NASSDOC has started getting the theses microfilmed.

The scholars visiting the centre can now consult the theses of various universities at one place and with availability of photocopying facilities at the centre, can get photo-copies of the relevant material. Indian Council of Social Science Research has six regional centres at -- Bombay, Calcutta, Chandigarh, Delhi, Hyderabad and Shillong. Each Centre has been authorised to purchase a copy of the theses in its respective regional language(s).

In the days to come National Social Science Documentation Centre is expected to collect a large number of theses at the Centre. It will strive to provide not only consultation facilities, but also provide microfilm or photo-copy of the document for loan and purchase. This will be possible only with the cooperation of concerned universities and scholars by taking steps on the lines suggested by SCONUL (Gt. Britain).

REFERENCES

1. Gidwani, N.N. and Navalani, K., Comp and ed. *A Guide to Reference Materials on India.* Jaipur, Saraswati Pub., 1974. p. 65-69.
2. Patterson, Geoffrey M. and Hardy, Joan E., ed. *Index to Theses Accepted for Higher Degrees.* V. 31, pt. 1. London, Aslib, 1982.
3. Peter, Auger C. Reports and theses, conferences and symposia, standards and patents, in Higgens, Gavin, ed. *Printed Reference Material.* New Delhi, Oxford and IBH, 1980, p. 223.
4. *Webster's third New International Dictionary,* and Springfield, Mass., G&C Merriam Co., 1967, p. 656.

APPENDIX

Bibliographical Coverage : Brief Survey

Great Britain

Bilboul, R. *Retrospective Index to Theses of Great Britain and Ireland, 1716-1950.* Santa Barbara, California, Clio Pr., 1976.

Index to theses accepted for higher degrees by the universities of Great Britain and Ireland and the Council for National Academic Awards. (Aslib, London). Semi-Annual.

U.S.A.

Dissertation Abstracts International. (University Microfilms Inc, Ann Arbor, Michigan.)-Monthly
Section : Humanities and Social Sciences.
Section: Sciences and Engineering.

Comprehensive dissertation index, 1861-1972. Ann Arbor, Michigan, University Microfilms International, 1973, 37v. The CDI data base also offers computerised service called DATRIX II. On request it will prepare cumulative inter-disciplinary listings of dissertations in any field.

India

Andhra University, Waltair. *Abstracts of the theses for D.Sc. and Ph.D., 1938-1972.* Waltair, Andhra University, 1972. 405 p,

Annamalai University. *Research in the Annamalai University.* Annamalai, The University, 1955. 36 p.

Asian Mass Communication Research and Information Centre, Singapore. List of theses. *Studies on Mass Communication in Asia.* The Centre.

Banaras Hindu University Library. *Abstracts of the theses accepted for the doctorate degree of Banaras Hindu University, 1927-1965.* Varanasi, Banaras Hindu University, n.d. 6V.

- *Documentation of doctoral theses in ancient Indian history, culture and archaeology in the Banaras Hindu University, 1930-1968.* Varanasi, Banaras Hindu University, 1970. v.p. (Documentation Series, 15).
- *Documentation of doctoral theses in economics in the Banaras Hindu University, 1943-1967.* Varanasi, Banaras Hindu University, 1969. v.p. (Documentation Series, 11).
- *Documentation of doctoral theses in geography in Banaras Hindu University, 1968. 21 p.* (Documentation Series, 2).
- Contains 21 annotated entries.
- *Documentation of doctoral theses in history in the Banaras Hindu University, 1949-1967.* Varanasi, Banaras Hindu University, 1970 C-V p. Covers 13 annotated entries.
- *Index to post-graduate and doctoral dissertations in political science in the Banaras Hindu University, 1930-1968.* Varanasi, Banaras Hindu University, 1970. v.p. (Documentation series, 16).

Bibliography of doctoral theses in... accepted by Indian Universitie: (Association of Indian Universities, New Delhi) 1930-34-Annua with cumulated supplement. Title Varies.

Bloomfield, B.C. Comp. *Theses on Asia, accepted by universities i the United Kingdom and Ireland, 1877-1964.*

- London, Cass, 1967., xi, 127 p. Lists 2571 titles arranged b country with subject sections.
- *Bulletin of research theses and dissertations in the Union of India* (National Archives of India, New Delhi). No. 1 (Jan. 1955)-Irr. 4 issues so far published covering the period up to 1966. Lists about 1670 titles which include theses in progress. Title varies slightly.

Case, Margaret H. Dissertations in Case, Margaret H. *South Asian history, 1750-1950: A guide to periodicals, dissertations and newspapers.* 1968. p. 385-4396.

Columbia University Libraries. East Asiatic Library, New York. *Columbia University Master's essays and doctoral dissertations on Asia, 1857-1956.* New York, East Asiatic Library, 1957, ii, 96 p.

Council for Oriental Research, Bhopal. *National register of doctoral dissertations accepted and in progress in social sciences and humanities in Indian Universities.* Bhopal, The Council, 1979-1980. 8V.

V1. *Economics, demography, agricultural, economics and econometrics.* 264 p.
V1-B. *Agricultural economics.* 56 p.
V2. *Political science, international politics, constitutional studies and public administration.* 102-36 p.
V3. *Educational and educational psychology.* 141 p.
V4. *Sociology, social anthropology and criminology.*
V5. *Commerce, business administration, business management, labour and personnel administration.* 280 p.
V6. *History and geography.*
V7. *Law and criminology.* 34 p.
V8. *Psychology.* 102 p.

Directory of research work in history in the universities of Madhya Pradesh. *Journal of the Madhya Pradesh Itihas Parishad* No. 5: 1967: p. 175-85; No. 6. 1968: p. 1-5.

Eelis, Walter Crosby. *American dissertations on foreign education.* Washington, Committee on International Relations, 1959, xxxiv, 300p. India: No. 1823-2133, p. 88-100.

Gautam, Brajendra Pratab. *Research in Political Science in India : A detailed bibliography.* Kanpur, Oriental Publishing House, 1965.

Gupta, Girija Prasad. *Economic Investigations in India : A bibliography of researches* (work for Ph.D. and D.Litt) in commerce and economics appeared and pending at Indian Universities with supplement. Ed. 3. Agra, Rama Prasad and Sons, 1966. 180 p. (Covers mostly the post-Independence period Ed. 3 is reprint of Ist ed. plus supplement.)

Haqqi, S.A.H. *Abstracts of dissertations in Social Sciences.* New Delhi, Sterling, 1979. 305 p.
Contains abstracts of doctoral theses in Geography, Political Science and Psychology.

Hart, Donn V. Comp. *Annotated bibliography of theses and dissertations on Asia,* accepted at Syracuse University, 1907-1963. N.Y. Syracuse University Library, 1964. xii, 46 p.

Indian Agricultural Research Institute, New Delhi. *Bibliography of theses, 1938.* New Delhi, The Institute, 1970. 172 p. (Covers 160 entries on Agricultural Economics, Rural Sociology, and Rural Social Psychology.)

Indian Council of Agricultural Research, New Delhi. *Classified list of theses.* Delhi, The Institute, 1967.

Indian Council of Social Science Research, New Delhi, *Indian dissertation abstracts,* Mar. 1973-Q.

Associate sponsor : Association of Indian Universities, New Delhi.

Indian Institute of technology, Madras. *Abstracts of Ph.D. Theses.* Madras, The Institute, 1980. 1070 p.

V II. *Technology, Humanities and Social Sciences.* Covers three titles in social sciences.

Inter-University Board of India, New Delhi, *Economics, commerce management : A bibliography of doctoral dissertations accepted by Indian Universities, 1857-1970.* New Delhi, Inter-University Board, 1073. 155p.

Inter-University Board of India, New Delhi, and Indian Council of Social Science Research, New Delhi. *Doctorates in Social Sciences awarded by Indian Universities up to 1967.* New Delhi, ICSSR, 1971. xii.401 p. (Research Information Series, VI, No. 1).

Jawaharlal Nehru Library, Saugar. Jawaharlal Nehru Library, 1967. vi, 72 p. (Mimeographed).

Jawaharlal Nehru University Library, Documentation section. *JNU dissertation index,* comp. by A.R. Sethi. New Delhi. JNU, 1975. 118, xxxvii.

Jayakar Library, University of Poona Pune. *Catalogue of theses and dissertations, 1950-1969.* Pune, The University, 1971. 249 p. (Lists 1,548 titles on all disciplines.)

Karnatak University, Dharwar. *A Compendium of Research, 1951-1976:* ed. by M.S. Chennaveeriah and others, Dharwar, The University, 1976. 386 p.

- *Synopsis of doctoral theses in social sciences*, 1955-1975. Dharwar. The University, 1978. 365p.

Kaul, Jagan Nath. *Dissertation in the Social Sciences by Indian doctoral scholars, 1933-63.* Ann Arbor, University Microfilms, 1955. (University Microfilms Publication, No. 12598.)

Krishna Gopal, comp. *Theses on Indian Sub-continent ; 1877-1971: An annotated bibliography of dissertations in social sciences and humanities accepted with the universities of Australia, Canada, Great Britain and Ireland and United States of America,* ed. by Dhanpat Rai. Delhi, Hindustan Pub. Corp. 1977. xix, 462 p. Covers 376 entries.

List of doctoral theses by Indian Universities. *University News 1,* 1963 - Monthly.

List of doctoral theses in industrial relations approved by the Indian Universities during 1960-63. *Indian Journal of Industrial Relations 1 (2) : Oct 1965: p. 231-37.*

Maharaj Sayaji Rao University of Baroda. Faculty of Education and Psychology. *Research Abstracts.* Baroda, The University, 1963. vi, 40 p.

Maulana Azad Library Aligarh. *List of theses approved for the B.Sc., Ph.D., M.Sc. and M.A. degree in the Aligarh Muslim University, Aligarh, 1920-1969.* Aligarh. The University, 1969. x, 68 p. (Its reference and research Publications, No. 1).

Mysore University Library. *Titles of theses and dissertations approved for the doctorate and master's degrees* deposited in the University Library. Mysore. The University, 1961. 26 p.

Indian Dissertation Abstracts Index, Vol. 1-10, 1973-1981, New Delhi, NASSDOC, 1985. (NASSDOC Research Information Series, No. 25).

National Council of Educational Research and Training, New Delhi. *Educational Investigations in India Universities: A list of theses and dissertations* approved for doctorate and master's degree in education. New Delhi, NCERT.

1939-1961 1966 286 p.

1962-1966 1968 304 p.

National Social Science Documentation Centre, New Delhi, *Theses in SSDC : A Bibliography*, New Delhi, NASSDOC, 1983.

(NASSDOC Research Information Series, No. 3).

National Social Science Documentation Centre, New Delhi. Foreign theses on India. (v.p) (Cyclostyled).

Punjab University, Extension Library, Ludhiana. *Punjab University doctoral dissertations, 1948-1964;* comp. by Ramesh C. Sharma and Raj Kumar Puri ; ed. by S.S. Lal. Ludhiana, PU. Ex Lib., 1965. 22 p.

-supplement 1965-67 comp. by Rajkumar Puri and M.S. Dogra; ed. by S.S. Lal. Ludhiana, 1968. 15 p. Main Publ and supplement contain 349 entries.

Rajasthan University, Jaipur. Jaipur, R.U.L. 1966. vii, 316 p. (Mimeographed). Contains 1690 entries.

Sardar Patel University. *List of theses accepted for the award of Ph.D. degree during the years 1960-1978.* Vallabh Vidyanagar, 39 p.

Shah, C.H., ed. *Dissertations in economics,* 1921-1971. Abstracts of M.A. and Ph.D. theses. Bombay University of Bombay, dept. of economics, 1974. 656 p.

Sharma, Baijnath. *Bibliography of research in indological studies carried on in various universities of India.* Maru Bharati 2 (2) : July 1963. p. 235-38.

Shulman, frank J., comp. and ed. *Doctoral dissertations on South Asia, 1966-1970 : An annotated bibliography.* Covering North America, Europe and Australia. Ann Arbor. Centre for South and South-East Asian Studies, 1971. 228 p.
(Covers 1,305 entries on India and Pakistan).

University of Chicago Library and far Eastern Library. *Doctoral dissertations and Master's theses on Asia,* 1694-1962. Chicago, University of Chicago Press, 1962. 52 p.
(Covers 145 titles on India and Pakistan.)

University of Delhi. Department of Anthropology. *Doctoral dissertations in anthropology, 1959-1978 : Summaries of theses...*Delhi, The University, 1981. xi, 99 p.
(Contains summaries of 45 dissertations).

University of Udaipur. Central Library. Catalogue of theses and dissertations available in the University Central Library. Udaipur, University Library, 1968. Mimeographed.

SIX

Government of India Documents

Government publication had been generally defined as a document published at the expense of the government and/or published under the authority of law.

In the present age of democratic set-up, the activities of the governments have increased manifold. This has resulted in generation of voluminous literature which interests the layman as well as the expert depending upon the thought content and the style of presentation.

In India, the biggest democratic country, a large number of official publications are brought out annually. The Department of Publication of Government of India singly handles 75,000 titles of 184 departments, ministries, attached and subordinate offices of the Central Government including semi-government and autonomous institutions and organisations. Another important department which deals with the publication and sale of official documents is the Publication Division of the Ministry of Information and Broadcasting and has so far brought out 5,200 publications. Parliament secretariat also markets a large number of publications.

Leaving aside publications brought out for publicity or for education of the layman, much of the material is rich in descriptive information and statistical data about the natural resources and development programmes of our country. They cover several of the key and significant areas of our national life. Their importance as primary sources of research is beyond doubt. Further the source is less costly in comparison to similar type of publications brought out by non-official channels.

In spite of their usefulness, these are not available to a large number of researchers. The paradoxical situation applies both to the publications of the Central Government and to the State Governments.

In the present paper, endeavour is made to present the prevailing situation and to identify bottlenecks and to suggest measures to remove them in the context of marketing and utilisation of Government of India publications. It is felt that the remedial measures applied in the case of Government of India publications can be fairly applied in the case of State Government publications as well.

Nature of Publications

Different types of official publications are brought out which can be broadly grouped as under:

1. Administration Reports
2. Research Reports (Census Reports, Survey Reports, Statistical Digests, Committees and Commissions Reports).
3. Law Reports (Judicial Decisions, Acts, Laws, Rules and Regulations).
4. Parliamentary Proceedings (Including Reports of Parliamentary Committees).
5. Periodicals.
6. Maps.
7. Leaflets, brochures, booklets, tourist guides, etc.

Generation Sources

1. Ministeries/Departments of the Government and their sub-offices.
2. Parliamentary bodies.
3. Statutory organisations like election commission of India, Office of the Comptroller General of India, Union Public Service Commission, Office of the Attorney General of India, Office of the Commissioner for Scheduled Castes and

Scheduled Tribes, etc.

4. Judicial Bodies like Supreme Court and High Courts.
5. Committees and Commissions appointed by the Government.

Bibliographical Control

The following important bibliographical tools provide current information about government publications :

Accession List-South Asia
(U.S. Library of Congress Office, New Delhi). Monthly
Catalogue-Govt. of India Civil Publications
(Department of Publication, New Delhi). Monthly
Catalogue of Govt. of India Civil Publications, corrected up to...
(Department of Publication, New Delhi). Annual
Indian Books
(Mukherji Book House, Calcutta). Monthly (Lists selected official titles in each issue)
Indian National Bibliography
(Central Reference Library, Calcutta). Monthly
Parliament Library Bulletin
(India. Parliament Library. Reference Research, Documentation and Information Service). Weekly

Resource Centres

Some of the government libraries in Delhi like that of Central Secretariat, Ministry of Home Affairs, Ministry of Finance, Parliament, and Planning Commission are depository libraries for Government of India publications. Besides this National Library, Calcutta; Connemara Public Library, Madras; Central Library, Bombay, and Delhi Public Library receive one copy each of the government publications under the Delivery of Books Act, 1954. A few research libraries in the country like the Indian Institute of Public Administration, Delhi; National Archives Library, Delhi; Archaeological Survey of India Library, Delhi; National Council of Agricultural research Library, Delhi; National Council of Applied Economic Research Library, Delhi, and Gokhale Institute of Politics and Economics, Pune, also keep a good number of government publications.

Research Facilities

The researchers can consult the available material in the departmental libraries. The Directory of Government of India Libraries, compiled by Government of India Librarians Association in 1984 can be helpful identifying the libraries retaining the desired specialised material and also the services offered by them. But it is not always easy to have access to theses centres due to entry restrictions. Further the primary objective of these centres is to serve their internal clientele, therefore outside scholars do not receive much cooperation and encouragement. It is the general experience of scholars that it is very difficult to locate the old official documents in these libraries and in case located, it is further difficult to have these on loan for study and noting. It may appear strange, but it is a fact that Indian scholars visit foreign libraries to consult the old records. Satisfactory reprographic facilities are also not available.

Marketing of Publications

The Department of Publication is the most important organ of the government responsible for publication and marketing of the largest number of the official documents. It is estimated that 75 per cent of the Government of India publications are handled by it through its 896 sales agents (including 24 foreign agents, 150 Sale and Return Agents and 365 employment exchanges). The other two important publication agencies are, Publication Division of the Ministry of Information and Broadcasting, and Parliament Secretariat (Lok Sabha and Rajya Sabha). Both the agencies have a network of sales depots, sales counters, agencies and distribution offices.

In the capital city, it is rather easier to get these publications on cash payment. But for institutions situated in far-off places, it is very difficult first to keep track of the new releases by various departments and when known, to acquire these from the concerned sponsors. The supply procedures are so slow that it takes one to two months and sometimes more to get an indented title. And it takes many months to get refund of the payment against non-supply of the material. The experience of the institutions in dealings with the Publication Department is not a happy one. Some of the books reported to be out of stock are later weeded out and find their way to the commercial market, and can be had at a premium. This can happen only with the connivance of some unscrupulous employees in the Department. To intimate the users about the new releases, the Controller of Publications issues a monthly, *Catalogue of Government of India Civil Publications*. But the number of printed copies is reported to be about 500 which is too small in comparison to the number of user institutions. Some of the new releases are also advertised in the national newspapers. *Accession List, South Asia* and *Indian National Bibliography* as listed earlier are the other two tools which list new arrivals. Most Ministries/Departments also bring out their own catalogues of publications.

Remedial Measures

It is extensively opined that in spite of large expenditure incurred on the compilation of the documents, these are not put to maximum use. Slow marketing techniques, lack of information and consultation facilities are greatly responsible for this. Following measures are suggested to alleviate the situation.

Bibliographical Control

Parliament Library at Delhi should be made responsible for full bibliographical control of publications. There are sound reasons for this. It has sufficient financial and manpower resources. It receives copies of all the official documents published/unpublished and priced/non-priced, emanating from any source as these are required to be placed in Parliament. Therefore, it is not faced with acquisition problems which others like the Department of Publication which compiles catalogue of Government of India Civil Publications and Central Reference Library, Calcutta, compiler of Indian National Bibliography (INB) face particularly in the case of unpublished documents.

It would not be unfair, if INB coverage is restricted to non-official documents and the bibliographical control of this material is taken up by Parliament Library.

Financial assistance should be provided to individuals/institutions who intend to take up documentation projects in this field. ICSSR, realising the importance of the work, provided financial assistance to the Indian Institute of Public Administration, New Delhi, for "Study of the publications, bibliographic and distribution mechanism of the State Governments and compilation of a select bibliography of State Governments publications". The Project Director, Shri Mohinder Singh, who has to his credit the publication *Government of India publications*, has brought out *State Governments publications in India, 1947-1982*, in two volumes, which is based on the above study.

Resource Centres

More resource centres in the form of Reference Centres/ Depository Centres/and Clearing House Centres are required for maximum utilisation of literature. Suggested Centres are:

National Reference Library for Government Documents

It should have the following activities:

i. Acquire one copy each of all the official documents (published/mimeographed).
ii. Provide facilities to bona-fide research scholars for consultation.
iii. Provide photo-copying facilities to the users. In case of out-of-prints, photocopy of the complete document may be provided.
iv. Get the old records converted into micro-form.
v. Compile machine-readable catalogue. The hard copies of it may be distributed among departmental libraries and other important resource centres.
vi. List of current additions may be circulated frequently.
vii. Provide computer search facilities for desired documents.

Departmental Reference Libraries

Each ministry/department should invariably have one library which should be designated as depository library for all its published and unpublished documents. The functions of these libraries should be similar to the National Reference Library but limited to the ministry's publications. Its additional responsibility would be to provide one copy each of the ministry's document to the National Reference Library.

Depository Centres

There are about 130 university libraries in India. In the initial stages all these libraries and those research institutes which are fully financed by the Government of India should be declared as depository libraries for government documents. After review of their functioning, more research libraries can be declared as depository centres. The maximum number by the end of the Eighth Five Year Plan should be around 500; in USA under the Depository Law of 1962, the maximum number of such libraries has been projected at 1,341.

NASSDOC-ICSSR took up depository activities by setting up Inter-Library Resources Centre in collaboration with Jawaharlal Nehru University in 1973. It invited libraries in Delhi to deposit on loan or gratis their less used serial material including government documents at this Centre. In this way it has collected a good number of government documents. However, faced with many hurdles, it has so far not fully succeeded in achieving its objectives.

Clearing House Centres

A large number of official documents are released every year. It is natural that it would not be possible for the libraries to keep permanently all the old files due to space problem as well as the diminishing utility of the material. But before the material is weeded out, by any library, a list of this may be sent to the Clearing House centre. A consolidated list with location sources the regularly circulated among the selected number of research libraries. Any library which requires a particular title(s) may contact the donor library. There should be 4-6 such clearing House Centres covering all the regions in the country.

NASSDOC initiated clearing house work through its Inter-Library Resources Centre. It asked libraries in Delhi to provide information about the material to be weeded out. Among the government departmental libraries, it received weeded out collection from the Department of Labour Library, Ministry of Finance Library, Ministry of Defence Library and Department of Publication. The availability of the material was intimated to the research institutes outside Delhi and on receipt of requests, the desired titles were despatched. The tempo of the activity, however, could not be sustained due to administrative problems. Nevertheless, the need for such activity put on a sound footing still remains.

Location Tools

The library catalogues and accession lists are important sources for locating the desired documents. Leaving aside those libraries, which bring out regularly accession lists, one has to go from one library to another for retrieving the official material. Union catalogues of official documents can make the search quite easier. NASSDOC-ICSSR took up a lead in this direction. It compiled Union Catalogue of serial Publications available in libraries throughout India, which also covered official documents of serial nature. Separate volumes for each state were compiled. For Delhi, two separate volumes covering Central Government and State Government Serial Publications available in the libraries were brought out. Rajeshwari Dutta has compiled "Union Catalogue of the Central Government of India publications held by libraries in London, Oxford and Cambridge". It covers serial and non-serial material. The catalogue for non-serial material are urgently required to be compiled in India. The proposed National Reference Library should take up this responsibility.

Research Facilities

The National Reference Library and Departmental Reference Libraries should be responsible for providing efficient information services like bibliographical, documentary, information retrieval, photo-copying, etc., to the non-official researchers.

Marketing of Publications

The marketing infrastructure can be a fully centralised, partially centralised or fully decentralised one. The centralised structure has been set up in Great Britain where H.M.S.O. is the sole agency for marketing of all official documents. Partially decentralised system is followed in the USA where Superintendent of Documents is the biggest agency for sale of publications, but distribution is also done (1) free by members of Congress,(2) free and by sale by the several executive agencies and (3) by sale by the Clearing House for Federal Scientific and Technical Information, Department of Commerce and (4) by the Photo Duplication Service, Publications Board Project of the Library of Congress.

In India we are broadly following the U.S. pattern. The Department of Publication is the main agency for publication and distribution of official documents along with other departmental and statutory agencies.

It is a matter of great consternation that though a large number of publications of research value are brought out by the Department of Publication and other agencies, only a few of them receive attention for review. The only possible reason can be that the review copies are not sent to the editors of academic journals and newspapers. Good review can attract more clientele. Publication agencies should think of distributing a good number of copies for this purpose. The reviews in the journals of library and information science would facilitate quick selection by the librarians.

Other measures which should be taken care of are:

i. There should be greater advertisement of selective titles in the leading newspapers and journals of India, quoting also from reviews, if any, appearing in the journals.
ii. More copies of catalogues be circulated among user institutions. The cumulated annual and quinquennial volumes should be brought out in time.
iii. Administrative and accounting procedures be streamlined to cut delays.
iv. The Controller of Publications should send one copy of all the documents to all the Depository Centres.
v. If possible, ISBN numbers in place of present identification number be given to the publications to keep in line with the in-

ternational practices.

vi. Pricing and marketing of government publications should follow a reasonable commercial pattern so that booksellers may take interest in supplying and selling the publications.

vii. Provide credit facilities to the research institutes.

viii. Arrangement may be made for reprinting the publications which are for a long time out of print but important.

Role of Universities and Organisations

Research organisations and universities can play an important role in the marketing of publications by acting as Sale and return Agents. ICCSR has encouraging experience about this. The Review Committee of ICSSR had recommended : "To overcome difficulties experienced by social scientists in obtaining government publications, ICSSR should prepare a monthly list of all government publications and send it out to universities and other research institutions." To implement this, a sales section was set up in NASSDOC in 1974 which started sending lists of selected titles of government documents collected from various official catalogues to the research institutions. It invited them to place orders for the desired listed items or for any other Central Government official document. Acting in the capacity of Sales and Return Agent of Department of Publication, it acquired material and supplied these to the research institutes. It got a very good response from the institutions. Similarly Publication Divisions of the Universities can shoulder the responsibility of meeting the demands of the clientele within their area. The commercial booksellers need profit motive to push up the sales, but no such motive is required for the research bodies.

CONCLUSION

The Controller of Publications holds the key to better supply of government documents. But, unless it improves its functioning by adopting scientific management techniques aided by modern information technology, spectacular progress cannot be expected. It is a pity that while stocks worth crores of rupees remain unsold with the Department those who need cannot procure them. Functioning of depository centres also depends upon quick supply of documents and dissemination of information about new releases by it. Research Organisations should, therefore, cooperate with the Publication Department in its efforts by creating more demand for its publications through extensive display at their centres and partaking in marketing activities. Extra efforts will be needed in keeping track of unpublished documents. There is every likelihood of their being lost after some time if not recorded at the appropriate time and place. The generation centres will have to extend their cooperation in this. A fruitful coordination is thus needed among those who generate, store, disseminate and use information. All efforts should be made to take jointly effective measures towards optimum utilisation of this important source of information. The main issues which require attention are:

i. Improvement in marketing techniques.
ii. Setting up of more resource centres like National Reference Library, Departmental Reference Libraries, Depository Centres and Clearing House Centres.
iii. Compilation of Local Union Catalogues of Government of India publications.
iv. Full Bibliographical Control through Parliament Library.

SEVEN

Document Supply System in Social Sciences: Delhi Libraries Experience

INTRODUCTION

The foremost objective of libraries is to provide documents demanded by scholars. It is not an easy task to cope with in the present conditions. This is because on the one hand there is a phenomenal increase in published and unpublished material, and on the other, increasing publishing costs have rendered libraries less and less self-sufficient. Developments in bibliographic sources are reflected in increased demand for access to documents. With all the efforts going into indexing, storage and retrieval of references, it will be utterly frustrating for both professionals and the users if the documents referred to cannot be obtained. Non-availability of a document, however, does not always mean that it is not physically available in a particular library or libraries but that it is not located on demand. We have, therefore, to devise ways and means to increase access to records and materials to two groups of people : librarians and users. Dr. Ranganathan emphasised this aspect of service when he said, "Every reader his book". It is, therefore, imperative that the information system as a whole should have a mechanism to ensure supply of a required document or a copy of it to the user. "Universal Availability of Publications" is now considered a necessary concomitant to "Universal Bibliographical Control of Publications". The aim of UAP is to provide a document in original or its copy in any form to the intending user in any part of the world.

Scope

The scope of the paper is to present a plan of document supply service for the capital city of Delhi, where a large cluster of libraries of different types exists. The experiment can also be followed in other metropolitan cities leading to a network of document supply centres in the country. Social sciences here include disciplines corresponding to the definition given by the *Encyclopaedia Britannica*, that social sciences "concern the disciplines that deal with human behaviour in its social and cultural aspects - economics, political science, sociology, social and cultural anthropology, social psychology and social and economic geography".

Organisational Models

The document supply service can be organised on the following models

(i) Centralised at a single institution with partial dependence on a small number of individual libraries.

(ii) Decentralised and spread over a large number of libraries but planned and coordinated and linked by location tools like union catalogue so as to achieve maximum coverage of source documents, and

(iii) Decentralised on several libraries without any access tool to each others' holdings.

All these models have been tried with varying degrees of success in different countries. To mention the activities of a few organisations will be relevant here.

United Kingdom

In the U.K. British Library Lending Division (BLLD) is an example of the first model. It has extensive acquisition programme which includes all significant periodicals regardless of language, all important worthwhile English language monographs and all available report literature. It supplements its own stock with a union catalogue of other libraries holdings and by cooperation with regional inter-lending organisations in the United Kingdom.

United States of America

In the USA (contrary to centralised practice in the U.K.) 300 networks, consortia and other cooperative library organisations, without any pre-planned central coordination, are engaged in document supply activity as their primary function. Some of the networks linked with union catalogue activity and supported by latest information technology, like Ohio College Library Centre (OCLC) Automated System, have facilitated interlending at reduced cost and greater speed of service. West Central Illinois Library Cooperative system works without centralised locational tool but is linked by a highly structured teletype transmission loop for the routing of request through central processing point in the Western Illinois University to the member libraries. An average of four to five days are taken in the delivery of a document. SUNY/OCLC (State University of New York/OCLC) is another network which provides fast and efficient State-wide delivery of inter-library loan material by using OCLC Inter-Loan Sub-System.

Union of Soviet Socialist Republics

In the USSR, Lenin State Library provides document supply service at national level. It also supplies copies of Soviet publications requested by other countries. Its stock includes Soviet publications collected under Legal Deposit Law and supported by periodical holdings catalogue. Since 1955, over 500 libraries have been contributing to the catalogue.

Federal Republic of Germany

Like the USA, document supply structure in FRG is decentralised but coordinated as a cooperative programme by the Deutsche Forschungs gemeinschaft which also provides financial assistance to the members to strengthen their stock. The system is based on identifying libraries specialising in specific subject disciplines like law, medicine, psychology, or particular form of publications like periodicals, official publications, newspapers, etc. Location tools available are seven Regional Union catalogues supplemented by Central Subject Catalogue (available also in microform). Berlin Periodicals Data Base and other union catalogue projects.

India

In our country, document supply is greatly confined to inter-library loan and supply of a photocopy of the desired document. The activity is taken up on an individual library level. There has so far been no organisational set-up at national or sub-national level to take up document supply as its primary activity, though location tools have been compiled in specific disciplines by various universities and documentation centres. In certain cities, sporadic efforts have been made to develop resource sharing activities to meet demands. The Indian National Scientific Documentation Centre (INSDOC) and the National Social Science Documentation Centre (NASSDOC) have taken up document supply service within their specialised disciplines at national level. *Insodoc* has been developing National Science Library to support the service. NASSDOC, to support document supply in periodical literature, has set up Inter-Library resources Centre (ILRC) in collaboration with Jawaharlal Nehru University. ILRC accepts as deposit/gratis from libraries in Delhi, serial material which is infrequently used but is important for research, i.e. Government reports, journals, newspapers, etc. The document supply system in Delhi generally works on "gentlemen's" understanding and few refuse to lend documents unless one is restricted for certain reasons.

In India organisational structure could be decentralised as in the USA and coordinated at national level forming part of national information network. The National Committee on Regional Library Cooperation in the U.K. suggested in its report on the future pattern of interlending "that the best pattern was for each to build on its special strengths and thus together provide a comprehensive service to the country. But for certain categories of material (e.g., serials, report literature, conference proceedings and official publications) concentration at national level is required to avoid wasteful and ineffective duplication".

For the present paper the above suggested model is chosen for structuring the Document Supply System in Social Sciences in Delhi. Interlending nodes could be identified in Delhi on the basis of subject specialisation and/or form of literature held by them.

LIBRARY SCENE IN DELHI

There are about 100 social science libraries in Delhi. These are attached to government departments, research institutes, universities, commercial enterprises, etc. Some illustrative examples with respective subject specialisation are : Economics -- Rattan Tata Library, National Council of Applied Economic Research, Indian Institute of Foreign Trade; Education -- National Council of Educational Research and Training, National Institute of Educational Planning and Administration and Central Institute of Education; History -- National Archives and Nehru Memorial Museum and Library; Labour -- Indian Labour Institute; Mass Communication -- Indian Institute of Mass Communication; Public Administration -- Indian Institute of Public Administration; Sociology -- Delhi School of Social Work. Delhi Public Library as deposit centre under law can play a great supporting role along with university and IIT libraries. For particular form of literature, NASSDOC can be a resource centre for Ph.D. theses, research project reports, and working papers and ILRC for serials. It can be safely assumed that these libraries between themselves, can fulfill at about 70 per cent needs of the scholars in Delhi. For the balance, other national resource centres in the country and outside can be contacted.

PREREQUISITE OF DOCSIS (DOCUMENT SUPPLY SYSTEM IN SOCIAL SCIENCES)

1. Government support and encouragement including formulation of a policy.
2. Adequate manpower and financial resources.
3. Computer and communication capabilities.
4. Reprography facilities.
5. Permanent organisation to ensure delivery of service.
6. Compilation of location tools like union catalogues.
7. Storage/Depository facilities for preserving materials less used in the libraries but important for research.
8. Carrier service to supply documents.
9. Coordinated acquisition policy to aim at availability of at least one copy of every worthwhile national publication in social sciences in the cooperative network.

SYSTEM DESIGN

The organisational structure of the system would consist of Central Loan Library, Specialised Material Delivery Centres and Discipline Oriented Centres. The system would be controlled by an Executive Committee and an Administrative Body with a small secretariat. Both of these will have members representing libraries and ministries/departments of Government of India.

Executive Committee

Its functions would be :

1. Formulation of a policy.
2. Formulation of plan of action.
3. Identifying bottlenecks and to take remedial measures.
4. Arranging necessary finances.
5. Maintaining liaison with government departments like Communications, Transport and Post and Telegraph for quick delivery of documents.

Administrative Committee

Its role would be :

i. To lay down rules for lending.
ii. To identify libraries for assigning responsibility of supplying documents within specific disciplines and to strengthen their resources accordingly.
iii. To fix charges for the service which may include micro-filming, photo-copying and documents delivery.
iv. To monitor the services from time to time and take corrective steps.
v. To frame rules for compiling union catalogues.

Central Loan Library

The functions of this library would be:

i. To coordinate the acquisition activities of other libraries vis-a-vis document supply service.

ii. To identify gaps in the overall collection and take necessary steps.
iii. To compile and keep updated union catalogues, preferably through computer.
iv. To create translation facilities for foreign and Indian regional language documents.
v. To provide micro-filming and reprographic facilities.
vi. To provide online access to computerised union catalogue data through terminals.
vii. To keep contact with national and international document delivery centres.
viii. To conduct surveys and sponsor seminars for improving the system.
ix. To acquire bibliographical tools to verify references for document supply.
x. To act as central point for interaction between the participating libraries.

Specialised Material Delivery Centres

Some libraries may be assigned responsibility to collect documents of special categories like theses, research project reports, working papers, newspapers, government documents, etc.

Discipline Oriented Libraries

These libraries would form the nucleus for document supply service in their disciplines and would shoulder major responsibility for its successful working.

WORKING INFRASTRUCTURE

We have a good number of document resource centres in Delhi and when properly coordinated in a network, with resource material duly identified, can provide a reasonable standard of service in document supply. For developing the system, the resources of the existing centres will have to be strengthened and new resource centres developed where necessary.

Executive and Administrative Committees Secretariat

The secretariat of the Executive and Administrative Committees may be set up in the Indian Council of Social Science Research (ICSSR). ICSSR is working at the national level for development of social science research and has taken up initiatives to support and develop a research information infrastructure.

Central Loan Library

The National Social Science Documentation Centre (NASSDOC) Library can act as Central Loan Library. Its resource material will be developed on cooperative acquisition concept. It will avoid duplication and fill up gaps where found. NASSDOC has good reprographic facilities and is already successfully providing photocopies of the documents to research scholars in the country and outside.

Specialised Research Material Centres

NASSDOC may be identified to develop specialised collections of Ph.D. theses, Research Project Reports and Working Papers.

a. *Theses Collection*: NASSDOC has already a running programme of acquiring Ph.D. theses approved by Indian universities and foreign theses on India on a token payment of Rs. 400 to the scholars. It has so far acquired 2,500 Ph.D. theses.
b. *Research Project Reports Collection*: ICSSR provides finances to research institutes and social scientists to conduct research in their fields. Consequently copies of the reports of aided research projects are received by NASSDOC as contractual obligation. It has, at present, a collection of about 1500 project reports. With additional manpower, it can collect reports from other research centres in the country. This material is particularly useful to our administrators and planners since it is relevant to the socio-economic development plans of the country.

Working Papers Collection

NASSDOC is building up a collection of working papers, which are useful as information source.

Government Documents Collection

Central Secretariat Library is a depository Centre for government documents. It is not only open to government employees but also to general public. Supported by resource material in Parliament Library and other departmental libraries, it can provide efficient service in government documents supply. Compilation of Union catalogue of Government Documents is, however, the foremost priority.

Periodical Literature

ILRC has succeeded in collecting 100,000 volumes of periodicals supplied by about 38 libraries in Delhi as deposit or gratis. It subscribes to most of the Indian social science research periodicals and a selective number of foreign periodicals. If the present resources are further strengthened, it can provide document supply service in periodical literature on the lines of BLLD. Union catalogue of periodicals, an essential element for the service has already been compiled, and with computerisation can be kept updated.

Newspaper Collection

National Archives of India Library and Nehru Memorial Museum and Library have a good collection of back files of old and new newspapers in hard copy and microform. NMML has brought out a catalogue of newspapers available in microform INASSDOC has also compiled a union catalogue of newspapers which records availability of 252 newspapers in 36 libraries and newspaper offices.

Discipline Oriented Libraries

Libraries rich in literature in specific disciplines can take up responsibility for supplying the documents in original or its photocopy within its specialised area. For this, it will be backed up by holdings of related discipline oriented libraries. They will fill the gaps where necessary and build up a core collection to meet their information needs. The resource material in such libraries as the Institute of Economic Growth, Indian Institute of Public Administration, Institute of Applied Research Manpower, National Council of Educational Research and Training, Rattan Tata Library, etc., will require to be further strengthened. Funds will have to be provided for additional manpower and equipment.

DOCUMENT DELIVERY

Rapid photo-copying facilities including facilities for making copies and enlarging microforms are an essential feature of Document Supply System. Developments in information technology and communication system have now made it possible to achieve this and deliver the same to the user in minimum time. Developed countries are now making use of electronic delivery systems. We, at present, cannot think of adopting such highly developed technology for this purpose. However, the minimum equipment we will require for the system would consist of carrier vans, telex and computer system (for central loan library only), telephones, photocopiers, microfilm/microficshe reader-cum-printer and computer terminals for participating libraries. In the long run, new technology will be gradually introduced to provide a faster service while taking into consideration the user requirements for speed and his willingness to bear the cost.

NETWORK MEMBERS

Successful inter-library lending depends on ready cooperation between libraries. Networks for this activity should restrict the number at first to libraries which have major collections and are willing to participate. Therefore, to begin with, 30 libraries in the city may be selected for the network. The holding data of these selected libraries, fully computerised at the Central Loan Library, will help in locating the desired document. Besides mutual contact, the central node will coordinate delivery schedules through its own carrier service. Efforts may be made to allow members of one library to avail loan facilities in other libraries in the network. This will reduce burden on inter-library loan system. After evaluating its working, more libraries may be allowed to join.

BARRIERS IN PROGRAMME OPERATION

i. Copyright laws.
ii. Restrictive condition on providing a certain category of material on loan to others.
iii. Greater burden on some selective libraries deterring them to part with their material.
iv. Weak resource collection of libraries.
v. Lack of sufficient manpower resources resulting in delay in locating and retrieving material speedily.
vi. Lack of proper equipment.
vii. Attitude of professional staff who tend to consider inter-lending an extra and unnecessary burden.

MONITORING AND EVALUATION OF THE SYSTEM

The following points may be taken into consideration while evaluating the performance:

1. The documents must be available.
2. Requests must be transmitted quickly.
3. Documents must be transmitted quickly.
4. Accounting must be simple.
5. Procedure and forms must be simple and standardised.
6. System in the long run should be self-supporting.
7. Running cost per document supply should be minimum.
8. Contribute to the maximum to Universal availability of Publications programmes/projects.

CONCLUSION

No matter how elegant an information system we may devise, its most important function will always be getting the information to the user. Document delivery is thus of prime importance.

To justify our professional existence, immediate concrete steps are needed towards setting up a suitable administrative structure with an appropriate fiscal foundation. A permanent organisation to ensure delivery of service is essential. Library cooperation is a difficult undertaking and, according to Evans, "requires a certain type of leadership, which can get results by persuasion and example rather than by demand and fiat. It requires careful participatory planning by those it will effect. It requires patience, understanding and faith on the part of administrators and legislators". Professional organisations at national and regional level like AGLIS, DLA, ILA, IASLIC and also professionals in the field will also have to face patiently the difficulties involved in the venture. Union catalogues in the missing areas will [illegible] be compiled. Catalogues already compiled [illegible] require to be [illegible]ted. We may start with manual procedures, but [illegible] complete mechanisation in the long run. The professionals attitude and involvement will, however, play a decisive role in the success of the experiment.

SECTION FOUR

HUMAN RESOURCE DEVELOPMENT

EIGHT

Information and Library Professionals in India

INTRODUCTION

Information is now regarded as a vital national resource to be developed and made available to all those who need it. It is increasingly being realised that development of capability in information handling and dissemination would help a country in knowledge advancement, understanding, decision-making, technology transfer, minimising duplication of efforts, conservation of resources, etc. The idea is gaining ground that the social and economic system of a country would function more efficiently, if availability of reliable information is ensured at the right time. Information, an intellectual resource as well as most valuable of all resources, is becoming the essential basis for the maintenance of modern society at whatever stage of development it may be. Most countries recognise today that better information services help to achieve a progressive society. They have, therefore, started examining the need for systematic planning of their present information infrastructure so as to utilise fully the information accumulated at the national level and to be able to participate in and benefit from existing and future world information systems in various fields of activity.

In India, information systems, services and facilities are being built up at various levels. It becomes necessary to work towards a general plan in agreement with all the principal information agencies so as to ensure that the world's specialised and professional knowledge is fully and properly used in guiding social evolution. The government, on its part, should be aware of the need for integrating the elements of information infrastructure in the overall development plans. The basic plan of action is to build an information network on the existing infrastructure by coordinating the present activities, articulating the various services, developing their strong points, encouraging private and public initiatives and filling in existing gaps.

India has made appreciable progress in the development of information facilities. The Government's support and assistance in building up information capability are quite evident. In the field of science and technology, the National Information System for Science and Technology (NISSAT) has already been ushered in. A National Informatics Centre has also been developed to handle data required for planning and decision-making by the government agencies. The medical and agricultural information systems are also being contemplated. Social sciences research in India has gained momentum after the establishment of the Indian Council of Social Science Research (ICSSR). It is a happy augury that ICSSR, even in its first year of establishment, had thought it appropriate to set up a National Social Science Documentation Centre (NASSDOC) to support the research and developmental efforts in social sciences. Later on the Council also established a Social Science Data Archives. NASSDOC has now successfully completed its developmental phase and is poised to step up its activities and to take up new programmes. Along side with the further development of NASSDOC, efforts have to be made to conceive of a National Information System in Social Sciences (NISS). In the field of social science, a number of libraries and information centres with differing functions, scope and efficiency have come into being under the auspices of academic institutions, research institutions, government departments, etc. In a stage of development, they have sprung up piecemeal without liaison between them, without plan and without cooperation. It is necessary at this stage, therefore, to coordinate or marshal such a large number of subsets of information services into a well-structured national information system or network. The impetus for an information network arises out of economic and time pressures which force organisations to share rather than duplicate information resources and facilities. The national system is not something new. It would be based on existing information facilities. It would make full use of the information potential of the country by coordinating the activities and by seeking the cooperation of individual information centres, according to well-defined guidelines and division of responsibilities. It may fill the existing lacunae in information services by establishing new ones. It may develop and apply compatible national standards for information techniques and methods to facilitate interchange of information and also introduce modern methods of information handling.

Guidelines in Planning

In developing a national system, it becomes necessary to work towards a general plan, in agreement with main information agencies, indicating the allocation of responsibility and the means it intends to employ such as specialised services, incentives, coordinating machinery, financial arrangements, etc. A framework reflecting the needs of all sectors of national endeavours is necessary to guide the establishment of a national information system.

The Social Scientists as well as Information Scientists are increasingly aware of the importance of the Data Archives services and that of Documentation services supported by Data Archives. Therefore, steps have to be taken to set up separate Data Archives Units. What, therefore, follows applies equally to Documentation services and Data Archives services as an integral part of Information services. The structure of a National Social Sciences Information System, quite obviously, will have the following main components:

1. Documentation and Library Services
2. Data Archives Services

To be effective, both these services are required to develop somewhat simultaneously in the vertical as well as horizontal planes.

In the matter of information resource development, guidelines are required with reference to (a) allocation of responsibilities to institutions for building up strong collections in special fields, (b) ensuring that there is in the country at least one accessible copy of every worthwhile publication for use by scholars, (c) provision of a national lending library service, (d) establishment of a data bank for socio-economic data (e) preparation of national union catalogues of holdings of libraries, and (f) establishment of regional dormitories for storing older, but important for research, material weeded out by service libraries.

As regards information users, the guidelines should cover (a) identifying the present and potential users of information and assessing their requirements, (b) creation of information consciousness among users, and (c) organising programmes for training of users of information.

The guidelines for offering information service should include (a) development of necessary tools, techniques and services adequate to meet users' needs and demands, as these change from time to time at different levels, (b) establishment of subject-oriented information grids, (c) establishment of referral services, (d) provision of translation facilities, and (f) provision of adequate computer facilities for information retrieval.

The guidelines with reference to manpower development cover (a) building up of expertise and provision for education and training for an adequate number of professional personnel, (b) supporting projects in information fields, (c) supporting research programmes, (d) sponsoring conferences, symposia, seminars, workshops, etc., and (e) securing adequate service conditions and status for library and information science personnel.

There should also be guidelines regarding cooperation with other national and international organisations engaged in information and/or related type of services.

Objectives

The objectives of NISSS may be stated in general terms as follows:

1. To facilitate the selection, processing and communication of ideas from the point of generation and availability to their potential users at all levels.

2. To ensure that the information made available is precise, exhaustive and accessible with a minimum delay, presented in a manner convenient to the users and services provided at a reasonable cost;
3. To promote the development and use of efficient tools and techniques of information handling; and
4. To make optimum utilisation of existing information systems and services and development of new ones.

Prerequisites

The following are some essential prerequisites for development of NISSS:

1. Government support and encouragement including formulation of policy for information;
2. Adequate manpower resources and potential for training manpower;
3. Information resources and facilities (libraries, specialised-documentation and information centres);
4. Publication capabilities;
5. Computer and communication capabilities;
6. Reprography facilities;
7. Good organisational machinery; and
8. Standardisation in materials, techniques and patterns of service.

STATUS OF SOCIAL SCIENCE RESEARCH IN INDIA

Social sciences as disciplines of study and research have already made recognizable developments since independence in this country. They are already being taken notice of as a resource by the government and other public and private organisations in promoting economic development and social change in this country. They have shown the capacity to grow and expand in terms of centres of teaching and research, manpower and professional organisations.

Although as compared to teaching and research in natural and applied sciences, social sciences have lagged behind in progress and financial support, their achievements and development during the past three decades are really encouraging. An idea about the present status of the social sciences in the country can be obtained from a number of indicators, i.e., number of post-graduate departments; number of doctoral theses; number of students registered for Ph.D.; number of professional institutions; volume of publications; social science manpower etc. Although up to date statistics about these indicators are not easily available, yet on the basis of the available information it can be pointed out that the number of post-graduate departments in social sciences in the universities and in the affiliated colleges is about 850; the number of students enrolled for the Master's degree in the various social sciences subjects is about 45,000 and the number of Ph.D. students around 2,300. Percentage-wise it may be relevant to mention that the total enrolment of students for the post-graduate work in social science disciplines is about 40 per cent of the total enrolment in the universities and colleges and the number of students registered for Ph.D. is around 25 per cent of the total registrations.

In addition to the Universities, there are about 1,000 institutions (including professional associations) engaged in research, teaching, training and counselling work in social sciences. These institutions are financed by the government and/or various private and public agencies.

As regards the social science manpower in the universities, it may be mentioned that the number of teachers of different categories in university departments and university colleges is about 2,500 already. In addition to this number, there is a substantial number of (more than 7,000) in the affiliated colleges. At the same time, technical institutions in various subjects such as engineering, medicine, agriculture, etc., have a substantial number of social scientists doing teaching and research work.,

With this increase in the teaching and research activities in social sciences as well as in the manpower potential, the need for research journals has already been felt in different subjects under social sciences and it is estimated that about 1,000 research journals are already being published in the country. In addition to the articles in these journals a large quantity of research material is being published in the country in the form of books, survey reports, seminars/conferences/workshops proceedings, etc.

It would be relevant to mention here that in addition to the increase in the quantity of the documents in social sciences, a significant change has also taken place in the structure of the subjects in social sciences because of inter-disciplinary and multi-disciplinary research in these fields. This research in social sciences has received considerable support from the Planning Commission which set up a Research Programmes Committee to fund plan-relevant research proposals submitted by research scholars. These research scholars get funds from various other organisations as well, like the Indian Council of Social Science Research, Indian Council of Historical Research, Indian Council of Philosophical Research and University Grants Commission, etc.

All these developments in the teaching and research activities in social sciences have made it essential that the information being generated through these activities is not only published properly but also stored and disseminated in the best possible manner so as to make this information resource really meaningful and productive. For that purpose a national information policy as well as network is much desired in the country.

DEVELOPMENT OF FACILITIES IN INDIA FOR DISSEMINATION OF INFORMATION

Historical Background

Parallel to the establishment and development of the Indian National Scientific Documentation Centre (1952), there has been considerable interest among professional circles for the idea of establishing a similar centre in the social sciences. This idea gained further attention after the establishment of the Unesco Research Centre in Social Sciences in India.

For the first time, professional opinion was expressed at the national level on the occasion of the Library seminar on research in the Social Sciences held under the joint auspices of the Indian School of International Studies and the Indian Council of World Affairs in 1959. The Seminar recommended the establishment of the Indian National Documentation Centre for Social sciences for promoting documentation services in the country. This initiative was carried forward next year at the Seminar on Bibliographical Organisation and Control in India held under the auspices of the Indian Library association in Calcutta in 1960. This Seminar laid stress on coordinating and supplementing the activities and programmes of various subject specialised centres by the proposed documentation centre. About 13 agencies were enumerated which were to take care of documentation in their respective fields of specialisation. It was thus for the first time the idea of sectoral information system was mooted but only implicitly. The plan for establishing a Social Science Documentation Centre almost became an annual affair, in the sense that the issue cropped up practically at every annual gathering of Librarians after 1960. The IASLIC Seminar held at Lucknow in 1964 took up the matter afresh by requesting the Central Government to take appropriate steps for the establishment of a Documentation Centre for Social Science. It was also suggested that a survey of existing documentation services in India be conducted. While the Calcutta Seminar favoured decentralisation, the Lucknow Seminar preferred centralisation for all practical purposes. The IASLIC Conference held in Trivandrum in 1965 did not favour centralisation. The Conference appointed a sub-committee for making recommendations to the Planning Commission before March 31, 1966, for their incorporation in the national plan.

The whole question came up again for a complete review on the occasion of the Seminar on Social Science Research and Library Development in India held in 1967 under the joint auspices of the Indian School of International Studies and the Indian Council of World Affairs. The Seminar considered very comprehensively the whole question and urged the establishment of a National Documentation Centre, with a provision that a number of other institutions were to be financially assisted under the national plan. The Seminar was of the view that the establishment of the Documentation Centre should be linked to a National Library of Social Sciences. The Seminar was thus a step forward to recognise the principles of viewing national resources and documentation services holistically.

The national debate that went on for a long time proved to be extremely useful and this finally led to the establishment of NASSDOC by ICSSR in 1969. The establishment of NASSDOC has been the most significant development in the information field. NASSDOC has launched several programmes and is now firmly established. ICSSR Regional Centres in cooperation with several universities as a decentralised activity were also established. NASSDOC has indeed provided a good foundation of building up NISSS.

Existing facilities in India for Dissemination of Information in Social Sciences

At the initiative of some libraries and institutions, it has been possible to develop indexing and abstracting services of the current literature in the field of social sciences. Perhaps there is need for a critical review now about the adequacies or otherwise of all these tools and services. That will help to improve the usefulness of these services to the social scientists, researchers, decision makers and managers. Some of the important indexing and abstracting services are :

1. *Accessions list - South Asia* (Library of Congress Office, Delhi).
2. *Annotated Bibliography on the Economic History of India*, 1500-1947 (Gokhale Institute of Politics and Economics, Pune, and ICSSR, New Delhi).
3. *Asian Social Science Bibliography* (Institute of Economic Growth, New Delhi). Presently suspended.
4. *Documentation on Asia* (Indian Council of World Affairs, New Delhi). Presently suspended.
5. *Documentation of Public Administration* (Indian Institute of Public Administration, New Delhi).
6. *Guide to Indian Periodical Literature* (Indian Documentation Service, Gurgaon).
7. *ICSSR Journal of Abstracts and reviews : Economics*.
8. *ICSSR Journal of Abstracts and Reviews : Geography*.
9. *ICSSR Journal of Abstracts and Reviews : Political Science*.
10. *ICSSR Journal of Abstracts and Reviews : Sociology, Social Anthropology*.
11. *ICSSR Research Abstracts Quarterly*.
12. *Index of Articles on Agricultural Economics* (computerised) (Indian Society of Agricultural Economics).
13. *Index India* (Rajasthan University Library, Jaipur).
14. *Index to Indian Economic Journals* (Calcutta).
15. *Indian Dissertation Abstracts* (ICSSR, New Delhi).

16. *Indian Press Index* (Delhi Library Association).
17. *Indian Psychological Abstracts* (ICSSR, New Delhi).
18. *Retrospective Cumulative Index of Indian Social Science Periodicals* (NASSDOC, New Delhi). In process.
19. *Samajik Vigyan Samachar* (NASSDOC, New Delhi) Social Science News (NASSDOC, New Delhi).
20. *Urban Documentation* (National Institute of Urban Affairs, New Delhi).

Many government and academic/research libraries are also bringing out their local documentation lists providing current awareness services primarily to their own clientele based on literature received by them individually.

SYSTEM DESIGN

Structure

The NISSS would be a multi-tier system. The main components are:

1. The NISSS Focal Point in NASSDOC.
2. The NISSS Network of Information Centres and Services.

NISSS Focal Point

The NISSS Focal Point would be advised and guided by an Advisory Committee. Under this, there will be an executive committee for overseeing and implementing the programmes and recommendations of the Advisory Committee. It would also be responsible for day-to-day decisions within the framework of the approved scheme. There will also be a number of ad hoc working groups and expert groups. These groups would be constituted by the Advisory Committee for carrying out special studies, surveys, preparation of reports, criteria, guidelines, standards, formats, etc.

A small secretariat would be set up to carry out the work of the NISSS Focal Point and to give support to the work of various committees and groups. In addition to a chief executive, there will be divisional heads for dealing with programmes, planning and policy and systems as well as specialists to look after different aspects of the schemes.

The functions of the NISSS Focal Point are:

1. Formulating of a policy for NISSS.
2. Formulating of plan of action.
3. Establishing mechanisms of implementing the policy and plans.
4. Allocating finances for various programmes.
5. Coordination of activities with national and international organisations.
6. Formulation of criteria, guidelines and standards.
7. Promoting and supporting research and development.
8. Promoting education and training programmes in information field and user education.
9. Monitoring and evaluation of the performance of the system.
10. Acting as a point of interaction with world information services, systems and programmes.

NISSS Network

The NISSS network would comprise:

1. National Centres of Information
2. Regional Centres of Information.
3. Sectoral System.
4. Other Specialised Services.

As stated earlier, in developing the system, the main consideration would be to make the maximum use of existing information resources and facilities. Wherever necessary, the existing centres would be upgraded by augmenting the infrastructure. Gaps in provision of information services, if any, would be identified and efforts will be made to fill them up.

National Centres of Information

The national centres would be responsible for conducting, organising and providing information at national level in an overall manner in the field of social sciences. They are mission-oriented information centres and would take care of mostly residual services not covered by the sectoral system. The following centres would constitute the national centres of information in the field of social sciences.

1. National Social Science Documentation Centre (Existing) (NASSDOC).
2. National Social Science Library (Proposed) (NSSL).
3. National Social Science Data Archives (Existing) (ICSSR Data Archives).

NASSDOC

NASSDOC has been in existence since 1970. It is now firmly established. It has been undertaking several major projects either directly or in collaboration with some selected institutions. It had also promoted implementation of many projects under its grant-in-aid scheme. Under the NISSS scheme the activities of NASSDOC would be stepped up several fold. The following programmes are mentioned in this connection.

1. Bringing out current awareness service on Indian social science literature as an indexing or abstracting service.
2. Bringing out current awareness service on selected social science foreign literature in fields which cover many sectors or where no sectoral information centre exists.
3. Bringing out state-of-the-art reports on selected subjects.
4. Centralised acquisition of commercially available foreign machine-readable bibliographic data bases and offering SDI and retrospective search services.
5. Creating data bases for socio-economic information and organising dissemination service therefrom.
6. Establishing of on-going research information service.
7. Developing of access tools such as directory of periodicals, research institutions, societies, specialists, information sources and facilities, etc., in the field of social sciences.
8. Offering referral services and answering technical enquiries.
9. Undertaking literature search and compilation of bibliographies against specific requests and in anticipation.

10. Procuring copies of documents, on request, from whichever source available.
11. Providing translation service from foreign as well as Indian regional languages.
12. Providing reprographic facilities for copying documents and distributing information.
13. Undertaking periodical surveys for assessing information needs and uses in the country.
14. Organising programmes for creation of information consciousness among users.
15. Organising user training programmes.
16. Organising training facilities in information science with special emphasis on social sciences.
17. Carrying out and supporting research in social science information.
18. Providing advisory services to other information centres in social sciences.
19. Developing relations and cooperation with national and international organisations engaged in social science information.

National Social Science Library (NSSL)

The development of NSSL is closely linked to the programme and activities of NASSDOC. It will be developed initially by the NASSDOC as an institutional project and later on it will become a separate institution. NSSL will be based on the cooperative acquisition concept. It will not duplicate material already available in the country. It will endeavour to supplement the national collection by way of filling up gaps. It will survey the information resources already available in the country and identify gaps in order to assume responsibility for filling them up. This concept would mean that as far as possible the materials will be located in actual places of use and this material should be bibliographically controlled through union catalogue to make it available to any user wherever he may be. The ultimate aim would be that NSSL and the other service libraries in social sciences will together ensure that at least one copy of everything worthwhile being published throughout the world in the field of social science will be available within the country, no matter where it will be kept, for use by scholars at all times to come. The main responsibilities of NSSL are:

1. To build a comprehensive world collection of social science material by way of supplementing the national collections.
2. To maintain a good collection of reference publications in the field of social sciences to enable carrying out of the bibliographical tasks.
3. To maintain a comprehensive collection of Indian material in social sciences including theses, government publications, reports, etc.
4. To offer consultation, reference and inter-library loan service as well as reprography services.
5. To maintain up-to-date national union catalogue of social science material in machine-readable form for promoting use of material as well as for following cooperative acquisition policy.
6. To maintain dormitories for storing older research material weeded out by service libraries.

Regional System

ICSSR has already established Regional Centres at Bombay, Calcutta, Chandigarh, Hyderabad, New Delhi and Shillong (see Appendix). These regional centres are assigned the responsibility of building up basic reference collection in social sciences not already available at the universities with which these centres are associated.

Under the new programme envisaged for the future, the role and functions of the regional centres would be modified considerably. The present regional centres are located in cities which have a heavy concentration of research libraries in social sciences and are well stocked with scholarly material. They are also attached to established universities. These regional centres also cover the various regions of the country adequately. They should be made use of essentially for utilising the literature resources available in the country for the benefit of the entire scholarly community. The main objectives of the regional centres are :

1. To survey the information resources of the region and to organise their mobilisation for meeting the information demands of the region.

2. To establish, maintain, update and publish regional union catalogue of literature resources.
3. To establish a strong reprographic unit and to serve the region with reprographic copies of information sources.
4. To procure, on request, documents within and outside the region.
5. To build and maintain a good collection of reference material for the benefit of scholars.
6. To collect and build a good collection of social science literature in the regional languages.
7. To provide a referral service to the users in the region.

Thus the regional centres would be set up, funded and administrated directly under the NISSS scheme. They will have separate physical facilities of their own, though housed in a university campus. They will be equipped with a good range of reprography equipment. They will be provided with vehicles for the purpose of inter-library borrowings. In a vast country like India, where the literature resources are widely scattered, the regional centres will be of help in mobilising the resources for the benefit of the entire scholarly community. In this manner, the development of information resources can be decentralised. While the collections, as far as possible, will be kept in actual places of use, they will be at the same time made accessible to any user in the country, through the document supply service of the regional centres.

Sectoral Information System

The sectoral system is the vital link in NISSS. Sectoral centres are discipline-or mission-oriented. They would be developed from the most suitable research institution in the discipline/mission concerned, which has already developed a strong information base. The facilities of the local unit would be augmented and it would be upgraded to provide service on a national scale. These sectoral centres would provide specialised services with a good amount of subject competence. They will be manned mostly by subject specialists trained in information work. Their services are expected to play an essential role in the flow of information by maintaining close touch with current research and practice and by keeping in close association with the users. They would select, evaluate and synthesise information in well-defined special fields, and/or in areas pertinent to scientific disciplines/missions and present it in a form best suited to the needs of users.

The sectoral system would consist of the leading centres chosen for the purpose as well as all other information centres, belonging to discipline/mission. They will together form a grid of their own and will take care of development of information resources as well as services in a holistic manner. The sectoral Information system is to provide the following services :

1. Specialised current indexing and abstracting services including SDI.;
2. Subject bibliographies.
3. Subject union catalogues.
4. Information retrieval.
5. Collection and dissemination of technical and socio-economic information.
6. Translation and document supply.
7. Preparation of surveys, state-of-the-art reports, forecasting reports, techno-economic and management information.

In addition, the sectoral centres would build up and maintain a document collection supplementing those of the institutions in the sector. They would coordinate the information services within the sector. They may offer advisory service and assistance to the local information units. They would build up data banks relevant to their scope and activity. They would envisage developing computer based information services for the sector in cooperation with national information centres and ensuring national and international compatibility. They would develop relations and maintain cooperation with foreign information centres, research institutions, professional bodies, etc., for evolving exchange of information.

The sectoral centres would be developed in major areas of national relevance and priority. At least eight centres could be developed during the Eighth Plan period. They will contribute a great deal towards building up the information infrastructure in the country in the fields of social sciences.

As mentioned earlier, the lowest level of information centres, called local information units, would operate in research institutions, academic institutions, government agencies, industrial enterprises, etc. They are expected to offer personalised services to users in their parent institutions. They belong to the sectoral system relating to their area of specialisation. They are responsible for feeding information generated by their institutions to the sectoral centres.

MAJOR THRUST AND ACTIVITIES

The ultimate aim of NISSS is to develop the national information infrastructure in so far as social sciences are concerned, for supporting research and scholarly pursuits. Towards this aim, certain major activities and services will be given a thrust.

Information Needs and Uses

Survey of information needs and uses as well as the resources available would be undertaken at national, regional, sectoral and institutional levels so that the functioning of the different tiers of NISSS network could be planned in relation to actual needs and uses and that adequate resources and facilities could be built for meeting them.

Information Resources Development

A policy for coordinating the acquisition of documents and their distribution among different libraries would be followed in order that libraries do not have an unnecessary stock, that there is no undue duplication of material among libraries and that the available book purchase fund of the country is made optimum use of for acquiring maximum number of titles. The acquisition policies and profiles of each institution would be clearly defined and coordinated within the sector, region and at national level. The coordination may include mutually agreed upon acquisition profiles of institutions and subscription to periodicals and serials.

In the matter of information resources development, a programme of decentralisation would be followed. Most important material would be available in the institutional libraries, that is, in the actual place of use. The sectoral centre would supplement the acquisition of individual institutions coming under its purview so as to ensure availability of an exhaustive collection in the area of the sector. The regional centre would maintain a general reference library, collect and hold theses and dissertations prepared in the region, maintain a depository of publications of regional languages and act as a dormitory for housing older research material weeded out by service libraries. NSSL would build up a national collection by complementing the local, sectoral and regional collections. There are many residual areas to be taken care of by NSSL.

In the matter of building up the national collection, the goal would be that NSSL, regional centres, sectoral centres and individual libraries taken together would ensure that at least one accessible copy is made available within the country, no matter where it is kept, for use by scholars at all times.

Union Catalogue

Setting up a decentralised network of collection building means that the constituent libraries must use common techniques for processing the collections and that there should be a union catalogue for the purpose of interconnection and for readily locating the documents in the libraries. Besides serving as a location tool, union catalogues help in revealing strong and weak areas in the national collection for the purpose of continuing the acquisition programme.

NASSDOC has already taken up the union catalogue work and achieved good progress. This programme will be stepped up. Efforts would be made to store the information in machine-readable form and establish a mechanism for constant updating. In addition to the total national union catalogue, compilation of regional union catalogues and subject union catalogues would be attempted.

Data Banks

Data Archives, NASSDOC and the sectoral centres would build up data/information bank relevant to their activities. The data bank will cover R&D activities, completed and ongoing projects, status of R&D abroad and country profiles, management information, manpower, techno-economic information, statistical data, etc. The sectoral centres would set up discipline-oriented data banks. They will select useful information, analyse it with user interests and store it in conventional or machine-readable form.

Current Awareness Service

Indian Literature

NASSDOC would attempt to bring out Indian Social Science Abstracts to provide not only bibliographical control of domestic output but also to act as a feeder for coverage of Indian literature by major international abstracting and indexing services. The sectoral centres would take care of the bibliographical control of unpublished literature.

Foreign Literature

Though in all major disciplines and branches of knowledge, international abstracting and indexing services are available, it would be desirable to prepare selective current awareness services with focus on the progress of work in the country. It would be the responsibility of sectoral centres to offer such selective current awareness services.

SDI Services

Indexing and abstracting services are now increasingly available in computer-prepared magnetic tapes. There are several such services available in social science fields also. But as they are costly, the acquisition of such tape services would be initially centralised at NASSDOC, which in turn would generate and offer services for SDI as well as for retrospective search. It may be possible for sectoral centres to obtain group profiles relating to the field of interest and, in turn select, evaluate and synthesise information for transferring it to the users. The SDI service provides information which, as closely as possible, meets the interest profile of the user. Sectoral centres can supply widely scattered users with the new knowledge they need to keep abreast with. They also constitute a means of making information conscious potential users, who had been unaware of its importance. SDI services are offered better using a computer for which expertise in software and hardware capabilities exists in the country.

Information Analysis, State-of-the-Art Reports, Surveys, Forecasts

Users today require carefully selected data and digested information which could be straightaway applied and assimilated. Information has to be analysed, synthesised and evaluated, keeping in view the interests of the users and served promptly. The users may not be satisfied with raw data and mere bibliographic citations. They may want the actual information for direct application. For this purpose, the source documents have to be analysed, pertinent information culled out, evaluated and served. This type of work is known as Information Analysis and the sectoral centres are expected to offer this service. Reviews, state-of-the-art reports, surveys, forecasts, etc., are products of information analysis.

Referral Service

Those who are in need of information should be able to know which source should give them the precise information and whom to consult for the purpose. A referral service who is doing what, where to get what, etc., should be set up to direct the inquirers to the sources of information for the purpose of establishing contact directly. The referral service should be organised at the national and sectoral levels.

Promoting Use of Information

Information ought to have its market so as to derive its fullest benefits. There is a need to create and step up demand for information. Ways and means have to be found to make potential users information-conscious. Programmes like organising group discussions, demonstrations, seminars, etc., will have to be taken up.

Proper facilities for training in the use of information have to be organised. The training will help to improve the users' attitude to information and would promote use of information.

Manpower Development

Proper training facilities specially oriented to social science information should be organised in order to take care of the manpower requirement of developing NISSS. This would be by way of supplementing the existing facilities and with particular emphasis to social sciences. Regular courses, short-term courses, refresher courses, in-service training, etc., should be available for meeting various requirements.

Provision should also be made for carrying out research in social science information. Organising symposia, seminars, workshops, etc., should also be taken care of by NISSS to enable the information scientists to share and exchange their experiences.

Budget and Strategy

The total outlay (capital and recurring) for development of NISSS over a period of five years is estimated at Rs. 5.43 crores, as given in the enclosed statement. This includes provision for the NISSS Secretariat, strengthening of NASSDOC establishment of NSSL, setting up of six regional centres, and eight sectoral centres and carrying out some centralised services. The estimates have been based on the analogy of the science and technology information system but for development on a reduced scale. For example, the non-Plan budget of INSDOC is now about Rs. 50 lakhs and only half of this input is proposed for stepping up the activities of NASSDOC. The National Science Library is being planned to be established at an estimated cost of Rs. 125 lakhs whereas an investment of Rs. 60 lakhs is proposed for NSSL. Under the NISSAT Scheme, each regional centre would be provided with about Rs. 25 lakhs in a period of five years. In the NISSS Scheme, about half of the amount is proposed for developing the regional centres. Similar is also the case with the sectoral centres. If we compare the existing level of investment in the science and technology information system, it would be seen that the proposed investment for NISS is not only realistic but also modest.

SUMMARY

The Ministry of Human Resource Development, through ICSSR-NASSDOC should be responsible for the NISSS scheme. The ICSSR-NASSDOC should be invested with appropriate powers to coordinate the information activities in social sciences. It should also be provided with adequate funds. The nucleus of developing NISSS would be the existing resources and facilities available in a number of organisations and institutions, universities, government departments, etc. The functioning of the system would be at several levels, viz., national centres, regional centres, sectoral centres and local information units. Active participation of all the constituent institutions is a *sine-qua-non* for achieving an integrated National Information System for Social Sciences. This national system will enable research workers, scholars, academicians, management personnel, etc., to have access to information economically, efficiently and expeditiously.

Broad Indication of the Financial Outlay of NISSS

(in lakhs of Rs.)

	I Year	II Year	III Year	IV Year	V Year	Total
National Focal Point NISS Secretariat	1.000	1.500	2.000	2.500	3.000	10.000
National Centres						
NASSDOC	25.000	28.000	30.000	32.000	35.000	150.000
NSSL	15.000	15.000	10.000	10.000	10.000	60.000
Regional Centres						
6 Centres (2 in I Year; 2 in II Year; 2 in III Year)	8.000	16.000	22.000	18.000	14.000	78.000
Sectoral Centres						
8 Centres (3 in I Year; 2 in II Year; 2 in III Year; 1 in IV Year)	15.000	40.000	45.000	50.000	45.000	195.000
Centralised Services	5.000	8.000	10.000	12.000	15.000	50.00
Total	69.000	108.500	119.000	124.500	122.00	543.000

[Based on Draft report submitted to ICSSR,]

APPENDIX

ICSSR Regional Centres

1. ICSSR Eastern Regional Centre
   10, Jadunath Sarkar Road
   Calcutta (West Bengal) 700 029 Phones: 466472; 467958
2. ICSSR North-Eastern Regional Centre
   NEHU Library Building, Mayurbhanj House
   Shillong - 793 003, Phone: 3941
3. ICSSR Northern Regional Centre
   Jawaharlal Nehru University
   New Delhi - 110 067 Phone: 387343
4. ICSSR North-Western Regional Centre
   Punjab University Library Building
   Chandigarh - 160 014; Phones: 25023; 29582
5. ICSSR Southern Regional Centre
   Osmania University Library
   Hyderabad (Andhra Pradesh) - 500 007, Phone: 71756
6. ICSSR Western Regional Centre
   Vidya Nagari, Kaling,
   Bombay (Maharashtra) - 400 098, Phones: 554943; 532241

NINE

Library and Information Science Education in India: Achievements and Perspectives

Information as a resource has become a key factory in the socio-economic development of the countries and the degree of its effective utilisation distinguishes the highly developed societies of the world from those that are still developing.

Development is a very complex and multi-dimensional process involving information and knowledge inputs of scientific and technological research and their applications, dovetailed with other societal information such as political, economic, demographic, health, etc. The developing countries have to accept this fact. The earlier these countries, individually and in unison, make effort to plan for optimum utilisation of this important resource, the sooner they would achieve their long-cherished objectives of removing poverty and illiteracy as also of developing self-reliant economy.

Regional Asia-Pacific Information Network in Social Sciences (APINESS) launched on 12–16 May 1986, is laudable as it would facilitate exchange of experiences and sharing of resources and facilities for tackling socio-economic issues which are mostly common to all the countries of the region. The achievement in this area will usher in a new international socio-economic order, which would ensure their sovereignty along with international peace and security.

The successful functioning of regional networking quite naturally would depend upon the efficient system of national networks and, within that, the local networks. This would require survey of present-day activities and existing resources-human and physical-to be strengthened, rationalised, and coordinated, creating new capabilities and facilities.

The structural/institutional framework of national networks, to form part of APINESS, may be suggested as under :

NATIONAL NODE

The National Social Science Documentation Centre (NASSDOC) in the Indian Council of Social Science Research is now the national focal point or national node for the regional network as it has the necessary resources, infrastructure and programmes to carry out the functions expected of a node. The financial resources are being met by ICSSR. The existing infrastructure includes documentation units at six ICSSR regional centres, mostly located in university campuses at Bombay, Calcutta, Chandigarh, Delhi, Hyderabad and Shillong, 24 ICSSR financed leading social science research institutes and other cooperating libraries/institutions. The documentation and data services programmes include providing financial assistance for (a) documentation and data archives projects, (b) holding of professional seminars, conferences and training programmes, (c) strengthening documentary and data resources in the research institutions, (d) promoting networking activities, among documentation and data centres, and (e) publication of documents on library and information science and data management.

NASSDOC–ICSSR in association with Data Archives is thus capable to act as a national node, and take up responsibility to promote the concept of network and coordinate, encourage and monitor the progress of national networking. Both these centres are at an advanced stage of providing documentation and data services and have already taken up a number of programmes to encourage resource sharing and networking. Some of the activities are as under:

NASSDOC Networking/Resource Sharing Activities

i. Compilation of union catalogue of serials/periodicals of libraries in India, 32 vols. 1972-76;

ii. Compilation of union list of current periodicals being received in Delhi, Revised 1985;
iii. Retrospective indexing of about 240 Indian social science periodicals from their inception to the year 1970 (in progress);
iv. Compilation of bibliographies on the States/Union Territories of India (in progress);
v. Compilation of bibliographies of social science research material in the regional languages of India including English (in progress);
vi. Setting up of Inter-Library Resources Centre at Delhi in 1976 in collaboration with Jawaharlal Nehru University, inviting libraries to deposit their less used serial material at the Centre. Thirty libraries have so far deposited about 1 lakh volumes of periodicals;
vii. Acquisition of unpublished Ph.D. theses in social sciences approved by Indian universities. It is thus on the verge of becoming the largest centre of this grey material throughout India (collection to date : 2500);
viii. Provision of bibliographic services to the scholars;
ix. Acting as input centre for Indian material for ICSSID International Bibliographies; International Bulletin of Bibliography on Education (BIBE Project, Madrid); International Geographical Bibliography (Paris) has updated information on behalf of Unesco Social Science Documentation Centre, Paris, in respect of research institutions and periodicals in social sciences in India for Unesco DARE DATA BANK;
x. Exchange agreements with well over 2000 Indian and foreign institutions for exchange of publications;
xi. Inter-library loan facilities; and
xii. Consultancy services in respect of setting up of documentation units.

The proposed new activities are

i. Central abstracting of social science literature produced in India;
ii. Compilation of South Asia Index;
iii. Continuing education programme leading to Associateship in Library and Information Studies in Social Sciences.

NETWORKING ASSOCIATE PROGRAMMES

NASSDOC has been developing close relations with international library and documentation organisations to promote the networking concept. The Director (NASSDOC) is a member of the National Committee and the Social Science Information and Documentation Committee of International Federation for Information and Documentation (FID) to pursue collaborative documentation programmes in the region.

NASSDOC has also developed relations with the International Federation of Library Associations and Institutions (IFLA). In a meeting recently held at NASSDOC and addressed by Dr. J.S. Soosai, Chairman, Asia section, IFLA, measures were suggested for IFLA to outreach more information centres in the Asian region so that certain priority programmes may be taken. In this context, taking up of training programmes and exchange of personnel within the Asian region found favour with the participants and Dr. Soosai.

Besides exchange relations with international organisations, NASSDOC has similar relations with a large number of institutions all over the world. Selective list of institutions in Asia and the Pacific region is given in the Appendix to indicate close relations already achieved for mutual benefit and the potential for further links in networking.

Data Archives Networking/Resource Sharing Activities

i. Compilation of an inventory of data generated by different research institutions in India since 1951. Data from 26 research institutions on 488 studies collected.
ii. Developing general purpose application programmes for statistical processing for research scholars and institutions;
iii. Serving as Regional Secretariat of the International Association for Social Science Information Services and Technology. A plan for exchange of data and software with many archives in India and abroad is being worked out;
iv. Compilation of *National Register of Social Scientists in India,* which covers more than 7,500 scholars working in the university departments, colleges and research institutes. The whole data

has been computerised.

SPECIALISED CENTRES

There are a number of specialised centres, discipline-oriented and mission-oriented, in the country. Their participation on a voluntary basis in the network will ensure its successful functioning.

As most of the countries in the region are giving priority to solving issues of socio-economic nature, it would be appropriate to identify networking potentialities in the above field and in the first stage enlist libraries and information centres specialising in development research literature for networking.

The resources of some lead centres, supplemented by a list of few others, arranged under sub-disciplines, is given below to explore their willingness to participate in the network.

Lead Centres

Centre for Development and Instructional Technology (CENDIT). New Delhi. 1972.
Specialises in education, development and communication technology subjects. It has holdings of 3,700 books and 1,237 microfilms, 10,000 product literature and data bases on magnetic tapes. It is the input centre for documents produced in India for DEVSIS data base. Compiles *Devindex India.* It has installed ISIS package.

Centre on Rural Documentation (CORD), Hyderabad. 1958.
Specialises in development sciences. Holds 45,000 books and bound periodicals and 10,000 reports. Provides reprography, translation and audio-visual facilities. Compile *Cord Index* (M). The index covers 600 journals and 13 newspapers. The indexing slant is towards policy-making.

Giri Institute of Development Studies Library, Lucknow, 1973.
Specialises in development sciences literature which include Government reports and World Bank publications. It has computer facilities.

Gokhale Institute of Politics and Economics Library, Pune, 1930.
Specialises in the disciplines of economics, sociology, statistics and political science. Holds about 200,000 books and 1,000 microforms. Depository centre for UN publications and special collection includes British Parliamentary Papers and government documents of the USA and Commonwealth countries. Provides reprography and translation services. Brings out *List of additions* and *Fortnightly list of articles on India.*

Indian Council of World Affairs Library, New Delhi, 1944.
Specialises in the disciplines of international affairs, international law and economics. Holdings include 110,000 books and 11,500 microfilms. Special collection includes Press clippings and UN documents. Compiles *Weekly List of Articles* and *Documentation of Asia.*

Indian Institute of Foreign Trade Library, New Delhi, 1964.
Specialises in trade literature. Holdings include 50,000 books and about 5,000 UN documents. Brings out *Documentation on Foreign Trade.*

Indian Statistical Institute Library, Calcutta, 1931.
Specialised literature in statistics, computer science, economics, etc. Holdings include about 200,000 books and periodicals, 375,000 maps and 3,500 microforms. Provides current awareness services, bibliographical services and SDI services.

Institute of Applied Manpower Research Library, New Delhi, 1962.
Subject specialisation in manpower, economics, statistics and management. Holdings include 14,000 books and 15,000 bound periodical volumes. Brings out *List of Additions* and *Manpower Documentation.*

Institute of Public Enterprise Library, Hyderabad, 1964.
Subject specialisation in public enterprise studies, policy studies, and management. Special collection includes annual reports of state and Central Government public undertakings. Brings out *List of Additions* and *List of Parliamentary Reports.* Compiling *Annotated Bibliography of Public Enterprises.* The Institute is financially assisted by ICSSR.

National Council of Applied Economic Research Library, New Delhi, 1956.

Specialised literature covers economics, agriculture, transportation and energy. Collections include 18,147 books, 20,938 reports and 1,053 microforms. Brings out *Artha Suchi : Index of Indian Economic Literature* on HP 3,000 computer, using MINISIS software package. Besides this, compiles topical bibliographies.

National Informatics Centre (NIC), New Delhi, 1977.

Specialises in developing interactive data bases in network of computers for the Government of India and State Governments. In the field of documentation it has undertaken development of the bibliographic system on techno-economic information documents. It developed a Pilot System for the National Medical Library for providing medical retrieval service as also Legal Information Retrieval System, based on the Constitution of India for the Ministry of Law, Justice and Company Affairs in 1984. Provides online bibliographic service for documents in the library and for news items on electronics and computers. Brings out *Weekly Current News Update*. MINISIS Application Package is used for bibliographic services.

Parliament Library, New Delhi, 1921.

Holdings contain 500,000 books consisting of Central, State and Foreign Government reports, UN and allied agencies publications and gazettes, debates, acts, rules, etc. Documentation activities cover compilation of *Journal of Parliamentary Information, Abstracts and Index of Reports and Digest of Legislative and Constitutional Cases*. Brings out topical bibliographies.

Planning Commission Library, New Delhi, 1950.

Holdings include 150,000 books, periodical subscription 800; special collection consists of 5,000 pamphlets, 10,000 plans and 1,000 maps. Compiles indexing and abstracting journal *Doc - Plan* and a list of *Recent Additions to the Library*.

Regional Information Centre for Development Policy Modelling, Pune, 1984.

Specialises in economic modelling to help policy-makers to choose a suitable one. Present collection includes 2,000 documents. The Centre has computer facilities and proposes to automate library procedures. The centre will work as a regional focal point for modellling in Asia.

Research and Information System for the Non-Aligned and Other Developing Countries (RISNODEC), New Delhi, 1984.
Set-up on the recommendation of NAM countries in their meeting at New Delhi. Priority research areas are (a) Wage and payments problems of the developing countries, (b) money and finance issues and (c) analytical digest of current trends in the world economy. On the documentation side, networking with other research institutions, government departments and UN bodies is contemplated. Compiled *Directory of Research Institutes/Information Systems.* The institution has computer facilities.

Small Enterprises National Documentation Centre (SENDOC), Hyderabad, 1970.
Provides comprehensive technical, economic and financial management information services to small industries. Special collection includes 5,000 product profiles and 5,000 trade catalogues. Brings out *SENDOC Chronicle, SENDOC Bulletin* and *Appropriate Technology Documentation Bulletin.* Conducts short-term training courses in information storage and retrieval systems.

Tata Institute of Social Sciences Library, Bombay, 1930.
Specialised disciplines include social work. Personnel management, rural and urban development, etc. Holdings consist of 58,000 books, 2,000 pamphlets and 500 reprints. Brings out monthly *Documentation list.*

Supporting Centres

Socio-economic Development

A.N. Sinha Institute of Social Studies Library, Patna.
Centre for Economic and Social Studies Library, Hyderabad.
Centre for Development Studies Library, Trivandrum.

Centre for Policy Research Library, New Delhi.
Centre for Regional, Ecological and science Studies in Developent Alternatives, Calcutta.
Centre for Research in Rural & Industrial Development, Chandigarh.
Centre for Social Studies Library, Surat.
Centre for Studies in Social Sciences Library, Calcutta.
Centre for the Study of Developing Societies Library, New Delhi.
Council for Social Development Library, New Delhi.
Delhi School of Economics Library, New Delhi.
Delhi School of Social Work Library, Delhi.
G.B. Pant Social Science Institute Library, Allahabad.
Gandhian Institute of Studies Library, Varanasi.
Giri Institute of Developmental Studies, Lucknow.
Gujarat Institute of Area Planning, Ahmedabad.
Indian Institute of Economics Library, Hyderabad.
Indian Social Institute Library, New Delhi.
Institute for Social and Economic Change Library, Bangalore.
Institute of Development Studies Library, Jaipur.
Institute of Economic Growth Library, Delhi.
Institute for Studies in Industrial Development, New Delhi.
L.N. Mishra Institute of Economic Development and Social Change Library, Patna.
Madras Institute of Development Studies, Madras,
Ministry of Finance Library, New Delhi.
National Institute of Public Finance & Policy Library, New Delhi.
National Institute of Social Defence Library, New Delhi.
Sardar Patel Institute of Economic and Social Research Library, Ahmedabad.

Agriculture

Indian Agricultural Research Institute Library, New Delhi.
Indian Council of Agricultural Research Library, New Delhi.
Indian Society of Agricultural Economics Library, Bombay.

Cooperation

National Cooperative Development Corporation Library, New Delhi.

National Cooperative Union of India Library, New Delhi.
National Institute of Public Cooperation and Child Development Library, New Delhi.
Vaikunth Mehta National Institute of Cooperative Management Library, Pune.

Demography

International Institute for Population Studies Library, Bombay.

Foreign Trade and Investment

Indian Investment Centre, Library, New Delhi.
Indian Council for Research on International Economic Relations Library, New Delhi.

Human Resources

Centre for Human Development and Social Change Library, Madras.
Centre for Women Development Studies Library, New Delhi.
Labour Bureau, Shimla.
Labour Documents and Reference Centre, New Delhi.
National Labour Institute Library, New Delhi.
Sri Ram Centre for Industrial Relations and Human Resources Library, New Delhi.
Xavier Labour Relations Institute Library, Jamshedpur.

Industries

Bureau of Public Enterprises Library, New Delhi.
Centre for Studies in Decentralised Industries Library, Bombay.
Institute of Public Enterprise, Hyderabad.
Small Industries Extension Training Institute Library, Guwahati.

Rural Development

Centre for Research in Rural and Industrial Development, Chandigarh.

Ministry of Rural Development Library, New Delhi.
Rural Institute Library, Amravati.
Rural Institute, Gandhigram Gandhiji-Lincoln Library, Gandhigram.
State Training Institute of Community Development Library, Bhubaneswar.

Statistics

Census Operations Library, Madras.
Central Statistical Organisation Library, New Delhi.
Indian Statistical Institute Library, New Delhi.

ADMINISTRATION

ICSSR has set up Committees, viz., Committee on Documentation Services and Research Information, Committee on Data Archives, and Committee on Training to advise and recommend programmes for documentation and data services. All these Committees consist of professional experts and renowned social scientists in India.

The infrastructure for National Network Advisory Committee thus exists. It may consist of members from these committees and representatives from participating institutions.

The secretariat may be located at the NASSDOC-ICSSR, 35 Ferozshah Road, New Delhi.

ACTIVITIES

Priority could be given to the following activities:

Training Programmes

The impact of information technology has forced librarians to think of new information management techniques. The professionals at managerial level need introduction to mechanised methods of management for creating efficient systems for storage, retrieval and dissemination of information. Library training programmes, covering the above aspect, have become more urgent. These would help in better management of network activities too.

Keeping in view the need for the above, NASSDOC is undertaking library courses leading to Associateship in Library and Information Studies in Social Sciences for professionals at managerial level. Concurrent with this, short-term courses under Continuing Education Programme are also being conducted.

Compilation of Inventory of Documentation Resources

Most of the libraries and information centres bring out indexing and abstracting journals without any coordination and standardisation. This results, on the one hand, in overlapping in coverage leading to wastage of money and manpower, and on the other, leaving some disciplines uncovered.

The documentation lists in existence may, therefore, be identified. Their coverage, presentation pattern and financial sources may be looked into. Lead libraries may be assigned responsibility of bring out indexing and/or abstracting journals in their respective fields. International standards for compiling documents will have to be followed in order to facilitate exchange among network members. Priority could be given to compilation of data in machine-readable form.

Bibliographical Control of Non-Doctoral Research, in Progress and Completed

A large number of developmental research programmes are under way in the country. To avoid duplication and to have optimum use of the information created, the bibliographical control of research is very essential. Networking partners will have to join hands for this, obviously not overlooking international standards for compiling such tools.

Incidentally NASSDOC has been bringing out documents covering ICSSR financed research projects, completed and in progress, and also the projects undertaken by twenty ICSSR financed research institutes. These documents require to be revised and updated according to international bibliographic standards and further the data is to be computerised for exchange and online services.

Compilation of Directory of Research Institutions

Directories of above nature are available, reference can be made to those brought out by NASSDOC-ICSSR, but these require to be updated and standardised.

Compilation of Union Catalogue of Books and Union Catalogue of Periodicals/Serials

The Union Catalogue of Periodicals/Serials has been compiled by NASSDOC, covering material available in libraries up to 1972. The catalogue is now being updated and requires to be computerised. Further NASSDOC has taken steps to bring out discipline oriented union catalogues. A Union Catalogue of Library and Informatics Publications in Delhi libraries, has already been released.

Exchange of Professionals

A system is required to be devised for exchange of professionals as partners in the network, to observe functioning of national networks in other countries of the region. This will facilitate personal contact for exchange of experiences and develop close affinity between them.

FINANCIAL SUPPORT

Financial support is required for providing micro-computer systems to lead centres which, in the initial stages, may not be more than ten. The compilation of different tools for resource sharing will also require initial investment. The other items of expenditure will be training programmes, exchange of personnel and subscription to foreign data bases. The approximate budget as per the following statement will come to Rs. 70 lakhs (i.e. $ .62 million). This expenditure can be spread over three years.

Expenditure Estimate for Three Years

	Item	*User Centres*	*Application*	*Amount*	
				Rs. (in lakhs)	US dollar (in lakhs)
1.	Main-frame Computer	National Focal Node	Centralised Storing of data relevant To: (a) Union Catalogue (b) Indexing & Abstracting Services (c) Directory of Research in progress and completed (d) Directory of Research Institutions (e) Inventory of Data Sets	25.00	2.00
2.	Microcomputers	Specialised Centres 10	(a) Creation of data bases (b) SDI Services (c) Online searches of existing data bases within and outside the region	20.00	1.75
3.	Initial Investment in Creation of Data Bases			10.00	1.00
4.	Training Programmes	National Focal Node	Holding of workshops within the region	5.00	·50
5.	Exchange of Personnel		To exchange experiences and first-hand observations of working of existing networks	5.00	·50
6.	Subscription to Foreign Data Bases	National Focal Node and Specialised Centres	SDI Services	5.00	·50
			Total : Rs.	70.00	$6.25

APPENDIX

NASSDOC Exchange Partners in Asia and the Pacific

Bangla Desh

Association of Development Agencies in Bangla Desh.
Bangla Desh Institute of Development Studies.
Centre of Integrated Rural Development for Asia and the Pacific.
National Library of Bangla Desh.
Social Science Research Council.

Bhutan

National Institute of Education.

China (People's Republic)

Academy of Social Sciences.
National Library of China.

China (Republic)

Institute of International Relations.
Resource and Information Centre for Chinese Studies.

Hong Kong

Chinese University of Hong Kong.
Social Research Centre.

Indonesia

Centre for Strategic and International Studies.
National Library of Indonesia.
Perpustakan Museum Pusat.

Iran

International Institute of Adult Literacy Methods.

Iraq

Ministry of Culture and Information

Japan

Centre for East Asian Cultural Studies.
Hitotsubashi University Library.
Institute of Developing Economics.
Japan Statistics Bureau.
Japanese Psychological Association.
Keio Economic Society.
Research Institute for Economics and Business Administration.

Korea (Republic)

Institute of Economic Research.
Korean Social Science Research Council.
Research Institute of Asian Economics.

Malaysia

Malaya University.
Rubber Research Institute of Malaysia.
UN Asian and Pacific Development Centre.

Nepal

Research Centre for Nepal and Asian Studies.
Tribhuvan University Economics Instruction Committee.

New Zealand

Conterbury University Library.
Massey University Library.

Pakistan

Institute of Economic Studies.
Pakistan Institute of Development Economics.
Punjab University Library.

Phillipines

Phillipines Social Science Council.
Phillipines University Asian Centre.
Population Centre Foundation.

Singapore

Asian Mass Communication Research and Information Centre.
National Library.

Sri Lanka

Centre for Development Information.
Sri Lanka Centre for Development Studies.

Thailand

National Institute of Development Administration.
Unesco Regional Office for Education in Asia and the Pacific.

TEN

Distance Education in India with Reference to Role of Library and Information Science Organisations

A definition of Distance Learning adopted in IFLA Circular, "as a delivery system for continuing education which enables people to study at home or in an other place of their own choosing, in their own time and at a time which suits them while still pursuing their normal job" (Dale, 1986) is not comprehensive enough. To explain it further, we may include teaching devices, like print, mechanical or electronic, for effective communication of knowledge.

Need

Near unanimity of opinion prevails about the need for this innovative form of education because it provides access to learning to people who otherwise may not have been able to gain knowledge through traditional educational infrastructure due to factors which may be identified as :

i. Geographical isolation;
ii. Social and economic isolation;
iii. Sex discrimination;
iv. Age factor.

Teaching Media

The multi media approach is adopted towards teaching techniques. These may consist of :

i. Lectures;

ii. Printed material;
iii. Audio media (radio, audio cassettes);
iv. Visual media (posters, slides, graphs, facsimile)
v. Audio-Visual media (television, video cassettes)
vi. Machine stored information (computers).

Source: Director, National Social Science Documentation Centre, 35 Ferozeshah Road, New Delhi (India) - 110 001.

These media, however work more effectively, when supported by well developed communication system (postal, telephone and satellite).

Some educational experts feel that certain disciplines like medicine and engineering, where a lot of practical work in laboratories and in the fields under expert supervision is required, teaching through distance educational techniques is not effective. The same opinion is held by some library professionals regarding their own discipline also. The opinion, however, is not borne out by facts as one sees many institutions imparting distance education in these very disciplines. According to a directory of resource materials used in distance teaching by institutions in Asia and the Pacific Region, 34 institutions cover disciplines like electronics, engineering, education, economics, psychology, sociology, languages, etc. It is not the discipline that matters in the successful results as according to Taylor and White, "The basic necessities are that the instructional materials be well designed". Moreover greater attention needs to be paid to the training of teachers, the most crucial link in the system, who are not always well equipped for the job.

Distance Education in India

In India, in spite of expansive educational infrastructure, consisting of 140 universities, 5000 colleges, 52279 schools (1982-83) about 24.8 crores (1981) of people are illiterate. It will not be possible for long to bring these people nearer to the fountain of knowledge unless Central and State Governments expand frontiers of education through open schools, correspondence courses, extension lectures, non-formal education, etc. The need for these has been fully realised as one observes the course of events during the last two decades.

Higher Education

In the field of higher education, University of Delhi (1962) was the first to start the correspondence course. The idea caught up by others and now 22 universities provide facilities for correspondence education at under-graduate and post-graduate level in various disciplines. University of Madras, among other disciplines, provides degree level instruction in Library and Information Science (LIS). The distance education programme in its true meaning, however, started with the opening of the Andhra Pradesh Open University in 1982 and the Indira Gandhi National Open University (IGNOU) in 1985. Rajasthan Open University is on the planning board.

The former covers Library and Information Science discipline and IGNOU proposes to do so from 1988. More open universities likely to be set up in the near future.

School Education

A few states have Institutes/Directorates of Correspondence Education at secondary education stage. The experiment of open school launched by the Central Board of Secondary Education has been very successful. Some of the innovations such as flexibility in the choice and number of subjects offered, accumulation of credits, team approach to curriculum formulation and script writing, learning centres, etc. are important departures from the rigid formal system.

Educational Technology

After an year's successful satellite Instructional Television Experiment (1975-76), there have been many developments. In collaboration with the University Grants Commission, television centres telecast educational programmes for university students. For non-literates and neo-literates, special programmes in different formats and ways are presented. Andhra Pradesh Government with the help of educational experts and media people has produced visual programmes of great educational value for young kids. To give impetus to distance education activities, Government of India's steering Group on Education, Culture and Sports for 7th Five Year Plan has suggested setting up of Sound Studies in 20 States and Television Production Centres in 7 States, and each university is to be provided with a library of software with VCR facilities for playback of programmes. The computer literacy programme is being implemented in 250 secondary schools.

Library and Information Science Education Under Distance Education Programme

Role of Universities

As described above, only University of Madras and Andhra Pradesh Open University provide facilities for education in the discipline at degree level through distance teaching techniques. The latter arranges lessons using publications, radio talks, audio cassettes, class lectures (on holidays), etc. It has set up study centres to make use of these media. IGNOU has also chalked out the syllabus for this subject. Jamia University also starts post-graduate diploma course in LIS through correspondence from 1988. The correspondence education is also provided at under-graduate level by few universities.

Role of Professional Organisations

There are a large number of professional organisations in the country. These can be categorised according to the geographical area covered, field of activities, nature of objectives, etc. Some of the well known organisations at national level are : Indian Library Association, Indian Association of Special Libraries and Information Centres, Government of India Librarians Association, Indian Association of Academic Libraries, Medical Libraries Association of India, Society for Information Science, Computer Society of India and Micro-Graphic Congress of India. In most of the 23 States, there are State Library Associations.

So far as their role in LIS education is concerned, they are more preoccupied in the field of Continuing Education rather than in the Distance Education. State level associations provide education professionals required to work at lower level in the libraries, through traditional ways i.e. lecture method.

Continuing education for professionals is pursued through holding seminars/conferences/workshops, short term courses, study tours and publication of journals and newsletters. In this way, they assist practitioners in maintaining and strengthening their competence through updating their knowledge, improving their skill and influencing attitudes. The topics currently being chosen relate to application of modern technology to information services.

These organisations have not ventured in the distance education field because they do not have the necessary financial resources and infrastructure required for this type of work. It is better that this domain should be left to universities and government departments which have the required facilities.

CONCLUSION

Our country has the necessary infrastructure consisting of network of radio and television stations (covering 97.5% and 52% of the population respectively), satellite system (INSATIB), Institutes of Educational Technology and network of educational research centres.

There is more scope for improving and expanding library and information services in the country for which we would need trained manpower. It is desirable that distance education techniques should be utilised for imparting library and information science education to people in remote areas, far removed from educational centres. The local people can work more enthusiastically and with devotion than those who are sent from outside to work at such places. To conclude, the mandate of equality to which democratic society is wedded demands that opportunities for higher education should be available equally to all those who need, and to achieve the objective, distance education should be designed as a corner stone of our learning society.

SECTION FIVE

INSTITUTION BASE

ELEVEN

Social Science Research Institutions in India

Genesis

Social Sciences in India are of recent origin. Their growth and development, which is a post-war phenomenon, is of great significance and importance particularly in the developing countries. There is a virtual 'explosion', of social science in India as a consequence of this 'explosion', there is general awareness, acceptance and use by the common laity, organizations-governmental and otherwise, scholars and researchers, business and industry and so on. In fact, there is hardly a social, economic or political problem that social scientists are not required to study and provide solution. Social scientists help elevate such problems through a scientific social scrutiny and evaluation, particularly in industrially developed countries. The social sciences have, therefore become an indispensable source of guidance for administrators and professionals of all kinds. They enlighten the people on the progress of ideas and make them see things through a wider perspective. If people today perceive the problems and their solution differently, it is because they are exposed to the perspective of social sciences - they raise their children differently, they have changed attitudes towards their governments, friends, neighbours and family members. Social Sciences influence the assumptions on which their daily lives are based. They contribute to rational thinking, a secular outlook, free from the "disenchantment of the World", which people weave around themselves.

Expansion of the social sciences, availability of funds and opportunity of participation in large-scale empirical study and research have placed a heavy responsibility on social scientists today. The Indian Council of Social Science Research (ICSSR), a pioneer organization in the field of social sciences in India has provided financial assistance to social science institutions and has brought out a number of papers dealing with social science research in India. It is hoped that social scientists will profit by keeping themselves abreast of new ideas and developments.

Historical Perspective

There has been, of late, a rapid growth of social science research and training organizations in the country. A host of research organizations have come into existance outside the university system and are playing an important and significant role in the developmental activities. Their utility is being gradually realised and recognised with the progress and development of social science subjects. It is estimated that a large number of them are functioning as autonomous bodies, some receiving partial assistance, some full assistance, and some getting no financial support from the Government.

The first two research institutions, outside the university system, for purpose of research, teaching, training and policy formulation were formed as early as 1927, one of them working in the field of public administration (All India Institute of Local-Self Government, Bombay) and the other had an inter-disciplinary character (Indian Council for Africa, New Delhi). In 1935 two more social science research organizations came to be set-up one for economics and the other for statistics. Then came institutions in political science (1943), anthropology (1945), commerce (1946), psychology (1949), management (1949), demography (1956), law (1959), criminology (1961) and defence studies (1965). A good number of them are multi-disciplinary in their composition while others are department-based or are inter-disciplinary in their concern and approach. In addition to conducting research in various fields, they also function as training institutions for future researchers and administrators.

According to a list compiled by ICSSR in 1971, there were 59 professional social science associations in the country. The largest number of associations was in the field of geography (10), followed by anthropology (8) and economics (7).

The first professional association was set up in the year 1919 in history, followed by anthropology (1921), geography (1926), linguistics (1928), and economics (1929). By 1947, the year when India attained freedom, there were 16 such organizations; in ten year's time i.e. by 1957, their number rose to 25, and in the later decade, ending 1967, as many as 22 were further added. In 1970, the total number had reached 59.

The Table 7.1: shows the growth of research institutions periodwise and Table 7.2 subjectwise distribution. The analysis is based on the data collected for Unesco DARE from 178 institutions during 1982. This can serve as a sample survey of existing institutions in India.

Table 7.1: Periods of Foundations of Research Institutions

	Period	No. of Institutions
Upto	1900	8
	1901 - 10	1
	1911 - 20	1
	1921 - 30	9
	1931 - 40	2
	1941 - 50	13
	1951 - 60	36
	1961 - 70	49
	1971 - 80	54
	1891	5
		178

Analysis based on data collected for Unesco DARE System during 1982.

Table 7.2: Disciplinewise Distribution of Institutions

S. No.	Discipline	No. of Institutions
1.	Accounting	1
2.	Administrative Reforms	1
3.	Adult Education	2
4.	Agricultural Economics	6
5.	Agriculture	2
6.	America	2
7.	Anthropology	3
8.	Archeology	1
9.	Asia	3
10.	Assam	1
11.	Behavioural Sciences	1
12.	Business Administration	2
13.	Business Management	1
14.	Children	1
15.	Commerce	1
16.	Community Development	1
17.	Comparative Law	1
18.	Consumer	1
19.	Criminology	3
20.	Cultural Anthropology	3
21.	Demography	4
22.	Development	3
23.	Ecology	1
24.	Economics	8
25:	Economic Development	2
26.	Education	10
27.	Employment	3
28.	Environmental Planning	1
29.	Family	1
30.	Family Planning	2
31.	Family Welfare	1
32.	Gandhiana	4
33.	Geography	5
34.	Government	1
35.	Higher Education	5
36.	Housing	2
37.	India	1
38.	Indology	1
39.	Industrial Development	1
40.	Industrial Relations	1
41.	Industry	3
42.	Information Centres	17
43.	International Affairs	2
44.	International Law	1
45.	Islam	1
46.	Labour	2
47.	Labour Relations	1

48.	Law	1
49.	Local Government	1
50.	Management	11
51.	Marketing	1
52.	Mass Communication	2
53.	Mental Health	2
54.	National Income	1
55.	Nepal	1
56.	Nomadism	1
57.	Non-Violence	2
58.	Organization	1
59.	Parliamentary System	2
60.	Peace Research	4
61.	Pianning	1
62.	Political Science	3
63.	Political System	1
64.	Policy Making	1
65.	Population	7
66.	Productivity	1
67.	Psychology	6
68.	Public Administration	2
69.	Public Enterprises	1
70.	Regional Development	2
71.	Regional Planning	1
72.	Religion	1
73.	Research and Development	1
74.	Rural Development	8
75.	Rural Planning	1
76.	Science	2
77.	Social Change	2
78.	Social Problems	1
79.	Social Sciences	10
80.	Social Welfare	13
81.	Social Work	2
82.	Society	1
83.	Socio-Economic Development	1
84.	Sociology	11
85.	Statistics	3
86.	Teaching	8
87.	Tibet	2
88.	Tribes	1
89.	Urban Sociology	1
90.	Urbanization	1
91.	Women	1
92.	Youth	1

Analysis based on data collected for Unesco DARE System during 1982.

Broadly, the burden of assisting the social science research in India is shared by three important agencies - Government, Private Bodies and the International Organizations. The Government's contribution is the highest i.e. about 90 per cent. As against *ad hoc* financing, the proportion of regular grant-in-aid by the government is also the highest. In other words, most of the social science research institutions in India receive their regular grants from the government sources. However, the mode and procedure followed by each organization very from one another. For instance, the Central Government allocated block grants to autonomous bodies, which in turn, frame their own rules and procedures for distribution of money to institutions and individuals, wishing to conduct research in any branch of social sciences. But the sum spent on social sciences is meagre as compared to what is done on scientific and technological researches. According to the estimate made J.L. Sardana, country is spending annually about Rs. 2500 million on natural, technological and medical sciences and around Rs. 25 million on research in social sciences. Similarly, the international organizations, which have large amounts, provide grants for social science research either directly to the government or to research institutions after obtaining formal approval of the government. Here too, the amount spent on social science research is small as compared to what is spent on scientific research.

The existing sources, financing the social science research in the country are within the following three sector:

I. Public/Government Sector:
   (a) Ministries/Departments of Central and State Governments.
   (b) Autonomous organisations, sponsored and funded by the government.
   (c) National Banks and Public Financial Institutions.

II. Private Sector:
   (a) Private Research Institutions
   (b) Professional Organisations
   (c) Industrial Houses and Individual Companies

III. International Sector:
   (a) National Organisations sponsoring and funding research activities in the third world countries.
   (b) International Organisations.

ICSSR conducted a study in respect of financing the social science research in India with the following objectives in view:

(a) to identify institutions and agencies financing the social science research:
(b) to quantify their financial inputs and assess their relative contribution;
(c) to analyse patterns and procedures of financing;
(d) to observe the nature of studies and researches emerging from the expenditure;
(e) to make suggestions for coordinating the system of providing financial support.

The study covered all the three above funding sectors for the period from 1947/75-1977/78. A brief report of the study is detailed below:

Central/State Government Departments

The Government plays two distinct but related roles in the research sphere, those of sponsor and user. The impetus to planned economic growth has produced an awareness of and need for social science research and consequently government sponsored research is greatly devoted to socio-economic problems facing the country and mostly is of *adhoc* nature.

The study identified 55 departments of the Central Government - considered to be the possible agencies which could sponsor research and provide financial support to research organisations. The response received was encouraging. Among the central ministries, the following were found to be originator of large volume of research directly and indirectly by providing financial support to research undertaken by other institutions:

1. Ministry of Agriculture
2. Ministry of Finance
3. Ministry of Education and Social Welfare
4. Ministry of Health
5. Ministry of Labour
6. Planning Commission

Autonomous Funding Organizations

The study has identified the undermentioned funding agencies. It provides information about their various activities, aims and objectives organizational structure, field of research (priorities), research policy, method of research promotion, finance, area of research, lon-term plan, collaboration and coordination, research facilities available, seminar/workshops conducted, income and expenditure, procedure for making grants, etc. to social science research in India. It has also provided basic data about published and unpublished documents and other interesting features.

Funding Agencies

1. Central Social Welfare Board
2. Family Planning Foundation
3. Indian Council of Agricultural Research
4. Indian Council Child Welfare
5. Indian Council of Cultural Relations
6. Indian Council of Historical Research
7. Indian Council of Medical Research
8. Indian Council of Social Science Research
9. Indian Council of World Affairs
10. National Council of Applied Economic Research
11. National Council of Educational Research and Training
12. National Productivity Council
13. University Grants Commission

Banking Institutions

ICSSR as a part of its study approached 85 banking institutions including the Reserve Bank of India as to how far they have been able to equip themselves for the tasks assigned to them by undertaking or sponsoring research in various desired fields.

It was found that the research activities of banking institutions are problem oriented i.e. of a functional character suiting the requirements of the concerned institutions. Their studies are short term surveys of a particular area of region and thus are of adhoc rather than of a continuing nature. Reserve Bank of India and State

Bank of India were found to be the leading institutions in social science research.

Industrial and Commercial Houses

Link the banking institutions, research projects of industrial and commercial houses were also of functional character, suiting to the requirement of the concerned industry i.e. problem oriented and of an adhoc nature.

International Agencies

The ICSSR conducted a similar study in respect of financing the social science research in India by the following 12 international organizations:

1. United Nations Educational, Scientific and Cultural Organization (UNESCO)
2. United States Educational Foundation in India (USEFI)
3. Ford Foundation
4. World Bank
5. British Council Division
6. United Nations Children's Emergency Fund (UNICEF)
7. International Labour Organization (ILO)
8. American Institute of Indian Studies (AIIS)
9. Shastri Indo-Canadian Institute
10. World Health Organisation (WHO)
11. United Nations Development Programme (UNDP)
12. Food and Agricultural Organisation of the United Nations (FAO)

The main objectives of the study were to identify various international agencies, which directly undertake or provide financial assistance for social science research in India, to quantify the financial inputs provided for the purpose and to analyse the patterns and procedures adopted by the various foreign funding agencies for providing financial support for social science research. These agencies were approached to supply the requisite information on a set pattern, laid down in a questionnaire, as in the case of other studies, to supply information about their basic objectives, research programmes and other facilities available with them.

It may thus be seen that there exists a number of agencies financing the social science research in the country. However lack of coordination among the funding agencies created problems, on one hand, of depulication of research and on the other imbalanced research in the different branches of social sciences. More over research output by various research institutions is not fully utilised. Realising the need for a comprehensive information system for utilisation of research, ICSSR brought out two directories of social science research institutions and professional organisations in India in 1971-72. These directories soon became out of date as a large number of institutions came into being. In addition, the nature and type of research activities, administrative and financial management also underwent a considerable change.

As a part of its larger study - the financing of social science research in India, ICSSR collected useful data about the research institutions in the country. This resulted in compilation of updated directory of research institutions and professional organisations in India in memeographed form in 1981. Most of the research institutions or organisations listed in it are outside the university system but university institutions of national importance have been included in it. Information about each institution includes: Name and address, Year of establishment, status, Executive Head, History, Structure, Aims and field of research, staff, research facilities, data processing equipment, training programmes, finance, research projects and publications, Arrangement of the entiries is first by statewise and within state alphabetical by their official names.

Quite separately, UNESCO collected information in respect of social science research institutions for input in the DARE System. In view of the considerations mentioned above, the Council accepted the responsibility to update information available in DARE printouts. A preliminary list of research institutions and professional organisations was accordingly prepared out of the material available from a number of sources including particularly the two directories prepared by the Council earlier and the DARE print-outs. A total of 405 institutions were identified. These included research institutions/professional organisations in the field of social sciences which are set up by Central/State Governments, industrial and commercial houses and other private bodies. Most of these research institutions/organisations are outside the university system. However, some university institutions of national significance have also been included for the purpose of updating the information. Questionnaires have been sent to all of them. A state-wise break-up of the institutions and professional organisations is given in the Table 7.3

Table 7.3: Statewise Distribution of Institutions

S.No.	Name of the State/Union Tettitories	No. of Institutions
1.	Andhra Pradesh	27
2.	Arunachal Pradesh	2
3.	Assam	7
4.	Bihar	12
5.	Chandigarh	1
6.	Delhi	78
7.	Gujarat	27
8.	Himachal Pradesh	3
9.	Jammu and Kashmir	3
10.	Karnataka	20
11.	Kerala	14
12.	Madhya Pradesh	7
13.	Maharashtra	60
14.	Manipur	1
15.	Meghalaya	1
16.	Mizoram	1
17.	Nagaland	2
18.	Orissa	7
19.	Punjab	3
20.	Rajasthan	18
21.	Sikkim	2
22.	Tamil Nadu	29
23.	Uttar Pradesh	35
24.	West Bengal	45
	Total	405

Analysis based on ICSSR Survey of financing of Social Science Research in India for the period 1975/76-1977/78.

The updated DARE print-outs will, quite obviously, provide the useful basic information to the research scholars in social sciences about various research institutions and organisations; thus enabling optimum utilisation of facilities available with these research agencies, on the one hand, and on the other help research agencies to have an idea of the researches undertaken or completed and facilities provided by other similar bodies to build close links for the promotion of social science research and its utilisation.

India thus had a haphazard growth of social science institutions, but the situation has been improving. New institutions, including professional organisations have started coming up. Now it would be necessary not only to speed them up, but to make sure that their growth is brought about in a coordinated manner. Establishment of ICSSR has filled the institutional gap which had stood for a long time in the way of the development of social science research in India and a source for regular supply of finance to research institutions enabling them to plan their research work well ahead.

SECTION SIX

RESOURCE SHARING

TWELVE

NISSS: National Information System in Social Sciences

PROEM

"Human resources not capital, not income, nor material resources constitute the ultimate basis for the wealth of nations", maintains Frederick H. Harbison in his report based on the Project of the Inter-University Study of Human Resources in National Development. This becomes evident when we look at T.W. Schultz's comment: "Suppose that by some miracle, India, or some other low income country, acquired overnight, as it were, a set of natural resources, equipment, and structures, including techniques of production comparable per person to ours (i.e. the United States), what could they do with them, given the existing skills and knowledge of the people? Surely the imbalance between the stock of human and non-human capital would be tremendous."

DEFINITIONS

In order to facilitate understanding, certain related terms, even if not used in subsequent discussion, are defined below:

Population constitute the number of people living in a given place at a given time.

Workers are those who produce or transform goods or provide services for their own consumption and for that of others.

Labour Force in its most generalised form is conceived as that portion of the population which is economically active.

Working Force is used by some scholars as equivalent to labour force. However, the term working force may conveniently be used to refer to the workers or the employed.

Manpower is a broader term than working force; it not only includes the latter but generally also includes the potential or maximum available working force which might come into being in accordance with economic, social or political considerations.

Human Capital, forms as the inherited and acquired abilities of producers and consumers.

Human Resources, Population, when channelised and given a direction is manpower. Manpower equipped with skills and disciplined to creativity becomes human resource.

Human Resources Development is the process of increasing the knowledge, the skill and the capacities of all the people in a society.

PURPOSE OF THIS STUDY

In overall context, an analysis of main trends, approaches accomplishments, contemporary issues relating to Human Resources Development with reference to library and information professionals in India is presented.

Major Developments in Modern LIS (Library and Information Science) and its Practice

The following is a highly selective and very sketchy enumeration of the major developments; it does not pretend to be an exhaustive historical survey culminating in the advent of a modern LIS and its practice. Its aim is rather to emphasise some aspects of the recent history of our profession, which may closely affect the curricula for ET (Education and Training) of LI (Library and Information) personnel.

Emergence of Modern Librarianship

Librarianship, in the sense of collecting and storing books, has been practised for many centuries, but only within the past 100 years has it begun to take on the real characteristics of a profession. M. Dewey is considered the father of modern librarianship.

By the end of the last century, the basic technology of librarianship was elevated by Dewey and other eminent librarians.

Emergence of Information Profession

Manifold development of science and technology resulted in the development of division of labour in research and development (R and D).

Some of the basic features of scientific research and invariability, i.e., varifiable openness or being available to all those who can make use of it; relatability, i.e., inter and intrarelationship of subjects; applicability for material development; growth, i.e., capability of further extension of frontiers of knowledge. Communication is common to these features and information constitutes a vital input.

Information, because of its importance to national development, is considered a national resource. To make full use of this resource, it needs to be properly managed. It is an extension of the traditional library functions, with the collection emphasis moving from books and journals to articles, reports and other special materials. The services are geared to meet intensive individual and group information needs rather than general loan and reference needs. To succeed in this task, the intermediary must be resourceful, have sufficient subject background, understand the user and his needs, well acquainted with all the sources of information, and skilled in various information processing techniques.

Emergence of LI Education

Systematic and organized (ET) in LIS is a relatively recent development of the past two or three decades. ET of information specialists is organised and offered either independently or in conjunction with ET of librarians.

Emergence of Theoretical Investigations

Modern LI practice and the growing need for well-trained professionals soon required not only the elaboration of practical rules, methods and guidelines which explain how to work, but obviously generated the need for investigations into the theoretical aspects of LI work. S.R. Ranganathan contributed substantially to the recognition of LIS as a scientific discipline.

Extension of the Types of Documents Handled

There are a good number of documents in addition to traditional documents which are to be handled by professionals.

The Information Explosion

The information explosion is some what the other name of document explosion. The never ending increase in the volume of published and unpublished information sources posed growing difficulties in the handling of the mass of literature for librarians, information specialists and their institutions. It has given birth to secondary sources and more recently to the application of modern electronic and reprographic technology for information handling.

The Increasing Role of Consolidated Information

There has been spectacular increase in the publication of abstracting and indexing publications.

Emergence of Reprographic and Computer Technologies

Newly invented reprographic technologies have become current practices in the LIS profession. Due importance is given to the use of computer in LIS profession for storage and retrieval.

The Changing Role of the Librarian

The traditional image of the librarian has faded out. The new role of the service librarian is supplemented by the library technologist, information technologist and information specialist, whose main duty is to serve user communities. To justify his role, LIS professionals have to acquire requisite knowledge of LIS and practice.

AIMS OF HUMAN RESOURCE DEVELOPMENT

Thus the human resource development should aim (i) to develop professionals for assuming a broader role of providing effective information to users; (ii) to develop scientific outlook in their jobs; (iii) to impart knowledge, skills and attitudes to L and IS personnel which would contribute to productive and development programmes through effective information handling techniques; (iv) to develop adequate staff; (v) to enhance the aspirations and capabilities of staff; (vi) to place staff where he/she is best required; (vii) to provide for in-service training; (viii) to facilitate healthy working conditions; and (ix) to create cordial staff relations.

HISTORICAL BACKGROUND

The recognition of the vital role of libraries in the educational, scientific and socio-economic development of the country is a rather recent phenomenon which came into existence during the last two to three decades. Educated and efficient library staff is required to run these centres. In India before 1930 there was hardly any university or training centre to educate library staff. Today we have 42 universities in the country which conduct study at post-graduate level, i.e. Bachelor's degree in library science or Master's degree in library and information science.

Nine universities enrol students for Ph.D. degree. Delhi University started M. Phil programme in July 1978.

Library associations, namely, Delhi Library Association, Andhra Library Association, etc., offer certificate courses and some institutions such as Women's Polytechnics at Delhi, Chandigarh, etc., also offer diploma courses contributing to human resource development. In addition to these universities and associations, the Documentation Research and Training Centre (DRTC), Bangalore, and Indian National Scientific Documentation Centre (INSDOC), New Delhi, National Social Science Documentation Centre (NASSDC) also offer training courses in documentation and/or information science.

The vast expansion of library and information science education in the country after Independence has naturally raised numerous problems which have been talked about in library committees, seminars, conferences and workshops.

As indicated above, library education imparted to professionals and semi-professionals becomes an important consideration for the success of library organisation in India.

LIBRARY AND INFORMATION SCIENCE EDUCATION

Rapid expansion of library and information science in India after Independence noteworthy raises questions about:

1. Levels of education;
2. Vigorous selection at admission stage;
3. Richer curriculum;
4. Strengthening of faculty;.
5. Continuing education for the teachers;
6. Suitable aids in teaching;
7. Production of library science literature; and
8. Employment openings.

The Advisory Committee for libraries appointed by the Government of India in its Report (1958, 1960) made several important recommendations. However the Report of UGC Review Committee (1965) can rightly be considered as the first comprehensive document on the subject.

In addition, UGC has appointed a Panel of Library and Information Science to review periodically different aspects of the existing L and IS education programmes in the country and make recommendations for future developments.

The panel has already finalised its recommendations with regard to various aspects such as status of library schools, teaching faculty, financial support, physical facilities, syllabi for BLIS, MLIS, M.Phil programme, etc., and these have been sent to the library schools in the country for implementation.

A SUGGESTED PATTERN

1. Duration of the Education and Training course at BLIS should be extended;
2. Dissertation writing should be made a compulsory paper at post-graduate level;
3. Introductory course of library science at under-graduate level;
4. Post-graduate course in library science should be designed as an advance course of two years' duration;
5. Research undertaken at Doctorate level should be either fundamental or problem oriented (often-recurring problems);
6. In-service training and refresher courses should be given due importance.
7. Proper co-ordination between library science education in different universities in India;
8. Training of computer technology;
9. Application of audio-visual aids in teaching; and
10. Introduction of library science education by open universities.

We find that trends are not all that encouraging. Normally manpower resources do create bottlenecks. But in the case of library and information science it is not entirely so, if the past experience, achievements and performance of libraries are any indication. As we had often felt in this context, an awareness of the problems, approaches used in alleviating them, accomplishment, and contemporary issues in the context of human resources development is generally lacking in our country. The library and information profession has so far received only lip sympathy of those who matter. In this context we recollect and reproduce what George Gissing has said:

"It is because nations tend to stupidity and baseness that mankind moves so slowly; it is because individuals have a capacity for better things that it moves at all".

This aptly applies to Human Resources Development with particular reference to Library and Information Professionals. Administrators are generally too pre-occupied to pay heed to what human resources development concepts entail. Even intellectuals and professionals, when they happen to be at the decision-making level, neglect, rather tend to dismantle, whatsoever infrastructure is there, just for the sake of immediate short-term benefits and administrative convenience; and this, despite sufficient realisation that decision making should be done on the basis of proven result. For human resources in Library science and informatics, extensive linking of would-be professionals with those at decision-making level is, therefore, a pre-requisite.

THIRTEEN

National Network of Social Science Information and Documentation Centres in India

BACKGROUND

Our way of life has always attached greatest importance to the development and dissemination of knowledge in all walks of life. We are proud inheritors of a tradition where knowledge has come down to us through more than 3000 years in a form and details which is amazing. (Dr. Cherian, 1966). The Vedas for instance have been passed from generation to generation through oral tradition, known as *Shruti* and *Smriti*, i.e. to listen and to retain. Side by side, we had also the tradition of preserving manuscripts at place, called *Bharati Bhandaras* and *Saraswati Bhandaras*. These were usually attached to the temples. A work of king Trillokyamalle, a Western Chalukyan ruler, refers to librarians as *Saraswati Bhandarikas* and mentions that they were treated on par with the teachers. The tradition continued during the Middle Ages. The libraries attached to *dargahs* (tombs/shrines), *madrasas* (schools), and mosques were suitably maintained. (Mohamed Taher, 1986). Thus 'Librarianship' in the sense of collecting and preserving books and manuscripts has existed in India from times immemorial, but it has been only in the early part of the 10th century that it began to be treated as a distinct field of specialisation with its own normative principles, techniques, theories and practices.

LIBRARY EDUCATION

There is reference to in-service training in universities set up during the letter part of 19th century. (Neelameghan, 1974). However, the credit for starting a formal course of library education goes to William Alonson Borden and Asa Don Dickinson, both students of the great librarian, Melvil Dewey. Borden established a training course at Central Library, Baroda in 1911/1912, and Dickinson at Punjab University in 1915. The training school at Punjab University was considered to be the second known library school in the world, the first being the Columbia school. Dickinson was probably the first to use the term 'Library Science' (LS), for his training course in place of 'Librarianship'. (Konnur, 1986). Gradually other universities and library associations started setting up library schools. Madras Library Association (1929) and Bengal Library Association (1935) started certificate courses. Among the universities, Madras University under Dr. S.R. Ranganathan, took over the certificate course from Madras Library Association in 1931. The course was subsequently converted into post-graduate course of one year duration in 1937. Some more to follow were : Andhra University (1935); Banaras Hindu University (1941); University of Bombay (1944); Calcutta University (1946); University of Delhi (1947); and so on. University of Delhi in 1948, under the guidance of Dr. Ranganathan, started a course in Master of Library Science (MLS) and also provided facilities for research leading to a doctoral degree. It was again the first to start M. Phil course in 1977. Vikram University followed suit in 1973 again under the leadership of Dr. Ranganathan. Some professionals had reservation about the utility of this course as it had been felt that MLS should be regarded as an intermediate research degree leading towards the Ph.D.

Present Position

At present 5 LIS Departments provide education at certificate level, 70 at degree level, 38 at master's level and 27 provide research facilities leading to award of doctoral degree. Education through correspondence is provided by two LIS departments at degree level, one at diploma level and 5 at certificate level. Besides this, Documentation Research & Training Centre (DRTC), Bangalore, and Indian National Scientific Documentation Centre (INSDC) Delhi, have been providing advanced training in Library science with emphasis on documentation and reprography, since 1962 and 1964 respectively.

Contribution of Dr. Ranganathan

One can not but acknowledge here the signal contributions of that erudite scholar and an able administrator, Dr. S.R. Ranganathan. He was one of those renowned librarians who contributed substantially through their theoretical investigations to the recognition of Library and Information Science (LIS) as a scientific discipline (Lazar, 1984). As university librarian, as a professor in library departments and later on as a national professor, and chairman of library committees, he incessantly worked to the last for elevating status of libraries, library education and library profession in India.

EDUCATIONAL FRAMEWORK

Course Title		*Sponsors*
Certificate Course	:	Library Associations; University affiliated Colleges; and University Departments.
Diploma Course	:	Women Polytechnics; and Library Associations
Degree Course	:	University departments;
Master's Course	:	University departments;
Associateship Course	:	Autonomous institutions;
In-Service Training/ Short Term Courses	:	Libraries, documentation centres, and professional associations.

Overview

In addition to formal teaching courses, some universities have introduced correspondence courses at various levels of education. M.L. Sukhadia University and Kashmir University provide correspondence education at certificate level, Punjabi University at diploma level and Madras University both at certificate and degree level. An important development in non-formal teaching is starting of a degree course by Andhra Pradesh Open University in 1985, thus taking education to the doorsteps of the people. Indira Gandhi National Open University equipped with multi-medium instructional system also plans to do so from 1987. This would provide facilities to professionals working at lower level to improve their qualifications and up-date their limited knowledge and skills and also to those who could not get admission to formal courses earlier.

Associateship Courses

To provide advanced training in documentation and reprography, DRTC, Bangalore and INSDOC, New Delhi have started 'Associateship' courses. The Associateship award is considered equivalent to MLIS degree. National Social Science Documentation Centre (NASSDOC) proposes to start Associateship course from 1988.

Refresher Courses

Inservice training courses, known as refresher courses, short courses, workshops, demonstrations, etc., on various library aspects like computer application, machine assisted indexing techniques, information management, preservation of material, etc, are now being conducted. The promoters are library associations, teaching departments/institutes, libraries and information centres, etc. University Grants Commission also provides funds for this to the university departments. National Institute of Small Industry Extension Training (NISIET), Hyderabad conducts short term intensive training programmes in specialised fields of librarianship not only for Indian students but also for students from other developing countries. NASSDOC has also decided to take up short term programmes at regular level. The first such programmes has been conducted on "Management Information System in Libraries and Documentation Centres" from 11-18 May 1987. There is however, need to seriously consider varying opinions expressed by scholars about such courses. To quote one, "The most important positive aspect is, that it updates the knowledge and competencies of practicing professionals... The most negative aspect is the relative shallowness of offerings (mostly because of time constraints) and relative lack of commitment or pressure for learning by participants".

(Saracevic, 1984).

Accreditation of Courses

There is no accreditation agency in India like American Library association, Committee on Accreditation in United States to ensure reasonable standards and quality of output. The Report of the Committee on National Policy on Library and Information System (1986) has stressed the need for such a body.

So far departments of LIS in the universities have broadly adopted the scheme of papers recommended by UGC Review Committee (1965). But its other recommendations regarding staff requirement, physical facilities required, and maintenance of departmental libraries have not been faithfully followed. The Review Committee considered a minimum staff of one reader and two lecturers for BLS course and one professor, two readers and four lecturers for MLS course. Few universities, who have introduced these courses have provided full strength of recommended staff. The situation is indifferent in case of other recommendations.

Regarding composition of 'Accreditation Committees', some have suggested that it should consist of representatives from UGC, AIU (Association of Indian Universities) and library associations. But how far it will succeed in enforcing standards and quality of output in our educational system is a question mark and will require serious consideration. It is better not to have an agency rather than to have a redundant one.

ADMISSION CRITERIA

The admission criteria in general for different levels of courses is as under :

Certificate Course	:	Matriculation/Higher Secondary
Diploma Course	:	Matriculation/Higher Secondary
Degree Course	:	Degree in Arts or science with minimum 45% to 50% marks.

Master's Course	:	Degree in Arts, or Science with a degree in Library Science.
Associateship Course	:	Master's degree or degree in professional discipline like Engineering, Medicine etc. and two years experience in a specialist library.

Overview

The main admission criteria adopted is achievement of certain percentage of marks. But some departments conduct admission test and interview as additional selection criteria.

The objective of entrance test is to measure the aptitude, motivation and potential of applicant to render library service, so that, "Those who are admitted" have not merely the academic qualifications, but also the mental and social attitudes necessary for successful career". (Danton, 1949). These tests are, however, to be conducted very carefully. An evaluation of entrance tests conducted by Osmania University for BLIS and MLIS courses, revealed that only 10 per cent of questions were slanted to libraries.

The minimum educational qualifications prescribed for BLS course is second class bachelor's degree, but due to tough competition for admission, most of the admitted students have master's degree and some even possess doctorate. The strong academic background, never the less, proves an asset to the professionals working in the specialised libraries.

It has been observed that majority of the entrants possess academic background in Arts. To rectify this imbalance, some universities like University of Delhi have reserved seats for different disciplines.

NOMENCLATURE

The names of the training courses continued to change according to to the developments in the LIS field. The courses started earlier were titled as Certificate in Library Science (Short term course) and Diploma in Library Science (One year course after graduation). On the recommendation of UGC Review Committee (1965), the Diploma Course was later termed as Degree Course with almost the same curriculum content. Later on, when the term 'documentation' became more current as a result of increasing number of special libraries offering documentation services and the need for providing training in documentation was recognised, one university changed the name of its course to "Bachelor in Library Science and Documentation". The recent developments in informatics and their revolutionary impact on library services necessitated change in the curriculum contents. The papers on information communication, computer application in libraries, use of micrographics, and duplicating equipments, etc. have been introduced. To reflect this change in syllabii, the UGC Panel on Library and Information Science (1982) recommended that all library schools might consider changing the nomenclature from Bachelor of Library Science (BLS) and Master of Library Science (MLIS) and Master of Library and Information Science (MLIS) respectively. The change has been effected by many university departments. DRTc & INSDOC award Associateship in Documentation and Information Science. The proposed training course at NASSDOC will lead to award of Associateship in Library and Information Studies in Social sciences (ALISS).

DURATION OF COURSE

1. Certificate Course	:	Six to twelve months
*2. Diploma Course	:	One to two years
3. Degree Course	:	One year
**4. Master's Course	:	One year
5. M. Phil	:	One to two years
6. Ph. D.	:	Two to three years
7. Associateship	:	Two years.

* Women Polytechnics provide two years course after matriculation.

** Calcutta University has two years part-time course.

ENROLMENT

The students strength for BLIS and MLIS classes varies from university to university. In 1983, Mysore University admitted 20 students for BLIS and Punjab University 61. Similarly for MLIS, Poona University admitted 3 students and Delhi University 22. Average turn out every year is about 2450 at graduate level (70 departments admitting on an average 35 students) and 380 at master level (38 departments admitting on average of 10 students). Department of Delhi University during the past 40 years have trained 1616 students in LS (1204 obtained post-graduate Diploma/Bachelor's Degree and 414 obtained Master's degree. At associateship level, the two institutes DRTC & INSDOC admit about ten to fifteen students per session. Students from developing countries seek enrolment for various courses in India.

MEDIUM OF INSTRUCTION

The medium of instruction at certificate and degree level is English, Hindi and regional languages. At master's level, and for higher specialised courses it is English only.

COURSE CONTENTS

The broad outline of course contents at different levels is given below:

Certificate Course

i. Library Management (Routine Operations)
ii. Library Organisation
iii. Library Classification (Theory & Practice)
iv. Library Cataloguing (Theory & Practice)
v. Bibliography and Reference Service

**Diploma Course*

i. Library and Society
ii. Bibliography
iii. Cataloguing

iv. Classification
v. Documentation
vi. Library Administration
vii. Library Correspondence
viii. Reference Service

Degree Course

i. Library Administration
ii. Library Organisation
iii. Physical Bibliography and Reference Service
iv. Classification (Theory & Practice)
v. Cataloguing (Theory & Practice)
vi. Documentation

Master's Course

i. Universe of Knowledge (its development and structure)
ii. Depth Classification (Theory)
iii. Advanced Cataloguing
iv. Library System
v. Literature Survey
vi. Research Methodology
(As conducted by Women Polytechnics)
vii. Information Systems
viii. Project Report

Associateship Course

i. Information Sources
ii. Information Processing and Organisation
iii. Information Communication
iv. Information Systems Management
v. Information Technology
vi. Research Methodology
vii. Project Report

Overview

The professional contents at various levels have been framed keeping in view the objectives to be achieved in each case, i.e. familiarisation with library routines at lower level. (Certificate Course), efficient performance of library operations at middle level (Diploma/Degree course), and holding managerial positions at higher level or taking up of consultancy and teaching jobs (Master/Associateship course).

The courses at Degree and Master's level in practice are broadly based on the course contents recommended by the UGC Review Committee (1965) and therefore are of uniform nature. But keeping in view the changing needs of the users in general and of the specialised groups in particular and also as the result of modern technological impact, some teaching departments/institutes have introduced new papers or given disciplinary slant to certain existing papers. Some of the significant changes can be cited as under:

Bachelor of Library & Information Science

Madras University	:	Sociology of Library Science
Guru Nanak Dev University	:	Asian Bibliography
Mysore University		Audio-Visual Library Methods
	:	Rural Library service

Master of Library & Information Science

Bombay University	:	Current Developments in Library Science
Calcutta University	:	Library Services for Children
Delhi University	:	Library Systems Analysis; Information Storage and Retrieval System; Computer Application in Libraries.
Nagpur University	:	Information and Communication Elements of Information Science Systems analysis and statistical methods. Evaluation of information systems and services. Computer Application in Libraries.

Associateship Course (Proposed)

NASSDOC	:	Associateship in Library and Information Studies in Social Sciences.

An outline of the course contents of some universities and institutions is appended to have fair estimate of the papers taught.

Course Trends

If one goes through the course contents at degree and master's level, one tends to agree with the conclusions (Lazar, 1984) arrived at on the basis of analysis of the 22 curricula of library schools in developing countries and which equally apply to the course trends in India. These are :

i. Traditional impact of historical and technical subjects;
ii. Little emphasis on modern information technology; and
iii. Less attention to consolidation, repackaging, assessment and evaluation of information; users needs; information system design; and management.

The criticism on similar line is by another expert. There is over emphasis on classification and cataloguing. These two together account account for four of the eight required courses at both the levels. (Inamdar, 1981).

Academics Vs Techniques

The order issue facing curricula planner is the dilemma over proportional course weightage to be accorded to academic contents and professional techniques. There is no doubt that the aim of the discipline is to develop service competencies rather than to pursue academic achievements. But as the professional has to serve different types of clientele; lay man and expert, a young and old, rural and city folk, he needs an insight into other disciplines like psychology, sociology, management, etc., so that he may perform his duties effectively within varied needs and environment. The librarian should not only fulfil the user's needs but anticipate them well in advance and prepare for them. (Foskett, 1985). Thus a proper balance between academic contents and training in skills is to be maintained in the curricula.

Tradition Vs Technology

While redesigning our courses, we should be careful as not to tilt too much towards the informatics aspects of the discipline of librarianship. It is to be kept in mind that India is still a country of villages with agriculture based economy. The extensive use of sophisticated technology, except at specialised centres, will still take a long time to materialise. The traditional methods of information handling will be practised for more time. Here also there is a need for keeping a balance between the local requirements and introduction of modern technological advances. This balance is to be reflected in the course contents as well. The end objective of education is to fulfil the need of the society. The training should develop in the professionals the quality of dynamic leadership, which may help them to understand user community, adopt innovative methods in providing services with minimum financial and material resources, and at the same time ensure people's participation in the spread of library movement.

Towards Change

We have been stuck took long to the traditional course contents, but the situation is gradually changing as more and more teaching centres are incorporating the expanding dimensions of the discipline in the course contents. The effort is still sporadic. There is a need for a national body to take up this job earnestly and recommend a model curricula for different levels of courses. This curricula should, more or less, keeping in view the local needs and resources, be uniformly followed throughout the country. The Regional Seminar on Curriculum Development in Information Studies held at Bangkok (1985) after a survey of 14 selected post-graduate programmes in library schools throughout the world has made some recommendations about a model curricula for a post-graduate course of the duration of two years for teaching centres in the developing countries. An outline of the recommended papers is reproduced below as this will be relevant to our curricula formulation efforts.

Core Courses

i. Information in its Social and Communication Context
ii. Information User
iii. Information and Data Sources and Information Services
iv. Organisation of Information
v. Design of Library, Information and Data Systems and Services
vi. Management
vii. Application of Information Technology
viii. Research Methods
ix. Dissertation

Elective

i. Planning and Development of National and Regional Information Systems and Networks
ii. Economic and Marketing of Information
iii. Sectoral/Subject Oriented Information Sources and Systems
iv. Community Information Services
v. Technical Writing
vi. Online Searching
vii. Planning and Design of Buildings and Facilities for Libraries and Information Centres
viii. Media and Micrographics
ix. Conservation and Preservation of Materials
x. Programming for Text Manipulation.

Research Activities

Library Science Students at MLISc and Associateship level are required to submit project report as partial fulfilment of course requirement. Besides this about 26 universities undertake registration to Ph.D. University Grants Commission (UGC) and Indian Council of Social Science Research (ICSSR) award scholarships, to doctoral students. National Commission on Science and Technology, Raja Rammohan Roy Library Foundation and ICSSR among others provide research grants for non doctoral research.

Teaching Methods

The lecture method is the generally practised method up to MLISc level. It is only at the Associateship level that lectures are reduced to a minimum. Here the teaching programme includes class discussions, tutorial work, group discussions and project work. This ensures active participation of the students in the learning process. The curricula at degree level too prescribe teaching hours for tutorials and group discussions but these are not attended to seriously by some lecturers.

As part of practical work, the university departments arrange tours to other libraries so that the students may observe a: close hand services provided by different types of libraries. But these are so loosely planned, that the very purpose of undertaking them is lost. Where as, "Visits to libraries and the invitations to visiting speakers are means of promoting relevance to the practical work in our courses, but to be useful, a great deal of time and effort must be invested in preliminary ground work and in post visit or lecture follow up". (Davinson, 1981).

New Techniques

There is greater need to accord due emphasis to the teaching techniques like seminars, role playing exercises, simulations, creativity, etc. as these develop self analytical attitude, and initiative capabilities, which are essential for adopting dynamic approach to the management of information services.

Teaching Aids

Not much use of audio-visual aids is visible in teaching lessons up to Master's level. "The chalk talk" teaching is the most popular method adopted by the teachers. (Kumar, 1986). Though the course contents at Master's level include a paper on "Computer application in libraries", students who opt for this paper, seldom got a chance to use the machine. Some departments even do not have the computer facility. In some universities, the situation is depressing. Here, even simple A-V aids like micro-film readers, over-head projectors and discs are not available to supplement teaching work. Their important role in the educational system cannot be over looked. Under the distance education programmes these aids will play a vital roll. Each teaching department should have at its disposal the equipment such as micro-computers and peripherals, terminals, micrographic and audio-visual hardware, to make teaching meaningful and effective.

TEACHING STANDARDS

Lack of Capable Teachers

Teaching standards are not uniform in the universities. While high standards have been maintained by some departments and institutions, same cannot be said of many others. The main factor responsible for this, as identified by the experts is the lack of capable teachers. Besides this, lack of financial and physical resources have also affected teaching standards. Some universities, without sufficient resources opened LIS departments, because of personal efforts by library professionals, so that they may improve their status, and not because of the actual need for the course. Ranganathan had long back remarked. "It has become a matter of prestige for some universities to open a department of Library Science with M. Lib. Sc courses too, without any thought on the availability of qualified teachers or to what should be taught or how it should be taught in a post-graduate course for a learned profession". There is thus greater need to have strict control over creation of new departments.

Invite Outside Experts

To improve quality of teaching, scholars and teachers from other university departments may be involved for topics of interdisciplinary nature. Documentation Research & Training Centre (DRTC) follows this practice by inviting experts from other institutions particularly for subjects such as computer programming, statistical analysis, reprography and translation services.

Continuing Education Programmes

To improve the knowledge base of the faculty members, continuing education programmes may be frequently organised. Facility may also be provided for training of teachers at some excellent teaching institute, which has sufficient expertise for this, either in the country or abroad. The latter may be attempted under international exchange programmes. The exercise in this direction at regional level like the one now being contemplated under ASTINFO and APINESS Programmes in Asian & the Pacific, will be worth to observe.

MANPOWER PLANNING

Need for a National Survey

To maintain high standards of information services, availability of highly qualified human resource is essential. UGC Review Committee had stressed the need for a national survey of available manpower to estimate prospective requirement, keeping in view of different types of libraries, nature of technology available and information demands of the users. But so far, no such survey has been conducted. The majority of trained manpower is proficient in routine library techniques only. This has led to unemployment. It has been observed that "447 BLIS graduates are on the live rolls of employment exchange in Andhra Pradesh (Eswara Reddy, 1986). The situation is not better in other States. In spite of this unhealthy situation, more universities propose to start similar courses.

Need for Initiation into New Areas

There is another side of the picture. We lack personnel which have been trained to experiment with modern information management techniques/systems. This is one important factor responsible for slow pace of automation in our libraries. There is need for training in the areas like 'Computer and its Application in Libraries', 'Information Centres and Systems', 'Information Storage and Retrieval', and 'Data Base': Their Generation and Management'. (Planning Commission Working Group Report, 1985).

Recruit People with Varied Backgrounds

Another disturbing aspect of the manpower situation as already mentioned is, that most of the students seeking admission to courses have background in arts and humanities. This makes them hesitant in taking up courses in informatics. To overcome this, talented students with background in various branches of science and technology may be provided incentives like scholarships or fellowships at the time of admission. It is encouraging that DRTC and INSDOC provide scholarship to attract better quality of students. This would go a long way in providing manpower needed for modernising our information services, and creating a balance between the type of professionals required and the educational facilities.

CONCLUSIONS

Many suggestions have been made by various professional experts and government committees to improve the quality of LS education. Some of these have already been referred to under the relevant heads. To briefly conclude, these are :

i. The syllabus at all levels should be updated and areas of 'Information Science' should be judiciously integrated with those of 'Library Science'.

ii. National Centre for Education and research in LIS may be established. It may plan and coordinate cooperative programmes like exchange of personnel, curriculum planning, extension lectures, continuing education programmes, etc., provide advanced training to teachers and practitioners; maintain national register of research in progress/completed; and support and guide research programmes.

iii. Howsoever rich syllabus one may plan, it will fail to produce desired results, unless handled by highly qualified and dedicated teaching personnel. There is thus greater urgency to improve the quality of teaching faculty. This would entail rigorous selection criteria and building up mechanism for inservice education of teachers for keeping up with new knowledge and technologies. The availability of a high calibre of teachers should be made a precondition for starting courses in LIS.

iv. Seminars, tutorials, assignments and field tours should be effectively integrated with curricula involving outside experts and agencies. These should be well planned and intelligently executed for producing substantive impact on quality of teaching.

v. Continuing education/in-service training facilities should be recognised as essential part of manpower development programmes and sufficient financial resources may be allocated for this. Such programmes of six to nine weeks duration or of more in the form of seminars, workshops, refresher courses on 'Information Management' 'Users needs' 'Users' 'Surveys', 'Computer application', etc. may be extensively conducted by libraries/documentation centres/professional associations for the teachers and practitioners.

vi. To improve quality of research, talented scholars may be provided financial assistance by research organisations.

vii. Manpower survey may be given top priority and training programmes for different levels may be planned according to the needs of different types of libraries.

Education is a field that needs continuous contemplation, discussion, experimentation, observation and feedback. There will be no single best model suitable for all times and situations. There is a need to experiment with different models and with proper evaluation select one which fulfills our needs to maximum. The issue about course weightage in regards to 'Academics Vs Specialisation' & 'Theory Vs Practice' would always remain in the forefront.

Inspite of short coming in our educational system, the professional competency of our working personnel is quite good. The teaching institutions here not only provide educational facilities to their own nationals but also to the students coming from several other developing countries in Asia & Africa. The professionals trained here occupy prestigious positions in regional and international organisations. The need is to improve and strengthen the existing infrastructure, so assiduously built-up through the efforts of many dedicated professionals led by the great stalwart Dr. S.R. Ranganathan.

APPENDIX

Cou.se Contents of Selective Universities/Institutes

Bachelor of Library & Information Science :

Banaras Hindu University: Library structure and Dev; Lib. Mgt; Lib. Classification (Theory & Practical) Lib. Cataloguing (Theory and Practical); Documentation on Information; Handling Reference Service and Bibliography.

University of Bombay: Mod. Lib., Dev; Bibliography Book Production and Mass Communication; Lib. and Mgt; Lib. Classification - Theory; Liar. Cataloguing - Theory; Reference Service; Documentation and Information Work. Practical exams in Classification and Cataloguing and an oral and a practical test in Reference Work.

University of Calcutta: Library Classification (Theory & Practical); Cataloguing (Theory & Practical); Library Orgn.; Library Admn; Bibliography and Book Selection; Reference Service & Documentation.

University of Delhi: Lib. Classification (Theory & Practical) Lib. Cataloguing (Theory & Practical); Reference and Information Sources; Reference and Information Services; Lib. and Society; Lib. Admn. and Mgt.

University of Madras: Library Mgt; Social of Library Sc; Literature Study; Classification and Cataloguing; Bibliography; Reference service; Documentation.

Open University Course Programmes

Andhra Pradesh Open University, Hyderabad: Library and Community; Library Management; Classification and Cataloguing (Theory); Bibliography and Reference Source and Services; Documentation and Information Service; Special Librarianship; Classification (Practice); Cataloguing (Practice).

Indira Gandhi National Open University, Delhi*: Library and Society; Library Management; Library Classification (Theory & Practice); Library Cataloguing (Theory & Practical); Bibliography & Reference Sources; Information Services; Computer Basics and Applications.

Master of Library and Information Science

Banaras Hindu University: University of knowledge; Research Methods; Depth Classification (Theory and Practical) Adv. Cataloguing (Theory and Practical); Lib. System and Services; Information Sources, Dissertation.

University of Bombay: Comparative Studies in Librarianship Research Methods & Documentation Techniques; Current Developments in Lib Sc. Dissertation : Viva Voce.

University of Calcutta: *Compulsory Subjects*: Classification; Cataloguing; Bibliography; Reference Service; Documentation and Information Retrieval; The book - its History and Development including Publishing and Book Trade; Lib Planning (Architecture and Equipment); Litt. of Humanities and Social Sc. & of Sc. and Tech; Practical; *Optional*: Any one of following: Pub. Lib. System; Academic Lib. System; Research and Special Libraries; Lib. Service

---

* Proposed to be introduced from 1987.

for children including Children's Litt; Manuscript and Archival Libraries.

University of Delhi: Universe of knowledge; Depth Classification (Theory & Practical); Library System Analysis and Elements of Statistical Methods; Bibliography & Literature in any one of the following: The Humanities; Natural Sc. Social Sc.; Medical Sc.; Agril. Sc.; Engg & Tech; Literature Surveys & Field Surveys; Adv. Library Cataloguing (Practice); Current Problems in Library and Information Sc. *Any one of the following*: Information Storage and Retrieval System; Reprography; Computer Application in Library. *Any one of the following*: Public Library System; Academic Library System; Research and Technical Library System; Medical Library System; Agril. Library System; Engg. and Technological Library System; Project Report.

University of Madras: Orgn. of Information Materials; Information Transfer & Dissemination; Research Methodology; Planning & Mgt; Information Technology Application; Guided Project. *Any one of the following*: Univ. & College Library System; Pub. Library System; Indl. Information System & Service; Social Science Information System; Health Sciences Information System; Government Publications.

Nagpur University: Information and Communication; Elements of Information Science; Information Control Techniques; Evaluation of Information Systems and Services; Systems Analysis and Elements of Statistical Methods; Computer Application in Library and Information Work; Practical/Observation Record; Project Work.

Source: Universities Handbook, 1985-86.
Associateship Course

Documentation Research and Training Centre, Bangalore (Award : Associateship in Documentation and Information Science).

Core Subjects

Foundations of Information Science
Information Sources and Communication Media
Information Systems and Programmes
Information Processing and Organisation
Information Transfer and Dissemination
Information Technology and Systems Design
Information Centre/System
Planning and Management

Guided Research Project

Two Research Projects to be submitted

Electives

Industrial Information Systems and Services
Information System and Services for R & D
Information System and Services for Planning
Management Information System
Health Sciences Information Systems and Services
Environmental Information Systems and Services
Social Sciences Information Systems and Services

Supporting Courses

Forms part of appropriate papers
Relevant selections from elements of
Mathematics, Statistics and
Operations Research (Paper I)
Research Methodology (Paper I)
Technical Report Writing (Paper I)
Communication (Paper 2)
Linguistics (Paper 4)

Source : Documentation Research and Training Centre
Courses in Documentation and Information
Science : Prospectus and syllabus

Indian National Scientific Documentation Centre, New Delhi
(Award : Associateship in Information Science)

Core Subjects

Information, Communication and Society
Technical Writing and Information Analysis
Information Sources and Media
Information Processing and Organisation
Information Systems and Services
Information Technology I : Concepts, Theories, Systems
Information Technology II : Applications
Information System Centre Management

Guided Research

Project Work and Dissertation

Electives

Information System for Planning
Information System for Industry
Bio-medical Information System
Energy Information System
Environmental Science Information System

Supporting Subjects

Appropriate and relevant selections from other disciplines
Research Methodology Mathematics, Statistical Methods,

Operations Research, Systems Theory, Information Linguistics, Behavioural Studies etc.

Source: Indian National Scientific Documentation Centre
Training Course in information science :
Prospectus and Syllabus.

National Social Science Documentation Centre*
(Award : Associateship in Library Information Studies in Social Sciences)

i. Information, Communication and Society
ii. Information and Data Sources in Social Sciences
iii. Information and Data Services in Social Sciences
iv. Organisation of Information
v. Design of Library, Information and Data Systems and Services
vi. Application of Information Technology
vii. Research Methods
viii. Library and Information Systems Management
ix. Dissertation.

REFERENCES

1. Cherian, P.V. Presidential address. *In*: Seminar on Library Education, 1965, Bombay. Report. Bombay, S.N.D.T. Women's University, 1966. p 8
2. Committee On National Policy on Library and Information System. *See*: INDIA CULTURE (Department of-), NATIONAL POLICY ON LIBRARY AND INFORMATION SYSTEM (Committee on-)
3. Danton J. Periam : *Education for Librarianship*. Paris, Unesco, 1949. p 46
4. Davinson (Donald) : Thoughts on a model syllabus for a two year Master's degree course. *In*: Mangla P.B. *ed. Library and information science education in India*. New Delhi, Macmillan, 1981. p 102-108.
5. Documentation Research Hand Training Centre (Bangalore) Courses in documentation and information science : Prospectus and syllabus. p 14. (cyclostyled)
6. Eswara Reddy, D B : Opinion expressed at "Seminar on perspectives in education and training of LIS personnel on 22-23 Nov. 1985 at Osmania University Library, Hyderabad".

---

* The training of one year duration is proposed to be started from 1987.

7. Foskett, D J : Address at "Seminar on perspectives in education and training of LIS personnel on 22-23 Nov. 1985 at Osmania University Library, Hyderabad".
8. Inamdar, N B and Riswadkar, M R : India. (*In*: Contemporary developments in Librarianship : An international handbook, *ed.* by Miles M. Jackson) London, Library Association, 1981, p 186.
9. India Culture (Department of -), National Policy On Library and Information System. (Committee on -) National Policy on library and Information System : A presentation. New Delhi. The Committee, 1986. p 30
10. India Planning (Commission). Modernisation of Library Services and Informatics for the 7th Five Year Plan (1985-90) (Working Group on -). Report. New Delhi, The Working Group, 1984. 123 p.
11. Indian National Scientific Documentation Centre, (New Delhi) Information Science (Training Course in -). Prospectus and syllabus, 1986. New Delhi, Insdoc, 1986. 29p.
12. Konnur, M B : Transnational library relations : The Indo-American experience.
Ph D Thesis. University of Poona, 1986, p 216
13. Kumar, P S G : Promoting the use of audio-visual aids : Paper presented at V National Seminar of IATLIS on Use of Audiovisual Aids in Library and Information Science Teaching, Lucknow, 9-10 Nov. 1986, p 18
14. Lazer, Peter: Some considerations on the education and training of librarians and information specialists. *Annals of Library Science and Documentation* 31 (1-2) : 1984 : p 1-12
15. Mohamed, Taher and Khan, Amin Ahmed and (Muhammed Burhanuddin) : Dargah libraries in India : A comparative study. *International Library Review* 18 : 1986, p 337-45
16. Neelameghan, A : Education for librarians in India. *In*: *Encyclopedia of Library and Information science*. Vol. II N.Y; Marcel Dekker, 1974, p 323
17. Ranganathan, S R : Education and research in library science. *Cultural Forum* (Libraries special number) 1967, p 10
18. Regional Seminar on Curriculum Development in Information Studies (Bangkok) (17-21 Sep. 1985). Final report. Paris,l Unesco, PGI, 1985. p 38 (PGI-85/NS/33)
19. Saracevic, Tefko and Others. Issues in Information science education in developing countries. *Journal of the American Society for Information Science*, 36(3) : 1984 : p 192-99
20. *University Grants Commission. (Review Committee on 1965 Library Science in Indian Universities : Report New Delhi, UGC. p 2-340
21. Working Group on Modernisation of Library Services and informatics for the 7th Five Year Plan (1985-90) *See*
India. Planning Commission. Working Group on Modernisation of Library Services and Informatics for the 7th Five Year Plan (1985-90)
*University Grants Commission Library and Information Science (Panelon). Recommendations. 1982 (Mimeographed).

FOURTEEN

Inter-Library Resources Centre: Projection and Constrains

INTRODUCTION

Although the tradition of teaching and research in social sciences in India is of recent origin, the concern over the outcome of rapid changes and the response of the Indian academic community to developments abroad have contributed to the speedy growth of social sciences in the country. In the face of ever-burgeoning materials, published and otherwise, it is almost impossible for a single library to cope with all the needs of its users.

To keep pace with the information explosion, various methods have been suggested or practised the world over. These include structured pattern of libraries leading to the development of repositories and resource sharing. In India, we have embarked on a new experiment, the Inter-Library Resources Centre, to collect reading matter and research tools for scholars, combining the salient features of inter-library lending and a repository for resource sharing in the process.

RESOURCE SHARING

Resource sharing is a term with wider connotations than cooperation. It is an essential element in providing library and information services, sufficient to meet the needs of a country's economic and social development.

The objectives of "resource sharing" can be achieved through various organisational arrangements called the consortium, the network or the cooperative. Generally, the term "resource" signifies a thing, a person or action; which is handy in times of need. "Resource sharing" involved reciprocity, "a partnership in which each member has something useful to contribute to others and which each is willing and able to make available when needed. Resource sharing denotes a mode of operation whereby functions are shared in common by a number of libraries".

The justification of resource sharing, particularly in India, is apparent from the fact that libraries organising research collections have to spend a lion's share of their acquisition budgets in purchasing materials that are seldom, if ever, used. The libraries, in this context, should strive more and more to realise "use" as well as "non-use" in terms of the acquisition budgets earmarked for each category. And this brings them logically to the resource sharing efforts.

INTER-LIBRARY LENDING

A traditional and tested method to this end is the "Inter-Library Lending System", but it has certain limitations. When the number of these transactions is small and not a daily occurrence, the inter-library loan system is both cheap and quick. But if the transactions are more frequent, they tend to be more complex and also costlier. Different libraries have different rules on loaning their materials. Some, for example, do not send out periodicals as a matter of rule, while some other stipulate that the loaned material must be used on the premises of the borrowing library. The security and care of the loan-material poses delicate issues, which are sometimes insoluble.

REPOSITORIES

The "repository" concept is generally equated with "the storage, preservation and continued availability of low-use material discarded by libraries through lack of space". Few libraries play the role of a repository exclusively, many of them continue, in themselves, the functions of a repository as well as the "usual" library.

Repositories are precluded from taking an active part in national inter-lending or acquisition systems because of a lack of ability or willingness to transfer library stock, paucity of suitable buildings and shortage of trained manpower, and also because of "user perceptions of their need for on-site access".

In the absence of clear-cut legislative guidelines there are sharp differences of opinion on what stock should be relegated to a repository, and the decisions have to be left to the whims of the relegating library, which is frequently weak in methods of transfer and in maintaining the catalogue and other records.

Repositories, it has been emphasised, are not glamorous. "They do not have the immediacy of on-line retrieval, the excitement of new techniques, even the human satisfaction of community information services. And yet, they are fundamental to all library and information activities, and it is shortsighted to concentrate on the techniques of information exploitation if the information itself is being slowly but inexorably lost."

RESOURCES CENTRE

Another method, which is of far-reaching significance in terms of sharing resources among several libraries, is to establish a Centre, where different libraries could deposit such research material as are not used frequently by them, and the Centre, in its turn, would be responsible for organising the materials and making them available to all visiting scholars. Obviously, the second alternative would be a great service to research workers. If the service is properly organised, researchers will not be required to visit different libraries in search of material now concentrated at the centre in a substantially large quantity.

A Centre of this kind has added advantages, some of which are:

i. The depositing libraries could have increased space on their shelves after their less used volumes are removed to the Centre. They can fill the vacuum with more recent books needed by their regular users.

ii. The authorities of the depositing libraries could also have the satisfaction that the research material acquired by them painstakingly over several years could now be used profitably and more frequently by a large number of local as well as out-station social scientists.
iii. The care and preservation of their materials ensured, the depositing libraries could have their budget allocations used for other purposes.
iv. Any lacunae in the collections from the depositing libraries could be filled up by the materials deposited by other libraries at the Centre. This is particularly true of the gaps in the back files of periodicals which are very expensive to fill, and
v. A spirit of active and meaningful cooperation would be generated among the libraries, which could vie with one another to extend their cooperation to other spheres, and all this could lead to a better service to their users. These libraries could, in the circumstances, share acquisition programmes to step up specialisation, cataloguing and programming to secure consistency and uniformity and micro-filming programmes.

The Centre may also undertake to establish and maintain a union catalogue of foreign monographs currently acquired by all or selected depositing libraries if each of them could send a card to the Centre for every new foreign monograph acquired by them. A union catalogue of this type along with the union catalogue of Social Sciences Serials would be yet another information tool on the growing resources for social science research in the libraries.

To establishment of the centre can help evolve a well-coordinated system, under which the unit libraries may overcome local difficulties of staff, space and budget.

DELHI SCENE

The capital has perhaps the largest cluster of libraries in India and they may be broadly divided into four groups:

i. Academic libraries include the libraries of the universities and colleges. These are naturally multifocal in their acquisition, i.e., they have acquired and preserved, over many years, printed materials in the form of books, periodicals and pamphlets in various disciplines of knowledge including social sciences for the needs of their students and faculties.

ii. The Government of India libraries are more restricted in their scope. Each of them has acquired and preserved, for several years, printed materials in the form of books, periodicals, pamphlets and also government publications primarily on such subjects as are within the scope of activities of its parent body, which is either the Ministry, its department or attached or subordinate office. Since the total governmental activities are comprehensive of all phases of social life, almost all Government of India libraries are resource bases for social research.

iii. The libraries of autonomous institutions are even more specialised than Government of India libraries. each of these institutions has very specific activities and most of them are devoted to study and research in particular branches of social sciences, e.g., the Indian Institute of Public Administration, Institute of Defence Studies and Analysis, Institute of Foreign Trade, Institute of Applied Manpower Research, Indian Law Institute, and so on.

iv. Public Libraries are established to cater to the needs of general public and often develop special collections, e.g., Delhi Public Library, Delhi.

The total number of libraries of all these categories in Delhi would be about 150. Many of them were established long before Independence, althougn quite a few have come into existence only after 1947. As reservoirs of research material, about half of these libraries are known to have large collections of social science material. A rough estimate is that they would have, between them, over 20 lakh volumes and their total annual intake by purchase, gift and exchange would exceed 100,000 titles. There are about 900 library trained personnel engaged in these libraries and annual maintenance cost including staff salary, book budgets and other services would be close to Rs. 3 crores. Delhi thus has a vast resource base for research in social sciences and it is expanding year after year by the establishment of new institutions and by additional funds becoming available.

An inevitable feature of such a situation is that a good deal of resource materials has become duplicated, some of it is available at only a few places and some needed material is perhaps nowhere available among the libraries in the city. None of these libraries has become, or will ever become, self-sufficient for its actual or potential needs. Moreover, most of these libraries have grown and are growing beyond their available space capacity. In consequence, the other material which is ordinarily less frequently used gets crowded on shelves in two or three rows and also gets relatively less attended to, as far as its maintenance is concerned. As a result, even the material which was once known to be available is not often located quickly for subsequent use. Yet another disadvantage to the researcher in social sciences is that he has to go from one library to another in search of his material and only in anticipation that the material required by him may become available to him on time in his pursuit of several libraries. In this, he faces some odd situations. Many of the government libraries require special passes to visit them. There are not always good reading facilities provided in some libraries. Most libraries function during normal office hours only and the paucity of staff and space in many of these libraries renders the use of the material somewhat difficult for a research worker visiting Delhi for a short period.

ICSSR with its primary objective to promote research in social sciences since its inception in 1969 took note of this situation and initiated several programmes, some time bound and some continuing, but all aimed at facilitating social science research. One such important programme has been the compilation of union catalogue of social science periodicals and serials. The Union catalogue enables a person to locate social sciences serials and periodicals available in important libraries of India. On the completion of the first phase of union catalogue project, the compilation of a retrospective index of Indian social science periodicals was taken up followed by "area studies bibliographies" and "languages bibliographies".

INTER-LIBRARY RESOURCES CENTRE

In 1973, ICSSR jointly with the Jawaharlal Nehru University established Inter-Library Resources Centre (ILRC). For this purpose, the University made available the library wing of its building at 35 Ferozeshah Road and the facilities of its hostel near by. The main office of ILRC at 35 Ferozeshah Road is very centrally located as far as the libraries having a large collection of social science research material are concerned and is open for use by the general public. To begin with, the Council invited a meeting of the librarians of the important libraries in Delhi and requested them to deposit only their back files of social science periodicals which are not too often in use in their libraries.

The response was very good. The Council, therefore, made formal arrangements to accept the deposits of back files of social science periodicals, newspapers and government documents. Under this scheme a dozen local libraries, to begin with, deposited materials non-current, infrequently used yet important from the point of research with ILRC. The idea caught on, and the number of participating libraries including NASSDOC has risen to 38. The deposits are accepted on condition that the proprietary right of each depositing library in respect of its material will be respected and the material will be preserved and made available for consultation on the premises. The depositing libraries can withdraw their deposits temporarily or permanently if they so desire. They may also gift the material to ILRC at their will. Several libraries have already gifted some material. The material is processed in a simple manner to enable its quick location for use. The depository collection has begun to attract visitors wishing to use this material because the back files of journals, research reports and government documents are now available for consultation under one roof.

Service

In setting up ILRC, the Council's objective has been not simply of accumulating social science research material at one place, but to provide a variety of services to the community of social scientists among which the following may be mentioned:

i. To the social scientists who are stationed in Delhi, ILRC is within easy reach. At present ILRC remains open on all days of the year except January 26, August 15, and October 2, from 9.30 a.m. to 6.00 p.m. In course of time, the working hours of ILRC would be extended to facilitate its use for longer hours on working days as well as Sundays and other holidays.

ii. For persons stationed elsewhere in India, a scheme of study grants provides for two-way travel and a modest allowance per day for lodging and boarding. Efforts are made to provide accommodation in the hostel near by.

iii. ILRC provides reprographic service so that readable photocopies of required articles from periodicals or of reasonable extracts from other documents in the centre are supplied on a cost-basis to local as well as outside scholars. The charges at present are Re. 0.40 per exposure.

iv. ILRC also provides short bibliographies on specific subjects on demand, tailored to the needs of the research scholar. There is a nominal charge of Rs. 10 for 25 entries or a part thereof.

v. For inter-library loan services, the Centre also maintains a carrier service so that the periodical volumes or documents which are not available in the Centre but are available in some library in Delhi can be obtained on loan for consultation in its premises. The 32 volumes of Union Catalogue of Social Science Periodicals and Serials which have already been published enable the location of periodicals volumes in any of the 65 libraries in Delhi.

It is proposed to connect ILRC in New Delhi with Regional centres set up by the Indian Council of Social Science Research, outside Delhi.

Constraints

Normally monetary and man-power resources create bottlenecks. But in the case of ILRC it is not so, if past experience, achievements and performance of ILRC are any indication.

The role of resource sharing in collecting available information materials, old and current, from various sources systematically, organising, preserving and making them available to the users speedily has been recognised. What probably is not appreciated is that no resource sharing network can perform this role if efforts lack sincerity of the purpose.

Unfortunately, an awareness of the requirements of resource sharing and networking as a base of the effective library services in the context of national planning and development is generally lacking in our country. Resource sharing concept has so far received only lip sympathy of those who matter and administrators are generally too preoccupied to pay heed to what resource sharing concept entails. Even intellectuals and known-to-be-library-lovers when they happen to be at the decision-making level tend to neglect, rather act to dismantle whatsoever structure is there, just for the sake of administrative convenience and immediate short-term benefits; and this despite sufficient realisation that decision-making should be done on the basis of proven results. Such patrons as the library set-up and resource sharing network had served so well in their research pursuits do not show the slightest hesitation in doing this disservice and that, too, giving the library set-up no chance to point out the likely negative results of such hasty unilateral action. Libraries and networking today are in fact laboratories for experimentation for such academics.

There is also the danger within inasmuch as we professionals help or hate the resource-sharing concept according to our own personal vested interests and future prospects, because of our ambitions rather than the institutional interest.

The attitude of starting a profit-sharing centre, and not resource-sharing centre also seems to have crept in. These disastrous attitudes are serious constraints which need to be debated. It would, therefore, not be out of place to draw the attention of all concerned-administrators, intellectuals, professionals and social scientists-to their obligations towards strengthening of the inter-library resources centre concept as also development and growth of ILRC to enable it to provide the services vis-a-vis the needs of the research community and the economy of country.

SECTION SEVEN

INFORMATION TECHNOLOGY

FIFTEEN

Information Transfer and Modern Technology

Libraries in India are still perceived as a *bonum librorium copia*; or a collection of books and the librarian as the custodian for these books. Before we start thinking of new library techniques and development of information transfer, we have first to see the library as a "convivial tool". Prof. Ivan Illich, in his *Tools for Conviviality*, explains convivial tools as "those which each person who uses them has the greatest opportunity to enrich the environment with the fruits of his vision". I also venture to recollect De Heinz von Forester's words who saw in a library the most awesome "manifestation of the traces of our civilisation and the librarian, in the role of a midwife or an obstetrician, helping people giving birth to new ideas, understanding and insights". If we, the library professionals in India do so, we will have to equip ourselves to meet the demands of the satellite age, and to come to grips with it so that like the piece of soap that continuously slips out of the hands of Dumpy in the fairy tale of "Snow-white" it does not slip from our hands.

Taking the spectrum of information transfer only, we find that there has been a transition from the traditional library service to electronic research systems. The transitional period had three major characteristics:

1. Computers were used to print on paper and the resulting product was distributed in a completely conventional manner through the mail.
2. Printed data bases and their machine-readable equivalents existed side by side but, by and large, the former had not been replaced by the latter. Before the end of the 1970's however, there were a handful of secondary data bases completely con-

verted from printed to electronic form.

3. The 1980's witnessed new data bases in machine-readable form only, without ever existing in paper form. The majority of these were actually data banks-files of numerical, statistical, physical, chemical data which could be regarded as essentially types of "paperless reference books" that emerged in electronic era.

While the developed world has greatly benefited from the computer technology, we in the Third World have still to strive for harnessing this developed medium. Taking a look at the development of information technology in India, Mr. P.V. Narasimha Rao, the then Union Minister of Education in his address at the 6th International Book Trade Fair, New Delhi, said "If it is not the old stone, it will have to be new chip (the micro-processor). The changeover is inevitable." In order to delineate the subject, an effort is made to determine its nature by checking off a short list of achievements and characteristics.

USE OF COMPUTERS IN INDIAN LIBRARIES/INFORMATION CENTRES

It has been estimated that in India there are nearly 216 institutions (all type) using computers. According to the state-of-art report by B. Guha, 35 libraries are using this technology. Let us have a look at the use to which they have been put:

1. BHEL at Hyderabad is providing an SDI service to 56 user groups; and the work for the compilation of a union catalogue of periodicals in different BHEL libraries and also a catalogue of available special materials is going on.
   Technical Information Centre (BHEL) has developed an acquisition system programme package for the library, which performs 17 functions.
2. The Central Food Technological Research Institute (Mysore) has conducted experiments for providing SDI service and also retrospective searches.
3. Computeronics India Ltd, Bombay, has developed a programme to list new additions to the library.
4. I.I.T., Delhi has experimented on the computerisation of textbook holdings in order to obtain their up-to-programme for cir-

culation of books also.

5. In INSDOC computer is being used for :

   (a) Preparation of indexes and their cumulation, e.g. Author & Keyword indexes of the Indian Science Abstracts and the corresponding indexes of the National Index Translations;
   (b) Preparation and processing of union catalogue data and directory type data; and
   (c) Processing of data bases for SDI service.

6. NASSDOC uses computer for compiling:

   (a) India 2000 : An annotated bibliography 1987;
   (b) Core list of social science periodicals;
   (c) Periodicals in NASSDOC; and
   (d) Programme for circulation control has also been developed.

ICSSR – DATA ARCHIVES

The Data Archives acquires data sets generated in ICSSR sponsored aided projects in machine-readable form. At present about 92 data sets are available for secondary analysis. The entire information contained in the "National Register of Social Scientists in India" has been maintained and updated through the computer.

Data Archives also prepares an Inventory of Data Holdings at different research institutes. So far 488 studies based on quantitative data from 26 institutions have been collected by it.

CENTRE FOR INSTRUCTIONAL TECHNOLOGY

It is working on research and training in communication technology. It has installed ISIS package at the Computeronics Data Processing Centre. DEVSIS gets input in respect of Indian published and unpublished documents through CENDIT. The by-product of this activity is the experimental issue of DEVINDEX-India produced through computer.

NATIONAL INFORMATICS CENTRE

It is playing a promotional role in developing a computer network for appropriate information systems.

So far more than 150 data bases have been created by NIC for various user organisations in the government of India. In addition, it has developed a nationalised social data bank to assist various users in the fields of social-economic statistics and statistics relating to foreign trade, agriculture, industry, etc.

In the field of documentation, NIC has undertaken development of a bibliographic system on techno-economic information documents.

INDIAN SOCIETY OF AGRICULTURAL ECONOMICS

It has produced through computer an index of articles on agricultural economics covering the period of 1950-70.

On reviewing the present situation, it seems that whereas the use of computers in Data Archives of ICSSR, CENDIT and NIC is at an advanced stage, the situation demands a thorough survey of the situation in other social sciences research libraries and information centres.

Problems

These libraries and information centres using computer facilities have developed systems independently resulting in inconsistency in programmes, record format, output format, etc. There is hardly any scope of sharing of programmes or programming efforts and skills. If a new library wants to introduce computerisation, it has to develop its own capabilities.

Forthcoming Plans

ICSSR - NASSDOC

The National Social Science Documentation Centre is working

on the details of computerising the union catalogue of social science serials available in various research libraries in the country. It also plans to put the Retrospective Index to Indian Social Science Periodicals into machine-readable form and computerise the library routline work.

The data regarding study grants to scholars to visit libraries has already been transferred on punched cards for the centralised centre and may be computerised in due course.

A committee appointed by ICSSR to prepare a plan for the development of a social science information system in the country has suggested an information network in social sciences comprising:

1. National Centres of Information,
2. Regional Centres of Information,
3. Sectoral System, and
4. Other specialised services.

The successful working of the network would greatly depend upon suitable modern technology support like the use of computers, microprocessors, microfilming equipments video tapes, teleprinters and photocopiers.

UGC

UGC has established information service centres in social sciences for teachers and scientists working in colleges and universities at SNDT University, Bombay, and M.S. University, Baroda. These Centres have been provided with computer facilities.

It has been estimated that over the next decade computer logic will drop 25 per cent per year and computer memory costs will decline 40 per cent per year. Advances in data base management systems and networking will make computer-based systems affordable even for the small library.

OTHER INNOVATIONS/TECHNIQUES

While the computers form the new frontline in information

transfer, there are some other modern techniques like microphotography, electrophotocopying and advanced telecommunication systems. Their application in Indian libraries requires to be assessed and investigated.

Microphotography

Micrographics greatly help in solving space problem in libraries. Even while a premier institution like the Nehru Memorial Museum and Library has a large collection of periodicals and newspapers on microfilm rolls (5,866) and on microfiche (10,588), there is not much evidence of their use in social science libraries. This may be due to lack of good quality indigenous equipment, scholars being long accustomed to using documents in hard form as also perhaps the inconvenience and fatigue felt by the users.

The National Social Science Documentation Centre is also getting its theses collection microfilmed and has acquired back volumes of journals in microform. To facilitate the use of microform material one Reader-cum-Printer and four microfilmfiche readers have been acquired. It is also proposed to set up a microfilming unit of its own to cater to the needs of other social sciences research institutions.

Electronic Photocopying

While we have not had to wrestle with copyright laws as yet, photocopying facilities have proved a boon in supplying the desired research material quickly and at economical cost. Good copiers are now being manufactured in our country with international collaboration. Research institutes realise the importance of plain paper copiers and in the very near future a copier in each library would be an aid to Laws of Library Science.

Video-Tapes

These can be used for information storage and dissemination. The day is not far off when they will take their rightful place in library holdings.

In India the facility is available in foreign information centres. Select research/information centres will have to study cost-use ratio and maintenance problems involved in their use.

Telecommunication

During the 1980s the worldwide satellite networks based on digital transmission emerged and made access to faraway data bases possible.

The Electronic Information Exchange System, USA, is a computer-based communication system which links 700 data bases all over North America and Europe.

With the advances in telecommunication, the time to scan any document will be considerably saved, the request for inter-library loan quickly processed, so on and so forth. Many libraries in the USA use telefacsimile service like LDX (Long Distance Xerox) for their inter-library loan activities.

Inspite of the fact that information technology has developed so much, we in India have hardly made 30 per cent use, mainly for the following reasons:

1. Lack of sufficient resources,
2. Lack of cheap indigenous equipment/technology,
3. Lack of co-ordination and cooperation among the information scientists and librarians.
4. Lack of enough trained manpower.

WORD OF CAUTION

It should not be inferred that modernised technology alone will solve the library's operational problems. There is a greater need to understand the fundamentals of service vis-a-vis nature of user needs. Professionals will have to know to differentiate between various models, to be more knowledgeable about consumer demand, the use of information as such and the value of information to the user.

The users of information are an integral part of and the final link in the information transfer. The information transfer and planning for new techniques in Indian libraries will have to be "national" first and then fully computerised.

SIXTEEN

Computers in Information Centres in India

The computer technology has revolutionised the work process in all societal fields which may be either research laboratory, production unit, information network or day-to-day public utility service (railways, schools, hospitals) and what have you. In a lighter vein, says Robens, "If the world is to disappear in a nuclear catastrophe, it will be a computer that will have worked out the day and the time and the place."

Computer Hardware

India, though a late starter, is second only to Japan in the Asian countries, regarding the number of computers installed. According to Jetly, the computer installation base is about 3,000 with the break-up as follows : imported, 600 and indigenous, 2,400.

The first digital computer, a British HEC 2, was installed in the 1950's at the Indian Statistical Institute, Calcutta. The first indigenous computer was developed at the Tata Institute of Fundamental Research, Bombay, in the late sixties. Since then, there has been a steady growth in the manufacture of computers.

At present the Electronic Corporation of India, Hyderabad, has been producing third generation computers of TDC Series. The talks are on with the U.S. Government for the purchase and manufacture under licence of super-computers. Thus within a short span of three decades, the computer industry has emerged from virtual non-existence to a stage of respectability. The prominent manufacturing units in the private and public sectors are ICL, ECIL, BEL, IDM,

IBM, HCL, UPTRON, KELTRON, WIPRO and DCM.

The progress in the micro-computer field is also no less creditable. The micro-computer market accounted for 30 per cent of the computer industry turnover notching up sales of Rs. 28.3 crores in 1983-84. There are about 25 manufacturers of micro-computers and more are planning to enter the field.

Computer Software

According to Jetly, 500 organisations are engaged in this activity These may be classified as :

1. (a) Consultancy organisations	
(b) Data Centres	400
(c) Software Houses	
2. Indigenous Computers	50
3. Educational Institute/R&D Labs, and development agencies	25
4. Distributors of foreign suppliers	25

India exported US $ 20 million worth of computer software and services in 1983-84. The software is available in most of the fields.

Computer Application

Computers are now applied to diverse purpose like accounting, communication systems, management control, methodology, public utility services, etc. During the Eighth Five Year Plan, some new computer networks are proposed and the existing ones are to be strengthened, like: NICNET (for government informatics), (ii) INDONET (commercial network for the entire country), (iii) RAILNET (computer network for railways), (iv) OILNET (computer network for oil sector) (v) BANKNET (computer network for banking applications). Availability of application packages has facilitated the use of the computers in these fields. But so far as the information field is concerned, computer application has been insignificant and even the little that is observed is mostly in science libraries. Moreover, the libraries and information centres do not have exclusive use of the computers. For, these are primarily meant for their parent organisations.

Pace of Computerisation

With the long tradition and experience in collecting, organising, storing and retrieving information, for providing a variety of services, information scientists are uniquely qualified to use and manage computers and machine-readable information.

In our country, in spite of having a strong base in both hardware and software, computerisation pace in information centres/libraries has been limited both in scale and type. The centres using computers can be counted on finger-tips. Some of the major developments in the field have been tabulated below.

Computerisation of Bibliographic Process
Highlights Since 1984

Year	Events
1964	INSDOC/IIT Kanpur attempts National Union Catalogue of Scientific Serials using IBM/1620 computer.
1968-69	INSDOC'S efforts for use of computers to the development of information products: i. Use of IBM/1620 model at Delhi School of Economics for "Roster of Technical Translators in India". ii. Author and Subject Indices for Indian Science Abstracts (ISA) using IBM 360/44 at Delhi University Computer Centre.
1970	i. Bhabha Atomic Research Centre (BARC) started participating in INIS. ii. TIFR library catalogues based on annual acquisitions. iii. DOCFINDER developed at DRTC, Bangalore.
1976	CHEM/SDI information retrieval system Jointly operated by INSDOC, New Delhi, and IIT, Madras.

1977 DRTC develops a package on ICL 1901 computer system for SDI service for BHEL, Hyderabad.

1978 Electronics Commission (IPAG), New Delhi, uses HP 21 MX mini-computer system and develops bibliographic data base for library books on an experimental basis for in-house utilisation.

1980 onwards Automatic thesaurus generation efforts at DRTC, Bangalore.

1980-81 Physical Research Laboratory, Ahmedabad, develops

i. Computerised Periodicals Management System and
ii. Computerised Books Procurement System. IBM 360/44 computer system on an off-line, batch processing mode used.

1981 "Union Catalogue of Scientific Conference proceedings: A pilot Fascicule", Brought out by INSDOC using IBM 360/44 computer system.

1981 Publication Information Directorate, New Delhi, brings out computerised keyword and author indexes of its journal, "Medicinal and Aromatic Plants Abstracts", using HP-1000 mini-computer with 64K main memory.

1982 Technical Information Centre of Bharat Heavy Electricals Ltd., Hyderabad, develops book acquisition system using TEXASTI 990 micro-computer.

1983 NIC's Library Data base accessed by NICNET (NIC Computer Network) members connected to Cyber System.

1984 Computer terminal installed at NIC Library for its routine information retrieval jobs.

The National Informatics Centre develops a Pilot System for the National Medical Library for providing medical retrieval service. A Legal Information Retrieval System based on the Constitution of India developed for Ministry of Law, Justice and Company Affairs.

Some of the recent developments in Social Science Centres are:

National Council of Applied Economic Research, New Delhi, brings out an indexing journal, *Artha Suchi,* using IBM HP-3000 computer on MINISIS Programme.

CENDIT brought out a preliminary issue of DFVINDEX-INDIA similarly using MINISIS Programme.

The Planning Commission Library undertakes convers on (f periodicals' holdings into machine-readable form.

The Data Archives of ICSSR has installed mini-computer system (SIRIUS-32 based on MC 68020). The system configuration comprises of CPU with 4 Mega Bytes Main Memory; three winchester Disk Drives of 188MB each; one 600 l.p.m. Line printer, two 9 track tape drives, and two Alpha numeric Terminals. The system is to be used for storing and analysing quantitative social data.

The National Social Science Documentation Centre (NASSDOC) has installed Eagle PC-XT and UPTRON PC-XT Micro-Computers for automation of its bibliographical services. Besides this, abstracting and newspaper indexing activities are going to be computerised by using REYAD-1020 computer available at the Centre for Social Development, New Delhi.

Besides these, some of the libraries of the universities, Government of India departments, research laboratories and IITs have undertaken automation programmes by using computers available with their parent organisations.

Prohibitive factors

The factors responsible for slow progress can be stated as:

1. High cost of equipment, though in comparison to the rates prerevailing a few years ago, they have shown a downward trend. This has to be judged in the light of the situation, where libraries have to cope with inadequate resources doing things on a shoe-string, with an inadequate infrastruc-

ture and often in an unsympathetic environment.

2. Lack of availability of suitable software which may cover all or nearly all the library activities/services.
3. Lack of manpower with knowledge of computer and modern management procedures, to guide and implement the automation programmes in the libraries.
4. Information consciousness is still at low ebb in the country, relegating information fields to back bay.
5. There has been no organisation at national level to guide and document the ongoing computerisation activities so as to help new entrants with experience and in programming efforts and skills. We should in this respect follow the methodology adopted in the Federal Republic of Germany where, according to Woods, specific tasks were allocated to particular institutions, and the resultant systems were adopted everywhere else. This method if judiciously applied will naturally reduce development costs.

REMEDIAL MEASURES

Problems thus identified, efforts are now being made at national and international levels to alleviate the situation. These are :

National Efforts

The Government of India is fully aware of the useful role that the computer technology is capable of playing in the socio-economic development of the country. The Planning Commission set up a Working Group on Modernisation of Library Services and Informatics to recommend measures for implementation during the Seventh Five Year Plan (1985-90). According to the Working Group:

1. There are around 1,200 small libraries (with a collection of less than 10,000 books), 600 medium libraries (with a collection around 30,000) and large libraries (with a collection of more than 40,000). During the Seventh Plan, it was proposed to computerise 20 per cent of the small, 40 per cent of the medium and 50 per cent of the large libraries with a total investment of around Rs. 75 crores.

2. More universities and institutions such as INSDOC and DRTC have included computer application aspects in their courses. Indira Gandhi National Open University, New Delhi, and the National Social Science Documentation Centre, New Delhi, also propose to provide computer education as part of their Library and Information science Teaching Courses.
   These have to be augmented by organising continuing education and training programmes to absorb the existing manpower into the mainstream, preferably through self-training computer programmes.
3. India is a multi-lingual country. It would need hardware that accepts programmes covering data in non-Roman alphabets too. Computers accepting data in English and Hindi and Telugu languages at a time have been manufactured by the Computer Maintenance Corporation, Hyderabad, by using INTEL 8088 chip. The research to cover more Indian languages is on.
4. The Department of Electronics set up a National Informatics Centre in 1977. This Centre has developed data centres for various government departments. It is expected further to play a useful role in accelerating the computerisation pace in the library and information science fields.
5. The Society for Information Science and the Computer Society of India have been holding workshops /seminars on informatic aspects to speed up computer literacy among professionals.
   The Department of Electronics has also launched a programme, Computer Literacy and Studies in Schools' (CLASS), on an experimental basis. The British Government is assisting in the programme which aims to make computer literacy an integral part of school education.
6. A Library of Software requires to be developed by collecting, from various sources, various softwares available for mutual exchange.

International Level

At international level, software packages like CDS/ISIS, and MINISIS are available free to developing countries but these are run on specific machines like IBM and HP-3000 series of computers. The cost of these machines is still prohibitive for the developing countries like India.

Right now what is engaging the attention of many is the work done on micro-computer based software package iv+v, at the Institute for Machine Documentation (IMD) in Austria. According to Lohner and Koch, Unesco has now taken the decision to accept the generous Austrian offer to use the iv+v software system and the expertise of the IMD for information system projects in developing countries. The pilot projects using this package will be executed in a number of countries including India. With Unesco assistance, some modal centres for computer application may be set up.

CONCLUSION

Micro-computers with their low costs and multifarious service capabilities have made it even possible for small libraries to utilise these for providing better services to the users. In our country, we have indigenous know-how, prominent documentation centres already using computers and technical manpower. All these can be helpful in accelerating computerisation pace. The only thing that is required is, new approach to education, software development and coordination efforts. The task is a formidable one but worth pursuing.

REFERENCES

India. Planning Commission. Working Group on Modernisation of Library Services and Informatics for the 7th Five Year Plan, 1985-90. Report. 1984 (Restricted Circulation)

Jetty, D.N. Software development and export. In: *Society for Information Science,* Annual Convention, 5th, 1986, Bombay. Souvenir. p. 9-12.

Lohner, Wolfgang, and Koch, Walter. Probable software packages for micro-computers to be installed in developing countries under Unesco's sponsorship. *IFLA Journal* 11(2): 1985: p. 124-28.

Robens of Woldingham. Foreword. In : Avebury, Lord, and others, eds. *Computers and the year 2000.* Manchester, National Computing Centre, 1972. p. 1

Woods, R.G. Library automation. *British Library Research reviews* No. 2 : July 1982: 32p.

SECTION EIGHT

LINKAGES

SEVENTEEN

National and Public Libraries in India

INTRODUCTION

India is at present confronted with several vital problems. The population explosion and information explosion, not unmixed with the technological pace, are the two major problems that need immediate attention. Aggravated by illiteracy, both have a bearing in our country's development programmes. Population problems can be tackled successfully through educated and well-informed citizens. It is here that public libraries can play the twin role of educating the people and controlling the information flow from the source to the user, wherever he may be, in a remote village or metropolitan city. As a public institution, it opens its collections, facilities and sources without distinction to all the citizens". Recognising its potentials, *Unesco's* public library manifesto of 1949 described it "as a living force for popular education".

The positive role public libraries play in education, research, spread of literacy and the overall socio-economic development of a country has been well recognised already both in the developing and developed countries. Soon after Independence, the National Government in its programmes for national development and reconstruction did lay emphasis on the development of public library services in the country.

FUNCTIONS

The public libraries, depending upon their respective resources, clientele and area of activity are required to perform the following functions:

i. advice on use of materials;
ii. answers to complex and simple questions;
iii. offering books on loan to users and arranging inter-library loans;
iv. current awareness service;
v. bibliographies on specific subjects;
vi. referral to community sources;
vii. provision of translations;
viii. provision of mobile libraries and mobile film vans;
ix. organisation of seminars and conferences and workshops, craft demonstrations, screening of educational and social films, etc. For these, facilities such as auditoriums, lecture rooms, conference/meeting rooms, reading rooms, and photocopying equipment may be provided,
x. use of folk media-puppetry and other folk art for dissemination of information on social themes;
xi. service to special groups of the society including children, rural youth, physically and mentally handicapped, etc.
xii. bring out a publication (house journal).

GROWTH

Today India has a library system that serves a population of 684 million (1982 figures) in an area of 3.3 million square kilometres. The population is spread over in 2,643 towns and 575,000 villages.

Important public libraries at national level include the following:

1. *National Library, Calcutta (Formerly Imperial Library)* (1902): This is one of the oldest libraries in India that caters for the needs of lay readers as well as research scholars. It has a holding of 1,800,000 books out of which about 200,000 are Indian languages; 75,000 maps; 3,010 manuscripts and 2,000 microfilms. It is a depository library under national legislation and has a monumental collection of official Indian publications from the early British days and personal collections of the great statesmen of India. It provides bibliographical and documentation services of current and retrospective material, photocopying service and acts as a centre for international book exchange and international loan.

2. *Central Reference Library, Calcutta:* This is mainly responsible for the following continuing schemes:
   i. the compiling, printing and sale of *Indian National Bibliography;*
   ii. the setting up of a National Book Exchange Centre.
   iii. the compiling, printing and sale of *Index Indiana.*

   It needs to be reorganised as a National Bibliographical and Documentation Centre.

3. *Central Library, Bombay:* This is presently managed by the Asiatic Society, Bombay, to which grants are released by the Government of Maharashtra and the Central Government. It is rich in oriental arts, science and culture and has an excellent collection of maps. It acts as a depository library for Indian publications.
4. *Delhi Public Library* (1951): This was established in collaboration with Unesco; it consists of a Central Library, four branches and 24 sub-branches. It has four book mobile vans, each with a carrying capacity of 30,000 volumes, two hospital libraries, one prison library, a Braille department and depository library and a children's section.
5. *Khuda Baksh Oriental Public Library, Patna* (1891): This contains over 14,000 manuscripts and 65,000 volumes including rare manuscripts in Arabic, Urdu and Persian.
6. *Connemara (State Central) Public Library, Madras* (1896): This is a depository library for all Indian publications and also for publications of the U.N. and Unesco. Its collection includes 337,990 volumes.
7. *Central Secretariat Library, Delhi* (1890): This is a departmental as well as a public library. The organisational structure comprises main library, branch library and a separate unite for holding material in regional languages.

Looking at the over-all number of public libraries in India we find that 15 out of 22 States (65 per cent) have central libraries; 291 out of about 400 districts (73 per cent) have district central libraries; 1,798 development blocks out of 5,027 blocks (36 per cent) have village libraries and 1,280 towns out of 2,643 (48 per cent) have town libraries. Out of 29 metropolitan cities, of which four (14 per cent) Madras, Hyderabad, Bangalore and Delhi have city public library systems with central libraries, branches and deposit centres.

It is estimated that only about 20 per cent of the literate population has access to the public library system. Thus, we have much leeway to make up in the development of public libraries in the country.

It will be relevant to have a comparison of public libraries in India with the U.K. and the USA as analysed in Table 17.1

TABLE 17.1:Public library network in India, U.K. and USA

Item	India	U. K.	U. S. A.
Population	684 M (1981)	55.93 M (1970)	226.5 M (1980)
Literacy (in percentages)	36.17010 (1981)	99.010 (1977)	99.010 (1977)
Number of actual library users	180 M	55 M	155 M
Total expenditure on education per annum	Rs.1100 Cr (1971- 72)	Rs.878.9 Cr (1970- 71)	Rs.38337 Cr (1970)
Annual expenditure on public libraries	Rs. 3 Cr	Rs. 60 Cr	Rs 1248 Cr
Provision of books for public library per 100 citizens	1	145	100
Number of citizens per 100 registered with public library as borrowers	01	37	25
Number of books borrowed per year per every 100 persons	1.6	512	263
M Million	Cr Crores		

PERFORMANCE REVIEW

Looking into the statistics we find that a number of public libraries at rural and urban levels have been set up. Raja Ram Mohan Roy Library Foundation was established in 1972 at Calcutta to give impetus to library movement in the country by providing adequate library services and popularising the reading habit among the people. It took up certain schemes of assistance like assistance towards (i) building up of adequate stock of books and visual materials, (ii) development of rural book deposit centres and mobile library services, and (iii) organisation of seminars, workshops and book exhibitions.

The government of India has appointed several committees to asses the needs, performance and prospects of public libraries. These include the K.P. Sinha (Advisory) Committee for Libraries (1957): the study team for Selected Educational Schemes (Committee on Plan Projects) (1963); and the Working Group on Libraries (1964). The recommendations of these Committees included development plans, library legislation and that a percentage of educational outlay should be incurred on public libraries development. But do the existing libraries provide the services expected of them? A brief review of their growth and functioning would show that we still have a long way to go, especially with regard to the following.

1. *Inequitable Services:* (i) Public libraries in India are unevenly developed, (ii) Most of the rural and sparingly inhabited areas do not have public library services at all, (iii) No serious attention has been paid towards providing services to children in the public libraries.
2. *District Libraries:* Only 50 per cent of the districts have libraries at district level. But most of these libraries function in a rather haphazard manner with no proper planning for their growth and development. There is no fixed library fund to replenish their stocks or to provide reasonably comfortable seating arrangements for the users and also to organise various other activities. These are usually manned by staff who are not properly qualified and have poor salary scales.

3. *Block and Village Libraries:* Except for a few branch libraries in villages as part of certain city library systems most of them can hardly be called libraries. These are in general reading Rooms where a few local and national newspapers are purchased for the users. The book material is confined to a small number either donated by a charitable society or provided by the State Education Department. The material has no relationship to the local needs.
4. *State Libraries/National Library:* At the State level the State Central Libraries wherever in existence function as depositories. Excepting those in certain States such as Karnataka, Andhra Pradesh and a few other States, they hardly perform the various functions expected of a system. Similarly, the National Library in Calcutta hardly plays any role of leadership in the future of the library system in the country as a whole.
5. *Public Libraries Cooperation:* There is no coordination between the libraries at horizontal and vertical levels, i.e., between various local libraries and between the libraries at village, block, city, district and State levels.

ACTION PLAN

Administrative Infrastructure

The Ministry of Human Resource Development at Central Level should assume the responsibility for the leadership role. It should create an office of Director of Public Libraries, similar to the Director of Field Publicity in the Ministry of Information and Broadcasting, who will be responsible for formulating and implementing the national policy of the network of public libraries as outlined by the library commissions and committees appointed from time to time and for co-ordinating the library movement and services in different States and Union Territories of India.

The above infrastructure should be extended to State level too.

Co-ordination among the different departments may be attempted through periodical meetings and seminars of the concerned officials and librarians. Overlapping in management of the affairs of libraries in states should be eliminated.

Library Legislation

Central legislation on libraries be enacted to provide for the National Commission for Library and Information Services and also to embody therein the national library policy.

At State level, each State should have library legislation ensuring proper development of libraries according to a pre-planned infrastructure.

At present there are five States, "Tamil Nadu (1948), Andhra Pradesh (1960), Karnataka (1965), Maharashtra (1967) and West Bengal (1979), which have enacted the Public Library Act. However, the organisational structure is not uniform. If necessary concerned heads and senior knowledgeable librarians from states, where Public Library Acts exist, could be invited for a free and fruitful discussion to suggest draft model Bills for the remaining States and Union Territories.

Library Resources

The mere existence of public libraries will have little impact unless due attention is paid to the form and nature of material to be acquired. As a large percentage of the population is illiterate, it would be desirable to acquire maximum material in the audio-visual form, which in addition to being entertaining should relate to the users' vocational interests. This may consist of posters, film slides, cassettes, radio, television, etc.

Cassettes have a special role to play. In view of a long tradition of Sruti and Smriti, (oral communication) cassettes recorded in the local dialect can greatly contribute to informing the masses about national development programmes like family planning and community development and persuading them to adopt new technology in their respective vocational fields. It is a psychological fact that it is easier to convince a person if talked to in his own simple language than to approach the matter through scholarly discourses or printed media.

The books could be of the "how-to-do" type boldly printed story books and like the series *Samaj Shikshan Mala* brought out from Pune. Selective use of other innovations like micrographics, and photocopiers be extensively made in library services.

Resource Utilisation

To make optimum use of available resources, it is necessary to have co-ordination among libraries at local level and above. College, school and public libraries in one locality may pool their resources and make them available to the local residents. In this context the recommendation of the Secondary Education Commission (October 1952–June 1953) is pertinent, that

> Steps should be taken to keep the school library open during the vacation and long holidays for the benefits of the students as well as the local community, if possible. In places where there is no public library, the school should also consider the possibility of throwing the school library open to the public, outside the school hours.

It is a pity that the suggestion made so long ago has not yet been implemented.

Depository Libraries

Four public libraries in the country have been designated as the depository libraries under the Delivery of Books Act, 1954. The objective is to collect all the national publications at the designated places and make them available to all users. The purpose, however, has not been fulfilled. Libraries working under constraints fail to process the material for use, resulting in creation of uncared dumps. Two alternatives to overcome this problem may be considered:

i. The depository libraries should receive publications only in their respective regional language(s). For this the number of depository libraries can be increased, or
ii. The depository libraries after receiving the material may transfer it to regional libraries on the basis of their specialisation in particular regional language(s).

This will promote greater use of collected material.

Resource Sharing

To promote resource sharing, clearing house centres may be set up. These centres would receive material of serial and non-serial nature from libraries of universities, research institutes and government departments, which have either duplicate sets or intend to weed out due to space problems. Such material properly screened may be distributed to various public libraries keeping in view location, readers' interests and available shelving space.

Public Library Clientele

It is now admitted that the library has a social role. In India 40 per cent of the population is in the category of "Youth", both male and female. Efforts, therefore, should be directed towards fulfilling the needs of the youth, especially the rural youth, and also neo-literates, children, women and disadvantaged like the handicapped, the poor, prisoners and patients in the hospital. Backward and tribal areas will have to hand the first priority.

Role of Private Organisation

Besides Government supported libraries, private libraries carrying out useful work may be recognised as libraries of national importance. These may be provided with recurring grants for maintenance by the Central and State Governments, just as the Asiatic Society in Calcutta has recently received substantial assistance. Representation to their librarians may be given on the library committees at the government level. Manuscript libraries among these may be given special attention. The Government should seek the cooperation of voluntary agencies like Kishor Bharati and seek guidance from successful community efforts at Jamkhed, Uruli, etc., for setting up rural libraries.

Staffing Pattern

The role of the public library depends on the role of its professional staff. The fact remains that funds for library development in this country have always been extremely limited, which is reflected by the poor public library services. A uniform standard of service does not exist and poor pay scales, among other reasons, do not attract talented persons to the professional cadre.

The staffing pattern as recommended in the Report of the Advisory Committee of Libraries, Ministry of Education and Youth Services, Government of India (1969), with minor changes should be accepted at different levels. An outline of the staff structure is given in the Appendix.

Integrated library cadre and facilities for career development may be provided.

OTHER PROGRAMMES

Diagnostic survey

It is high time that a comprehensive survey at national level is organised which would provide data for future planning on scientific lines.

Monitoring, Evaluation and Statistics: A task force may be established at the national level to look into the work of setting up a statistical and information set up at all levels of library administration, i.e., from village to national level.

Training and Research: A National Institute of Library Planning and Administration should be set up at the national level to provide facilities for research, training, consultancy in the field of library services in the country.

Financial Resources

Governments both at national and state levels giving due consideration to socio-economic planning should spend 15-20 per cent of the total budget for informal education on public library service, or per capita expenditure on public libraries in the states which at present ranges from 5 paise to 35 paise, be raised according to the states' income.

Among the various suggestions made for mobilising financial sources, a suggestion to levy a tax on entertainment and even on liquor to support the public library movement in the country made by the Lieutenant-Governor of Delhi in 1982 is laudable and worth consideration.

Plan Target

The objective of the day, keeping in mind the demands, is that we should have a clear target to be achieved by the end of the Eighth Five Year Plan. The minimum achievement should aim at:

i. each state and Union Territory to have a Central State Library;
ii. each district in the State to have a District Library;
iii. each city or block with a population of 100,000 to have a City or Block library system, and
iv. public library law to exist in each state and Union Territory.

For this suitable funds have to be allocated. A proposed expenditure plan for 1985-89 is given in Appendix 1.

REFERENCES

India (1961). *Advisory Committee for Libraries: Report.* New Delhi: Ministry of Education.

India (1979). *Advisory Committee for Libraries: Report.* New Delhi: Ministry of Education and Youth Services.

India (1953). *Secondary Education Commission, 1952-1953: Report.* New Delhi: Ministry of Education.

India (1986). *Working Group on Libraries: Report.* New Delhi: Planning Commission.

Jakson, M.M. (ed) (1981). *Contemporary Developments in Librarianship: An International Handbook*, pp. 194-195. London: Library Association.

Jain, M.K. (1982). Public library development in India. In J.L. Sardana and others (eds). *Twenty-Eighty All India Library Conference, Lucknow, 20-23 October, 1982: Seminar papers,* pp. 30-35. Delhi ILA.

Misra, J. (1975). History of library legislation in India. *Libr. Hist. Rev.* 2(2), 13-62.

Ujlambkar, K.M. (1982). Post independence public library development. In J.L. Sardana and others eds. *Twenty-Eighth All India Library Conference, Lucknow, 20-23 October, 1982: Seminar papers,* pp. 43-51. Delhi: ILA'

APPENDIX-I

TABLE 1. Public libraries financial outlay, 1985-89 (Proposed): State Sector

Name of the State	Population (1977) (000)	Provision at the rate of 25 paise per capita (in Rs. Lakhs)	Provision at the rate of 35 paise per capita (in Rs.Lakhs)
Andhra Pradesh	48102		170
Assam	17073	40	
Bihar	63127	160	
Gujarat	30229	80	
Haryana	11469	30	
Himachal Pradesh	3888	10	
Jammu and Kashmir	5370	10	
Karnataka	32711		110
Kerala	23802	60	
Madhya Pradesh	48555	120	
Maharashtra	56623	140	
Manipur	1288	3	
Meghalaya	1181	3	
Nagaland	626	2	
Orissa	24667	60	
Punjab	15116	40	
Rajasthan	30010	80	
Sikkim	234	1	
Tamil Nadu	44596		160
Tripura	1859	5	
Uttar Pradesh	98131	250	
West Bengal	50660	130	
Union Territory			
Andaman and Nicobar Islands	160	0.40	
Arunachal Pradesh	558	1.40	
Dadra and Nagar Haveli	84	0.20	
Delhi	5210	13.00	
Goa, Daman & Diu	1026	2.60	
Lakshadweep	37	0.10	
Mizroam	500	1.25	
Pondicherry	549	1.40	

Total: (a) 1245.35 + (b) 440
Total: 1685.00 (approx.)
Cost escalation at 10% 170.00 (approx.)

Grand total 1855.00 (approx.)

Appendix-I (contd.)

TABLE 2. Public libraries financial outlay 1985-89 (Proposed) Central Sector

	Public libraries (central sector)	Figure in lakhs
1.	National Library, Calcutta, including Reference Library	250
2.	Regional Libraries (national level)	
	a. Bombay	20
	b. Madras	20
	c. New Delhi	20
3.	Libraries of Importance (national level)	
	a. Khuda Baksh Oriental Public Library, Patna (Bihar)	28
	b. Rampur Raza Library, Rampur (U.P.)	
	c. Thanjavur Maharaj Serfoji Saraswati Mahal Library, Thanjavur (Tamil Nadu)	
	d. Manuscript Depository Library (25 libraries at the rate of 1 lakh per annum	125
	e. Delhi Public Library	70
	f. Library of Tibetan works and archives (Dharamsala)	106
4.	Others	
	a. Assistance to voluntary organisations for development of public libraries	70
	b. Grant to Raja Ram Mohan Roy Library Foundation	70
	c. National Commission for Library and Information Services and the Director of Libraries	255
	Total	1034

Appendix-I (contd.)

TABLE 3. Statement showing State Public Library Act

Name of the State	Whether library legislation exists	Title of legislation	Date of enforcement
Andhra Pradesh	Yes	Andhra Pradesh Public Libraries Act (Act VIII of 1960)	3 April 1960
Assam	No		
Bihar	No		
Gujarat	No		
Haryana	No		
Himachal Pradesh	No		
Jammu and Kashmir	No		
Karnataka	Yes	Karnataka Public Libraries Act (Act X of 1965)	22 April 1965
Kerala	No		
Madhya Pradesh		Under compilation	
Maharashtra	Yes	Maharashtra Public Libraries Act (Act XXXIV of 1967)	1 May 1968
Manipur	No		
Meghalaya	No		
Nagaland	No		
Orissa	No		
Punjab	No		
Rajasthan	No		
Sikkim	No		
Tamil Nadu	Yes	Tamil Nadu Public Libraries Act (Act XXIV of 1948)	1 April 1950
Tripura	No		
Uttar Pradesh		Under consideration by State Government	
West Bengal	Yes	West Bengal Public Libraries Act, 1979	
Union Territories	No		

Appendix-I (contd.)

TABLE 4. Library Network in State and Union Territories

	Name of State	Whether separate central state library exists	Address
1.	Andhra Pradesh	Yes	State Central Library Afzal Ganj, Hyderabad-500012 *Regional Libraries* State Regional Library, Guntur-522001 State Regional Library, Visakhapatnam-530001 State Regional Library, Tirupati-517501 State Regional Library, Warangal-506002 State Regional Library, Nizamabad-503001
2.	Assam	Yes	State Central Library. Gauhati-781001
3.	Bihar	Yes	State Regional Library, (Sachchidananda Sinha Library), P.O.B. 62, Patna-800008
4.	Gujarat	No	Vidyapith Granthalaya, Ahmedabad-380014 (acts as State Central Library) *Regional Library* Central Library, Baroda-390001
5.	Haryana	Yes	State Library, Staff Road, Ambala City-133001
6.	Himachal Pradesh	Yes	Motilal Nehru State Central Library, Solan-173212
7.	Jammu and Kashmir	No	S.P.S. Public Library Srinagar-190001 (acts as State Central Library)

8.	Karnataka	Yes	Central State Library Seshadriyer Memorial Hall, Cubon Park, Bangalore-560001
9.	Kerala	No	Trivandrum Public Library, Trivandrum-605001 (acts as Central State Library)
10.	Madhya Pradesh	No	*Regional Libraries* Regional Library, Gwalior-474001 Regional Library Bhopal-462001 Regional Library Jabalpur-482001 Regional Library, Indore-452001 Regional Library, Rewa-486001
11.	Maharashtra	No	Asiatic Society Library Bombay-400001 (acts as Central State Library) *Divisional Libraries* Divisional Library, Nagpur-440001 Divisional Library, Ratnagiri-415612 Divisional Library, Aurangabad-431001 Divisional Library, Pune-410001
12.	Manipur	Yes	State Central Library, Imphal-795001
13.	Meghalaya	Yes	State Central Library. Shillong-793001
14.	Nagaland	Yes	State Central Library, Kohima-797001
15.	Orissa	Yes	State Central Library, C/o. C.P.I. Office Bhubaneswar-751001
16.	Punjab	Yes	State Central Library, Patiala-147001

17.	Rajasthan	Yes	State Central Library, Located in Maharaja Sarvajanik Pustakalaya, Jaipur-302001 *Divisional Libraries* Bikaner Divisional Library (Pradeshik Pustakalaya) Bikaner-334001 Jodhpur Divisional Library (Sumer Sarvjanik Pustakalaya) Jodhpur-342001 Kota Divisional Library (Pradeshik Pustakalaya) Kota-320001 Udaipur Divisional Library, Saraswati Bhawan Pustakalaya, Udaipur-313001
18.	Sikkim	No	
19	Tamil Nadu	Yes	Connemara (State Central Public Library), Egmore, Madras-600008
20.	Tripura	No	Birchandra Public Library, Agartala-79900 (acts as State Central Library)
21.	Uttar Pradesh	Yes	State Central Library, Allahabad-211001
22.	West Bengal	Yes	State Central Library, 56-A, BT Road, Calcutta-700001
Union Territories			
1.	Andaman and Nicobar Islands	Yes	State Library, Port Blair-744101
2.	Arunachal Pradesh	Yes	State Central Library Shillong. (Being transferred to Itanagar-791111 capital of the Union Territory)

Appendix-I (contd.)

3.	Chandigarh	Yes	State Central Library Chandigarh, Sector 17, Chandigarh-160017
4.	Dadra and Nagar Haveli	No	
5.	Delhi	No	
6.	Goa, Daman and Diu	Yes	Central Library, Panaji-403001
7.	Lakshadweep	No	
8.	Mizoram	Yes	State Library, Aizawal-796001
9.	Pondicherry	No	

Summary

	Total number of States and Union Territories	State and Union Territory having a State or Central library	State and Union Territory without Central library
States	22	15	7
Union Territories	9	5	4
Grand total	31		

TABLE 5

State	No. of districts	No. of district libraries	No. of blocks	No. of block libraries	No. of villages	No. of village libraries	No. of towns	No. of town libraries	No. of Children's libraries	No. of Nehru Yuvak Kendra libraries
Andhra Pradesh	21	21	324	324	27221	1623	207	207	2	4
Assam	10	8	130	-	21999	9	69	14	2	-
Bihar	31	17	587	58	67566	-	161	58	-	-
Gujarat	19	18	218	104	18275	4265	200	200	-	-
Haryana	11	5	87	-	6731	-	65	12	6	2
Himachal Pradesh	12	12	69	4	16916	25	35	-	-	4
Jammu and Kashmir	10	10	73	-	6503	2	43	9	1	1
Karnataka	19	19	175	175	26826	1498	230	230	1	6
Kerala	11	11	144	144	1268	1268	88	88	4	6
Madhya Pradesh	45	25	457	250	70883	23627	232	78	2	11
Maharashtra	26	26	340	195	35778	285	257	257	5	2
Manipur	6	5	26	26	1949	12	8	8	-	2
Meghalaya	5	2	24	-	4583	-	3	-	-	1
Nagaland	7	-	21	14	960	-	3	-	-	-
Orissa	13	14	314	10	46992	172	78	6	-	7
Punjab	12	6	117	-	12188	-	106	-	-	5
Rajasthan	26	26	232	9	33305	7	151	11	-	9
Sikkim	4	4	-	-	215	-	7	-	-	1
Tamil Nadu	15	15	374	374	15735	3427	241	-	1	4
Tripura	3	3	17	10	4727	600	6	3	-	2
Uttar Pradesh	57	13	868	-	112561	4400	293	27	1	18
West Bengal	16	16	835	48	38074	531	134	61	6	8
Union Territories										
Andaman and Nicobar	2	-	5	5	390	18	1	-	-	1
Arunachal Pradesh	5	5	43	10	2973	-	4	-	-	1
Chandigarh	1	-	1	-	26	-	1	-	-	1
Dadra and Nagar Haveli	2	-	1	-	72	-	-	-	-	1
Delhi	1	-	5	5	243	-	1	-	2	2
Goa, Daman and Diu	3	3	12	12	409	35	13	3	2	1
Lakshadweep	1	1	4	-	10	-	-	-	-	-
Mizoram	3	2	20	17	225	-	2	2	-	1
Pondichery	4	4	4	4	333	24	4	4	1	1
Total	401	291	5527	1798	575936	41828	2643	1280	36	102

TABLE 6.Proposed Staff Structure

	Librarian	Deputy Librarian	Assistant Librarian	Professional	Clerical	Class IV
Central State Library	1	1	2	21	20	32
Regional State Library	1	1	1	10	5	7
District Library	1	-	1	3	4	5
Block Library	1	-	-	2	2	5
City Library	1	-	1	3	2	6
Village Library	1	-	-	-	-	2

EIGHTEEN

Libraries for Children

The future of any country depends upon children because they are the leaders and builders of tomorrow. A sociologist, points out: "If Society is to control and direct its development, call the process social planning, social reconstruction or what you will – then the place to begin with is the incoming generation. The remaking of the world is essentially a process of trading in social futures. .. and the future is the Child." A Child has to learn about this world, about himself and his relationship with this world; and one of the means of learning is to develop the habit of reading books and absorbing them.

"Children, as a sector of the population, have an immature mind, not as a result of sickness, but because of natural conditions", says S.R. Ranganathan, father of the Library Science in India. "From the Library's point of view, the nation's children or, say, the nation's population under 16 to 18, should constitute a special sector of the people."

Child and the Book

Books are essential to children if they are to enjoy their childhood and satisfy their quest for knowledge. It is books which help to develop fine feelings, good habits and humanitarian values among the children. If children do not establish the right contact with good books then the loss suffered is irreparable. According to one scholar, "A child, who learns to read and understand and has wide access to books, has his own independent road to every kind of knowledge."

Importance of Children's Libraries

According to S.R. Ranganathan, Books for adults lose their utility for children on account of the latter's undeveloped minds. The first hurdle in their way is that the language of the books for grown-ups is beyond their elementary intelligence. Secondly, the thought contents of books for adults do not fit in with their simplicity. Thirdly, the minds of children, with their elementary knowledge, need something new instead of being crammed with conventional ideas. we may safely state on the basis of the simple natural knowledge of the children that their books should be more illustrative and attractive than books for adults."

But the problem is that most of the parents cannot purchase sufficient books for their children due to economic constraints and it is here that the library comes to the aid of the children and adults. The great virtue of a library is that it can provide books in an economical way because these books can be shared by many readers. The library can save the children from being attracted towards bad books, by providing access to a rich and good collection of reading material. It provides an opportunity to the child to choose books of his choice and interest. The child gets the opportunity to develop his natural inclinations in a library.

The major benefits of properly planned library services to the children are:

1. The children develop the habit of going to libraries and using their resources at their habit-forming age which helps them in choosing their careers and professions.
2. It is through the library that self-reliance and self-confidence can be instilled in a child.
3. The children develop the habit of seeking truth for themselves and getting at the facts in an unbiased manner, which is possible through children's libraries.
4. Libraries provide healthy means of recreation and fruitful methods of utilising leisure time.
5. Books in libraries increase the general knowledge of the child and widens his horizon of knowledge.

6. Children develop love for fine arts such as paintings, drawing, doll making, etc., with the help of library collection and extension programmes organised by the library.
7. Library imparts cultural values through drama, music and other forms of entertainment.
8. Debates, discussions, quiz programmes, essay competitions, etc., help to cultivate healthy competition and art of speaking in public.
9. Library guides the children to select books and other reading materials to fulfil the needs of the school syllabus as well as their personal needs.
10. The children acquire the necessary knowhow to locate and utilise the books in the library. This knowledge to use and consult library material is an important contribution as it develops faculties of learning and research in a proper way.

Children's Libraries in India

In India presentation of library material to children through institutional libraries on a wider scale is relatively recent. Jawaharlal Nehru, the visionary first Prime Minister of India, provided a perspective not only to our welfare philosophy but also to the placement of children in the welfare programme. In an International Seminar on "Development of Public Libraries in Asia" in 1955 he said: "All public libraries should provide services for children and young people as an integral part of their services to the community." Baroda Central Library, which remains a pioneering public library, initiated services to children. The Delhi Public Library with a section exclusively for children is making an important contribution. Another model children's library was opened in the National Library, Calcutta, in 1960. Other important libraries are: the Central Library (Chandigarh), the Public Library (Patiala), Shishu Niketan (Ahmedabad), Children's Book Trust and association of writers and illustrators for Children (Delhi).

Delhi Public Library

The Delhi Public Library, realising the importance of library services for children, set up a section exclusively for children. This section admits readers below 15 years of age. The membership of this department during 1983-84 was 4,041 and the members borrowed 69,224 books during the year. The attendance at the cultural activities organised by the section was 8,805. Some of the important programmes were - Balsabha, Kishore Sabha, Story Hour, News Hour, Appne Appne Vichar, Radio and T.V. programmes, film shows and annual competitions.

Essentials of Children's Library

Location

One important aspect about children's libraries is that they should be easily accessible to the children. Convenience and ease of access are very important for children than for adults. The child must not be required to go through crowded roads and heavy traffic. It is difficult for parents to accompany children every time they want to visit the library.

Timings

The timings of the library should also be convenient to the children. The library should remain open during holidays also so that children can enjoy their leisure time.

Collection

Books are the important element of the library. This collection should be very attractive to the children, to be able to evoke proper response from them. The collection of children's library should also, of necessity, include the following types of books:

Reference works like encyclopaedias, dictionaries, etc., specially written for children, so that they know how to consult them.

Fairy tale themes are essential to fulfil certain educational purposes. For example these fairy tales help the child understand literary allusions in the literature and poetry of the past. Some fairy tales have very appealing moral content of universal acceptability.

Folk tales also appeal to the children a great deal. Panchatantra, Arabian Nights, etc., are some of the books which provide great allurement to children.

Books dealing with patriotism, love of nation, and biographies of freedom fighters should be included.

Illustrated books written in simple style explaining scientific and technological advances made by man, books on geography, animal stories, etc., should find a place in such libraries.

The library should purchase books of humour and cartoon collections too. The popularity of comics among the children cannot be ignored. Some of our Indian publishers have done well to choose good subjects for their titles

Besides these conventional book materials, modern means of communication should also be available in the library. Emphasis should be given to maps, globes, charts, records, radio films, TV, and audio and video cassettes.

Librarian

The librarian with his staff brings the child reader into contact with books. The child's tomorrows depend upon the love and care we shower on them today. The love moulds the children into good citizens of tomorrow. Individual and personal attention needs to be given to to the children. The librarian should necessarily be very friendly and cooperative with the child. A child's visit to the library depends not only upon the collection but more importantly upon the inviting behaviour of the librarian. And as such, children's librarian, apart from being professionally well qualified, should have knowledge of child psychology, love for children and a sense of humour. He should also possess a pleasing personality and should be tolerant, practical, placid and patient. Berwick Sayers says that "Children's librarian must be a person of good education, solid nerves and attractive to youngsters". The librarian and the assistants should never assume an attitude of superiority which may create an inferiority complex in a child user's mind. The library personnel should treat the young library users, almost with motherly tenderness.

What Experts Say

In November 1979, an All India seminar on "Libraries for Children" was held in New Delhi to celebrate the International Year of Child. The major recommendations of this Seminar include:

1. Children's libraries should be established either on an independent basis or as a branch of the public libraries in the urban areas. In the rural areas they should be established as sections of the public libraries. Thickly populated areas should be covered by mobile library vans.
   The children's libraries should be adequately stocked with suitable books, magazines and audio-visual material for children, these libraries should be opened during hours convenient to them and should be adequately staffed and manned by librarians who have received training in children's librarianship.
   All public libraries should earmark at least 20 per cent of their budget for service to children and young people.

2. The existing courses in librarianship neglect due emphasis on library work with children...University Departments of Library Science as well as other agencies conducting the training programmes in librarianship in the country should give due emphasis, in their curriculum, to the special requirements of children's librarianship. Such courses should include, among other things, "methodology to work with children", acquaintance with juvenile literature and other reference sources.
   Selective bibliographies of children's books in regional languages should be compiled... by the experts in juvenile literature and should be updated. These bibliographies should include suitable children's periodicals and reference works.

3. The state governments, universities, writers of children's books and publishers should expand and assist the programmes of preparation and publication of good books for children by offering aid and incentives.

4. The Department of Public Libraries in the states may conduct a survey of the existing provision of library facilities for children by way of space, books and other materials, staff and services in their respective areas, evaluating the present services and recommending future steps for the improvement of these services quickly and adequately.

5. The Indian Library Association should add a new section on "Library Services for Children and Young People".

6. "Children's Book Council" should be organised at an all-India level comprising libraries, writers, publishers and booksellers to jointly work for and promote children's libraries movement.

7. Governments at the Centre and in the States, should make provision for a model children library, in Delhi and all the capitals of States and Union Territories.

The Education Commission (1964-66) deliberating on pre-primary education made a very important recommendation: "Another important experiment of this type, which has been tried with success in some parts of the country, is the establishment of children's play centres in close association with the primary schools. These are conducted by a specially trained teacher in the primary school, who is given an allowance for the purpose, or by a separate teacher. The programme, which lasts for about two hours a day, is simple and consists of group singing, story telling and games, with considerable attention being given to personal hygiene and health. These centres serve as pre-school classes and smoothen the transition of the child from its play-dominated world of infancy to the formal atmosphere of the primary school... Such Centres should be attached to as many primary schools as possible."

CONCLUSION

And finally, the beginning of child education is to be marked by the cooperation among parents, teachers, librarians and writers. The parents should bring the child to the library at least at the age of three. Teachers also should encourage the child to visit the library. The librarians should be able to attract the children with their pleasant personality. The authors should write for children with imagination to catch their eye and evoke their interest.

There should also be cooperation between school and public librarians because while the school library makes the child's classwork more interesting and fruitful, the public library looks after his leisure time, his individual requirements and tastes. There should also be cooperation between authors and children's librarians. The librarian may inform the authors about the interests, aptitudes of the children and suggest a field or topic which might have been ignored by the writers.

The mass media can help the movement for libraries by giving publicity to the theme in the Press, Radio and TV. This will not only attract the children and evoke an urge to visit the library but also make parents conscious of and alert to this important duty of theirs.

NINETEEN

Documentation Activities and Services in Social Sciences

Role of NASSDOC and ICSSR Regional Centres

INTRODUCTION

As the pace of research increases in any specific area, the need for supporting infrastructure is a natural corollary. This is desired to provide for – research directions, financial input, information flow, and substantive utilisation of research output. The Council of Scientific and Industrial Research (CSIR) took up this role in the field of Science and technology in 1946. Social Sciences had to wait for such an infrastructure will 1969 when Indian Council of Social Science Research was set up as an autonomous organisation under Ministry of Education. The objectives were the same, that is, to strengthen and expand the research base, improve its quality, and strive for its better utilisation. Besides this, it was to create facilities of documentation and bibliographical services for research scholars in the field of social sciences. The Social Sciences here covered disciplines like economics, education, geography, history, public administration, sociology, social and cultural anthropology, international relations and all other subjects of inter-disciplinary nature.

To decentralise implementation of its programmes, it set up six regional centres-Western Regional Centre, Bombay (1973), Southern Regional Centre, Hyderabad (1973), Eastern Regional Centre, Calcutta (1973), Northern Regional Centre, New Delhi (1976), North-Eastern Regional Centre, Shillong (1977) and North-Western Regional Centre, Chandigarh (1977). (Annexture 1 provides addresses and area jurisdiction). Besides this, ICSSR supports research institutes whose number has risen to 22 (1987) from, 9(1975). (Annexture II provides the list). The Regional centres and

Research Institutes combined look after needs of the researchers in all parts of the country.

S.P. Agrawal, Director, NASSDOC
Manohar Lal, Dy. Director, NASSDOC

GENESIS

The documentation and bibliographical services are a priority programme in ICSSR activities. Soon after its inception, it set up Social Science Documentation Centre, which because of its expanding role at national level was designated as National Social Science Documentation Centre in 1986. The credit for planning and growth of NASSDOC goes to Late Shri J.P. Naik, the first Member-Secretary of ICSSR. He always took keen interest in its activities. In this task, he was ably assisted by Shri N.M. Ketkar, the distinguished librarian, who was the Centre's first Director. Under the latter's guidance, the two ambitious programmes, i.e., Union Catalogue of Social Science Periodicals/Serials and Retrospective Indexing in Social Sciences were initiated.

OBJECTIVE

The main objective of the Centre is to provide full range of documentation and information services which include:

i. to inform scholars about the material available, current and retrospective, in his research field,
ii. to assist scholars in the procurement of research material,
iii. to strive for bibliographical control of research material,
iv. to assist research institutions in creating documentation and bibliographical services,
v. to maintain linkages with other documentation and information centres, and
vi. to bridge the gap between professionals and information technology.

ORGANISATION

Administrative and financial control over the NASSDOC is exercised by ICSSR.

The policy guidelines are provided by the ICSSR Committee on Documentation services and Research Information. It has at present membership of 14 leading social scientists, librarians and information scientists.

The Director, NASSDOC assisted by a team of 100 members, consisting of professionals-29, semi-professionals-4, machine operators-7, and non-professionals-60, looks after its multifarious activities and services.

NASSDOC has organised itself into various functional units as presented in the organisational chart.

The financial expenditure incurred by ICSSR on NASSDOC including expenditure on its staff for the last five years is given as under. It approximately comes to 5% of the total ICSSR expenditure.

Financial input for NASSDOC

Year	Amount (Rs. Lakhs)
1986-87	29.01
1985-86	20.76
1984-85	18.83
1983-84	15.74
1982-83	14.02

PROGRAMMES AND ACTIVITIES

- Building up a collection of reference materials and works on research methodology: collection (a) unpublished doctoral theses approved by Indian universities and foreign theses on India (b) research reports of the projects undertaken by ICSSR and other social science research institutions assisted by ICSSR (c) working papers presented at ICSSR funded seminars and conferences, and (d) Periodicals of research standard in social sciences.

- Providing bibliographical information about Indian publications in social science disciplines to international documentation agencies.

NATIONAL SOCIAL SCIENCE DOCUMENTATION CENTRE ORGANISATIONAL CHART

RESEARCH MATERIAL

LIBRARY SERVICES

DOCUMENTATION

FINANCIAL ASSISTANCE

BIBLIOGRAPHY

COMPILATION

COMPUTER APPLICATION

-Acquisition
-Cataloguing
-classification
-Binding

-Circulation
-Reading Room
-Reference & Guidance

-Retrospective Social Science Index
-Union Catalogue
-Area Study Bibliographies
-Language Bibliographies
-Unesco Projects

-Grants-in-aid
-Study Grants

-Scholars
-International Organisations

DOCUMENT DELIVERY AND REPROGRAPHIC SERVICE

CONTINUING EDUCATION PROGRAMME

INTER-LIBRARY RESOURCES CENTRE

COLLABORATION

PUBLICATION

SALES

ADMINISTRATION

-Associateship course
-Short term Courses

-National : Member-ship-Professional
-Regional : Asia-Pacific Information Net Work
-International-Membership-Professional Organisations

-NASSDOC Research Information Series
-NASSDOC Serials

-ICSSR Publications

-Policy & Planning
-Maintenance & Coordination
-Mail Room Service

- Striving for bibliographic control over social science materials by bringing out various documents under Research Information Series. About an hundred titles have so far been brought out. (A list of these is at Annexture III).

- Providing select bibliographies on request.

- Providing duplicating and reprographic services.

- Providing document supply services to scholars from outside Delhi.

- Awarding study grants to scholars for working at libraries of their interest in India.

- Providing consultancy to social science institutions in setting up documentation and information centres.

- Providing facilities for staff participation in professional seminars and conferences through contributing papers and taking active part in their deliberations and also deputing staff to attend short term refresher courses.

- Conducting professional training courses under Continuing Education Programme.

- Processing project proposals involving financial assistance to documentation and bibliographical projects for consideration by ICSSR Committee on documentation services and Research Information.

- Entering into agreement with national and international organisations for mutual exchange of publications. (At present 2000 institutions are on exchange list).

- Promoting sale of ICSSR publications, participating in book exhibitions and undertaking sale of Government of India publications to research institutes. A sales counter functions at 35 Ferozeshah Road, New Delhi.

COLLECTION

The guiding principle of acquisition policy is to acquire material which is not available in other libraries in Delhi. The objective is to fill up the gaps and avoid duplication. The exception is made in respect of reference documents, literature on research methodology, social indicators, library and information science and the material which is required in the context of ICSSR sanctioned projects as also for presentation to foreign scholars under international collaboration programmes. There has been steady growth in library collection. The number stands at 27,104 in March 1988. It includes 2500 Ph.D. theses and 1500 research project reports. The annual addition for the five years is as under:

TABLE.19.1. Annual Addition in Library Collection

Year	No. of Titles
1987-88	1295
1986-87	4400
1985-86	5322
1984-85	3718
1983-84	2285

The following table provides figures of financial expenditure on research material which include journals during the last five years.

TABLE.19.2. Expenditure on Research Collection

Year	Amount (Rs. lakhs)
1987-88	4.37
1986-87	6.42
1985-86	4.92
1984-85	3.87
1983-84	2.90

60% of the amount is spent on journals and 40% on the remaining material.

Type

i. *Books:* These are procured through purchase, exchange, gift and in lieu of ICSSR publication assistance. NASSDOC has rich collection of reference sources which include dictionaries, directories, encyclopaedias, bibliographies, indexes, abstracts, etc. and books on library and information science. "Reference sources in SSDC" "Social Science Research Methodology: A Bibliography," and "Library and Information Science Literature: SSDC Resource List" can be consulted for locating the desired material.

ii. *Journals:* The general acquisition policy also applies to procurement of journals. NASSDOC strives to collect all the worthwhile social science journals published in India, and a selective number of journals in library and information science. It currently receives about 3000 titles or journals. The subscription is made for 500 journals and 22 newspapers and the rest are received against exchange and publication grants. The ratio of Indian and foreign journals is 1:1.

The table below provides the number of copies of the ICSSR journals on exchange programme.

TABLE.19.3. ICSSR Journal in Exchange

ICSSR Annual Report	242
ICSSR Newsletter	1100
ICSSR Journal of Abstracts and Reviews: Economics	135
ICSSR Journal of Abstracts and Reviews: Geography	100
ICSSR Journal of Abstracts and Reviews: Political Science	87
ICSSR Journal of Abstracts and Reviews: Sociology and Social Anthropology	195
ICSSR Research Abstracts Quarterly	295
Indian Dissertation Abstracts	195
Indian Psychological Abstracts	89
NASSDOC Research Information Series	160
	2598

Under Inter-Library Resources Centre Programme (explained ahead), a collection of back files of about 1,00,000 volumes of social science periodicals has been made.

The two documents, "ILRC Holdings List" and "Periodicals in NASSDOC: A Current List" provide complete information about the periodicals holdings in NASSDOC.

iii. *Ph.D. Theses:* Of special significance to Ph. D. students and other researchers in social sciences in the Library's collection of unpublished Ph. D. theses and research project reports. Efforts are made to obtain a copy of unpublished doctoral thesis in social sciences accepted by Indian universities and also those by foreign universities on India. So far, about 2,500 Ph.D. theses have been collected. To furnish access to these, the bibliographical list entitled "Theses in SSDC" has been brought out and is updated from time to time.

iv. *Research Reports:* 1500 reports of research projects have so far been collected. These are received largely under contractual obligation to ICSSR for its providing financial assistance, and also against exchange and gratis from research institutions in India and abroad. The document "Research Project Reports in SSDC: An Annotated Bibliography" and its supplements provide information about holdings in NASSDOC.

The table below provides discipline-wise distribution of research projects sanctioned by ICSSR during 1980-81 to 1984-85.

Table 19.4.

Discipline	Number	Percentage
Economics	133	30.00
Political Science	52	12.00
Sociology	52	12.00
Inter-disciplinary	40	8.00
Psychology	34	8.00
Women's Studies	24	5.00
Commerce	21	5.00
Geography	20	4.00
Public Administration	13	3.00
Anthropology	9	2.00
History	9	2.00
Education	8	2.00

Law	7	2.00
Linguistics	6	2.00
Management	4	1.00
Statistics	4	1.00
Home Science	2	-
Criminology	1	0.22
Military Science	1	0.22
Regional Planning	1	0.22
Music	2	0.44
Total	448	100.00

Note: Percentages do not add up to 100 because of rounding of figures in this Table.

Physical Format

Hard copies form the major part of the collection. But to cope with the space problems, backfiles of journals, Ph.D. theses, research project reports, and ICSSR publications like annual report, newsletter, brochures, etc. are now being maintained in micro-form. Some of the titles in this format are: (i) Annals of Indian administration; (ii) Anthropological Society of Bombay Journal; (iii) Bombay Geographical Society Journal; (iv) Economic Working Papers (UK); (v) Gujarat Research Society Journal; (vi) Indian Linguistics; (vii) Psychological Abstracts; (viii) Social Action; (ix) A Bibliography of Mughal India, 1526-1707, by R.A. Sharma; (x) Castes and Tribes of Southern India, by E. Thurston and K. Ramachari (7 vols.) and (xi) NASSDOC Research Information Series.

Beginning has also been made in the acquisition and maintenance of documents in machine readable from i.e. floppy/disc/tape. Some of the publications available in this format are: Economic and Political Weekly Index; India - 2000 : An Annotated Bibliography (1987); List of Current Periodicals in NASSDOC; Core List of social science Periodicals.

INTER LIBRARY RESOURCES CENTRE (ILRC)

ILRC was set up in 1975, inviting local libraries to deposit their non-current, infrequently used but important for research, serials (i.e. Govt. reports, journals, newspapers, etc.) with this centre at 35,

Ferozeshah Road. 38 libraries in Delhi have so far deposited their periodicals/serials at the Centre. Due to lack of space, about 70 per cent of the volumes have been shifted to the space acquired at Noida.

DOCUMENTATION PROGRAMMES

Briefly described here are three broad categories of programmes (i) those undertaken directly or in collaboration with selected institutions (ii) those undertaken by ICSSR Regional Centres and (iii) those assisted by the Council under its Grants-in-Aid scheme.

Direct Programme

Union List of Social Science Periodicals: Four volumes of the Union Lists relating to periodicals currently available in Andhra Pradesh, Bombay, Delhi and Karnataka libraries were brought out in 1971-72. The Delhi list had been updated in 1978, 1982 and 1985. The latest one records the availability of 2,909 periodicals titles in 30 libraries in Delhi during 1985. The list is now continualy updated through micro-computer. Similar lists are now planned to be brought out from other cities as well. The first to come out has been from Lucknow.

Union Catalogue of Social Science Periodicals/Serials: The compilation of the Union catalogue was the first major project undertaken on April 1, 1970 and formally completed on March 31, 1976. 32 volumes giving location of about 31,125 serials and periodicals in 550 libraries in 17 States and two Union Territories, including a separate volume on National Library, Calcutta were published. The union catalogue helps to locate a recognised volume of social science periodical/serial if it is available in one of the participating libraries. The project has been revived for updating.

Union Catalogue of Newspapers in Delhi Libraries: To update data regarding availability of back files of newspapers in Delhi libraries, which earlier formed part of Union Catalogue of Social Science Periodicals - Delhi Libraries, a separate fascicule was brought out in mimeographed form in 1978, and revised in 1983, covered 252 newspaper titles available in 35 libraries and newspaper offices.

Inventory of Social Science Institutions and Organisations in India: It contains addresses of over 1000 institutions and was brought out in 1985. Prior to this, "Directory of Social Science Research Institutions in India" and "Directory of Professional Organisations of Social Scientists" were compiled in 1971-72. Subsequently a "Directory of social science research institutions and organisations in India" was compiled as part of the ICSSR Project of "Financing of Social Science Research in India" in 1981. In 1987 NASSDOC Source Book of Institutions was brought out. It provides information about directories of research institutions available in NASSDOC.

Mahatma Gandhi Bibliography: The first volume in the series Mohandas Karamchand Gandhi: A Bibliography devoted to monographs in English was released on October 27, 1974. This has been followed by volumes covering monographs in Bengali, Hindi, Sanskrit and Urdu. The remaining volumes are at various stages of compilation.

Retrospective Cumulative Index of Indian Social Science Periodicals: With the Union Catalogue project behind it, NASSDOC planned to prepare a retrospective cumulative index of Indian social science periodicals right from this respective first volume. 240 periodicals were identified for the project and 1970 was fixed as the cut-off year. So far, work relating to indexing of journals in education, psychology, anthropology and sociology has been accomplished. When the project is completed, it will offer bibliographical control of periodical literature published over the past hundred years or so of potential utility to social scientists. The first volume, Indian Education Index, has been greatly appreciated, reflecting the need of such work. The next one in the series, the Index to Indian Periodicals: Sociology and Psychology (1BB6-1970) was printed in 1987. The publication covers 35 periodicals in sociology (1886-1970) and 7 in psychology (1926-1970).

Area Studies Bibliographies: Started during 1979, the Area Study Project aims at bringing together all social science material of research value excluding articles pertaining to the different states and Union Territories of India. Under this project, it is intended to bring out series of bibliographies which will cover material in social sciences available in any form and language exclusively related to the area concerned. So far information about 10,000 titles in English and Indian regional languages has been collected.

Under the supervision of a project director in each State/Region, the compilation work has been completed for Andaman & Nicobar Islands, Goa, Daman & Diu, Madhya Pradesh. Punjab, Haryana & Himachal Pradesh, Rajasthan, Tamil Nadu, U.P. (Eastern Region) and is in progress in the remaining States and Union Territories.

Languages Bibliographies: The project is wider in scope and seeks to cover research materials in all disciplines in social sciences in Indian regional languages. The compilation work of bibliographies in Gujarati, Hindi, Kannada and Oriya is in progress. The bibliographical data of about 6,000 documents in Hindi, 2,000 in Gujarati and 300 each in Oriya and Kannada languages is in hand.

ICSSR Regional Centres Programmes

The last decade has witnessed the rapidly growing significance and importance of social sciences in the country. Side by side, there has been an increase in the knowledge and the information generated in this field through various researches and studies. It necessitates the formation of a kind of network system through which this knowledge can easily be made available to all the scholars engaged in research work or any one who wants to benefit from it. As described earlier, ICSSR has set up six Regional Centres (RCs) in the country each having its jurisdiction over a cluster of States. (Annexture I). Some of the RCs have been able to build fairly good infrastructural facilities that include library facilities, documentation centres and hostel facilities for visiting scholars. The libraries/documentation centres, besides providing books and journals undertake bibliographic and reprographic services which are useful to visiting scholars. These are expected to be repository of social science literature in the regional languages. RCs collect doctoral theses and research reports in their respective regional language(s), and are also required to undertake translation of important sources of information that may be available in English or any other language.

Programmes: The ICSSR Southern Regional Centre, Hyderabad undertakes documentation activities which include compilation of Documentation in Social Sciences (Bi-Monthly); (ii) Current Contents in Social Sciences (Monthly); (iii) List of Select Articles from Telugu Newspapers and Journals (Half-yearly); (iv) List of Selected Articles from Urdu Newspapers and Journals (Urdu, Half-yearly) (v) List of Select Articles from Kannada Newspapers and Journals (Half-yearly).

Besides these, a number of bibliographies covering material in regional languages and English have been brought out on various themes like women, reservation policy, state government and politics, area study, etc.

ICSSR Eastern, North Eastern, and Western Regional Centres have taken up NASSDOC sponsored project of compiling Area Study Bibliographies.

A bibliography on Mahatma Gandhi covering documents in Bengali has been compiled by ICSSR Eastern regional centre and published.

ICSSR Northern Regional Centre, New Delhi in collaboration with Jawaharlal Nehru University brings out Suchika, a monthly index to periodical literature in social sciences and area studies. A comprehensive bibliography on South and West Asia, 1967-82 has also been completed.

ICSSR North-Western Regional Centre, Chandigarh is preparing cumulative index of social science books in Punjabi language and social sciences material in Punjabi periodicals. It has compiled various documentation and bibliographical publications like "Bibliography of Ph.D. Theses in Social Sciences in Punjab Agricultural University, Ludhiana" and "Holding List of Social Science Periodicals in Libraries in Chandigarh, 1963-1984".

ICSSR Assisted Projects

The third category of programmes relates to indexes and bibliographies, libraries aided with grants and scholars assisted to visit libraries.

Documentation Assistance: The financial assistance has been provided for a number of documentation projects. Some of the current project are given at Annexture IV. The financial expenditure incurred during the last five years has been tabulated below:

TABLE. Expenditure on Documentation Projects

Year	Amount (Rs in lakhs)
1987-88	1.20
1986-87	1.38
1985-86	1.35
1984-85	2.43
1983-84	2.43

Publication Assistance: Publication of good reference works has also been promoted by bulk purchase of copies. (1) Hindi Sandharbh, (2) Index India, (3) Index to Calcutta Review, (4) Indian Behavioural Science Abstracts, (5) Indian Education Index (1948-1978), (6) Indian Political Movement (1919-1971), (7) Kesari Centenary Index, (8) Library and Information Services in India, (9) Indian Press Index, (10) Second Handbook of Psychological and Social Instruments are some examples in the category.

Financial Assistance to Libraries and Documentation Centres: Grants-in-aid has been provided to the Indian Council of World Affairs, New Delhi, towards the maintenance of the library/documentation activities including subscription of journals and to the Indian Renaissance Institute, Dehra Dun for maintenance of M.N. Roy Archives.

Study Grants: Under the scheme, the scholars are financially assisted to visit libraries in India for consulting research material.The scheme is conducted from six ICSSR Regional Centres and ICSSR assisted Sardar Patel Institute of economic and Social Research, Ahmedabad and coordinated by National Social Science Documentation Centre. The assistance consists of payment of Rs. 30/- per day subject to maximum period of 56 days in a financial year and second class to and fro (from place of residence to place of work) rail fare.

The table below provides data about the number of scholars provided assistance and the total grants disbursed during the last five years by NASSDOC-ICSSR Northern Regional Centre.

Table. Study grant Programme

Year	No.	Amount (Rs. thousands)
1987-88	65	53.1
1986-87	97	73.252
1985-86	95	50.288
1984-85	86	39.147
1983-84	121	70.368

SERVICES

During brief span of two decades, the services of NASSDOC have been well appreciated by academicians, researchers and professionals. The centre won first D.R. Kerala Award in 1983 for all round achievements in documentation and library services fields. The services have branched into as under:

Consultation Facilities:

The library provides facilities to bonafide scholars to consult research material in the Reading Room, through out the year except on three national holidays. Its rich collection attracts scholars from all parts of India and abroad. About 10,000 scholars annually visit the Library.

Bibliography Compilation:

The bibliographies are the prime need of the scholars. NASSDOC prepares short bibliographies for scholars on the topic of their research. About 300 bibliographies are compiled annually. These are reported in ICSSR Newsletter, NASSDOC Bibliographies on Tap and NASSDOC Bibliographic Reprints. The copies of these bibliographies are frequently demanded by the scholars.

Information Dissemination

State of the Art Reports: ICSSR brings out periodically survey reports in the various disciplines of social sciences. Thirty volumes have so far been brought out under the series.

Abstracting Journals: The seven abstracting journals in the field of social sciences are brought out. These have been listed on page... under the table Exchange Programme.

NASSDOC Serial Publications: NASSDOC brings out eleven serial titles, disseminating information about its various activities, services and programmes like acquisition, current awareness service, bibliographical service, indexing service and resource sharing. These are:

- Acquisition Update (Monthly)
- APINESS Newsletter (Quarterly)
- Bibliographies on Tap (Irregular)
- Conference Alert (Quarterly)
- Indian Diary of Events (Quarterly)
- NASSDOC Dockets (Monthly)
- Paging Periodicals (Bi-Monthly)
- Samajik Vigyan Samachar (Monthly)
- Social Science News (Monthly)
- Social Science Research Index (Irregular)
- Bibliographic Reprints (Irregular)

NASSDOC Adhoc Publications: A number of adhoc publications nearing hundred have also been brought out by NASSDOC. Some of these have been mentioned in the present document. These can be broadly categorised as: Research material resources in NASSDOC and other institutions; Directories; and Indexing and bibliographical documents (A complete list is at Annexture III).

Continuing Education Programme

Training Courses: Undertaking one year library course from

August 1988 leading to award of *Associateship in Library and Information Studies in Social Sciences* and also short term courses on various topics of interest.

Short term courses have been conducted on the various topics of interest. The courses organised so far are:

- Management Information Systems (MIS) in Libraries and Documentation Centres

- Computer Application to Indexing in Social Sciences
- Application of Word Star Package (For Secretarial Staff)

The forthcoming courses are:

- Application of Micro CDS/ISIS package

- Application of d'Base III package

- Financial Management of Libraries

The courses have proved very popular. The faculty for these courses is drawn from universities, management institutes, and informatics field. The table below provides bird eye view of the type of participants in the first course i.e. MIS in Libraries...

TABLE. Participants in MIS Course

Total No. of Participants		23
Institutions Representation	:	14
Universities Representation	:	9
Participants Position	:	
- Heads	:	19
- Deputies	:	3
- Others	:	1

Staff seminars: The staff seminars are organised weekly where in either one of the staff members or a guest speaker from other institution delivers a talk on a topic of professional or academic interest, and this is followed by lively discussion.

Document Delivery:

To back up bibliographical services and even otherwise, NASSDOC provides copies of research material from journals/books/theses/reports to the scholars and the officers in ICSSR. The material not available with it is procured from other libraries. The number of exposures provided annually during the last five years proves the utility of the service.

Table

Year	No. of exposures
1987-88	11,43,499
1986-87	8,53,452
1985-86	3,13,259
1984-85	1,84,458
1983-84	53,000

Reprography:

NASSDOC has sufficient resources for providing services in electronic stencil cutting, duplicating and photo-copying. The supporting equipment includes photocopiers (4), microfilm reader printer (1), electronic scanner (1), duplicating machines (4), and offset printer (1).

Consultancy:

NASSDOC provides consultancy services to institutions regarding planning for library, documentation and information services. Some of the institutions which have availed of this service are

Office of the Regional Advisor-for Social and Human Sciences in Asia and the Pacific, Bangkok.

Family Planning Foundation Library, New Delhi.

Delhi Financial Corporation, New Delhi.

Centre for Women's Development Studies, New Delhi.

Translation:

Through arrangement with other institutes and translators, NASSDOC provides translation facilities to the scholars. The requests so far this service have not been much.

INTERNATIONAL AND REGIONAL LEVEL COOPERATION

International: NASSDOC provides input data regarding Indian publications to International Committee for Social Science Information and Documentation, Paris, International Bulletin of Bibliography on Education published from Madrid and for International Geographical Bibliography published from Paris.

It assisted UNESCO DARE Data Bank to update data about research institutions, journals and research projects, completed and in progress, in the field of social sciences in India. It has now been asked to extend geographical coverage to the Asia-Pacific region.

Regional: NASSDOC actively participated in the UNESCO Regional Meeting of Experts at Bangkok, held on 12-16 May, 1986 which launched Asia-Pacific Information Network in Social Sciences (APINESS). NASSDOC is the national contact point for the Network under APINESS programme. The projects assigned by UNESCO include: (i) India 2000: An Annotated Bibliography (Completed); (ii) Selective Inventory of Information Services (Completed); (iii) Collecting data from Asia-Pacific region for World Directory of Social Science Institutions (In progress); (iv) State-of-the-Art-Report on Social Science Research Trends in India (In progress); and (v) Publication of APINESS Newsletter (On going).

MEMBERSHIP

International: NASSDOC is represented in International Federation for Information and Documentation (FID); and International

Federation of Library Associations and Institutions (IFLA). The centre is planning an international seminar in India on "Professional attitudes and reading habits" for IFLA Round Table on Research in Readin-.

ational: NASSDOC holds membership of most of the professional organisations and associations in India. Some of these are: In- Library Association, Indian Association of Special Libraries and Information Centres, Association of Government Librarians & Information Specialists, Micrographic Congress of India.

Others: The Director, NASSDOC is member of IFLA Round Table on Research in Reading, International Committee for Social Science Information and Documentation, FID National Committee, FID Social Science Information and Documentation committee, Budapest, Academy of Library and Information Services, Trivandrum, Indian Association of Teachers of Library Science, Nagpur, Indian Standards Institution-Committees and panels etc., with regard to Documentation, Information and Library Science, New Delhi, etc.

FRESH INITIATIVES

(i) *Automation of services:* It is intended to create computerised data-bases of research material (books, periodicals, research reports, theses, working papers) and reference material (abstracts, indexes, directories of professional organisations and research institutions) in social science disciplines available in libraries in India.

(ii) *Research Projects Data Base:* The aim is to set up a data base of research projects in social sciences, completed and in progress, to avoid duplication and judicious utilisation of resources.

(iii) *SDI Service:* The compilation of interest profiles of scholars so as to provide selective dissemination of information services is being initiated.

(iv) *Resource Sharing:* With a view to conserve resources and put them to better use, a meeting of subject experts and library professionals in various disciplines is envisaged.

(v) *Micro-filming of Research Material:* Microfilming of theses, project reports and journals is contemplated to cope with space shortage and preservation problems.

vi) *Research Facilities to Scholars:* Quick document delivery services will be provided by adding more photo copiers and icrofilm reader-printers.

FUTURE PROGRAMMES

(i) *National Information System:* A national information grid has been on the planning board for some time. The system is expected to link centres of excellence in social sciences in the country and provide efficient service to the seekers of information. As a first step, it would strive for developing linkages with six ICSSR Regional Centres and twenty two aided research institutes by exchange of documentation outputs, preferably in machine readable form.

(ii) *Documentation programmes*

The forthcoming programmes include:

(a) Central Indexing Services in Social Sciences.
(b) Central Abstracting Service in Social Sciences.
(c) South Asia Bibliography.

ANNEXTURE I

ICSSR Regional Centres

Name and Address	Jurisdiction
ICSSR Eastern Regional 10 Jadunath Sarkar Road, Calcutta-700029 West Bengal Tel: 466472 467658	Bihar, Orissa, West Bengal
ICSSR North-Eastern Regional Centre, Nehru Library Building Mayur Bhanj House Shillong-793003 Meghalaya Tel: 3941	Assam, Manipur, Meghalya Mizoram, Nagaland and Tripura
ICSSR Northern Regional Centre, Jawaharlal Nehru University, New Delhi-110067 Tel: 387343	Delhi, Madhya Pradesh, Rajasthan, Uttar Pradesh
ICSSR North Western Regional Centre, Punjab University Library Building Chandigarh-160014 Tel: 25023 29582	Haryana, Himachal Pradesh, Jammu & Kashmir Punjab & U.T. of Chandigarh
ICSSR Southern Regional Centre, Osmania University Library	Andhra Pradesh Karnataka, Kerala & Tamil Nadu

Hyderabad-500007
Andhra Pradesh
Tel: 71756

ICSSR Western Regional Centre, Vidya Nagari Kalina Bombay-400098 Maharashtra Tel: 554943 532241	Goa, Gujarat and Maharashtra

ANNEXTURE II

ICSSR Assisted Research Institutes

A.N.S. Institute of Social Studies
Patna-800 001
Bihar
Tel: 21395

Centre for Development Studies
C/o. State Planning Board
Secretariat
Bhubneshwar, Orissa

Centre for Development Studies
Bakulam Road, Ullor
Trivandrum 695011
Kerala
Tel: 8412

Centre for Economic and Social Studies
Nizamia Observatory Campus
Begumpet
Hyderabad-500016
Andhra Pradesh

Centre for Policy Research
Dharma Marg, Chankyapuri
New Delhi-110021
Tel: 3014797

Centre for Regional, Ecological and
Science Studies in Development Alternatives
Chaturanga, Flat No. 3
32, Gobinda Auddy Road
Calcutta-700027

West Bengal
Tel: 491950

Centre for Research in Rural
& Industrial Development
2A, Sector 19A
Madhya Marg
Chandigarh-160019
Tel: 23136 33045

Centre for Social Studies
South Gujarat University Campus
Udhna-Magdhalla Road
Surat-395007
Gujarat
Tel: 86173

Centre for Studies in Social Sciences
10 Lake Terrace
Calcutta-700029
West Bengal
Tel: 466472

Centre for the Study of
Developing Societies
29, Alipur Road
New Delhi-110006
Tel: 231190

Centre for Women Development Studies
B-43, Panchsheel Enclave
New Delhi-110017
Tel: 665828

Council for Social Development
53, Lodhi Estate
New Delhi-110003
Tel: 611700

G.B. Pant Social Science
Institute
80, Tagore Town
Allahabad-211002
Uttar Pradesh
Tel: 53762

Gandhian Institute of Studies
Post Box 1116
Rajghat
Varanasi-221001
Uttar Pradesh
Tel: 62182

Giri Institute of Development Studies
Sector 'O', Aligan Extension Scheme
Lucknow-226020
Uttar Pradesh
Tel: 73640

Indian Institute of Education
128/2, J.P. Naik Road
Kothrud
Pune-411029
Maharahstra
Tel: 33336

Gujarat Institute of Area Planning
New Brahma Kshatriya Society
Pritam Rai Marg,
Post Box No. 2
Ahmedabad-380006

Institute of Development Studies
B-118, Mangal Marg
Bapu Nagar
Jaipur-302015
Rajasthan
Tel: 2609691

Institute of Economic Growth
University of Delhi
New Delhi-110007
Tel: 2522524

Institute of Public Enterprise
University Campus
Hyderabad-500007
Andhra Pradesh
Tel: 71148

Institute for Social and Economic Change
Nagarbhavi
Bangalore-560074
Karnataka
Tel: 607216

Madras Institute of Development Studies
79, Second Main Road
Gandhi Nagar
Adyar
Madras-600020
Tamil Nadu
Tel: 412202 412295

Sardar Patel Institute of
Economic and Social Research
Thaltej Road
Ahmedabad-380009
Gujarat
Tel: 441719

ANNEXTURE III

NASSDOC RESEARCH INFORMATION SERIES

1988. 75. Bibliography of Bibliographies.

76. Rajasthan: A Select List.

77. Directory of Encharge Services.

78. Bibliography Reprints: Management.

79. Recent Indian Books in Social Sciences.

80. Bibliographic Reprints: Education.

81. Abstracts of Research Reports (with analytical preface): Commerce.

1987. 39. NASSDOC Source Book of Institutions: Part I.

51. Madhya Pradesh: A Select List.

52. Bibliographic Reprints: Women.

53. NASSDOC: How it works.

54. Thesauri. Glessaries. Terminologies and Dictionaries in NASSDOC: A Rresource List.

55. Recent Indian Books on Economics, Education, Political Science, Sociology and Social and Cultural Anthropology, 1986.

57. Bibliographic Reprints: Tourism and Transportation.

58. Punjab, Haryana and Himachal Pradesh: A Select List.

59. Bibliographic Reprints: Labour and Labouring Classes.

60. Bibliographic Reprints: Scheduled Caste and Scheduled Tribes.

62. Bibliographic Reprints: Social Problems (Drug Abuse, Family and Health, etc.)

63. Bibliographic Reprints: Sychology.

64. Bibliographic Reprints: Economic Development.

65. Swatantrata Ke Paschant Bal Sahitya (Hindi).

66. Bibliographic Reprints: Banks and Banking.

67. Index to Indian Journals: Sociology and Psychology Rs. 700/-

68. Bibliographic Reprints: Foreign Collaboration. Rs 25/-

69. Periodicals in NASSDOC: 1987. Rs. 25/-

70. University of Delhi: Research in Library and Information Science: A Bibliographical Survey. Rs. 25/-

71. Bibliographic Reprints: No. 1, 1987. Rs. 25/-

72. Bibliographic Reprints: Industry. Rs. 25/-

73. Bibliographic Reprints: Commerce. Rs. 25/-

74. National Integration. Rs. 25/-

1986. 33. Bibliographic Reprints: Youth. Rs. 25/- (Out of stock)

40. Recent Indian Books in Economics, Education, Political Science, Sociology and Social Anthropology. Rs. 25/- per copy (Out of stock)

41. Indian Social Science Periodicals: Survey, Part-I, Pre-Independence period. Rs. 25/-

42. Mythic Society Library, Bangalore, Catalogue of Periodicals, 1985. Rs. 25/- (Out of stock).

43. Social Sciences in the Present Day World. (Out of stock).

46. Goa, Daman & Diu: A Preliminary List. Rs. 25/- (Out of stock).

47. Union List of Social Science Periodicals: Lucknow. Rs. 25/-

48. Bibliography on Student Teaching. Rs. 25/- (Out of stock).

49. Union Catalogue of Library Science and Informatics Publications-Delhi Libraries. Rs. 25/- (Out of stock).

50. Bibliographic Reprints: Children. Rs. 25/-

1985. 20. Inventory of Social Science Institutions and Organisations in India. Rs. 25/- (Out of stock).

21. Documents in Microform: A List of Resources at SSDC, JNU, University of Bombay, ICSSR Regional Centres, Calutta. Rs. 25/-

22. Library and Information Science Literature: SSDC Resource List Rs. 25/- (Out of stock).

23. Bibliography of Bibliographies: Supplement 3. Rs. 25/- (Out of stock)

24. Periodicals in SSDC: A Current List. Rs. 25/- (Out of stock).

25. Indian Dissertation Abstracts Index Vol. 1-10: 1973-1981. Rs. 25/-

26. Dr. S.R. Ranganathan: A Bibliography. Rs. 25/-

27. Distance Education: A Reading List. Rs. 25/- (Out of stock).

28. Union List of Current Social Science Periodicals: Delhi Libraries. Rs. 25/-

29. National Integration: Literature in SSDC. Rs. 25/- (Out of stock).

30. Bibliographic Reprints: Library Science and Informatics. Rs. 25/- (Out of stock).

31. Family Walfare Education in India: A Bibliography. Rs. 25/- (Out of stock).

32. Statistics and Data Sources: Part I, SSDC Resources. Rs. 25/- (Out of stock).

1984. 10. Bibliography of Bibliographies: Supplement. Rs. 25/- (Out of stock).

11. Recent Indian Books in Economics, Education, Political Science and Sociology. (Out of stock) Rev. in 1985.

12. Social Science Institutions and Organisations in India. (Out of stock).

13. Andaman and Nicobar Islands: A Bibliography. Rs. 25/- (Out of stock)

14. A Guide to Books & Journals Aided/Published by ICSSR. Rs. 25/- (Out of stock)

15. Inter-Library Resources Centre, Holdings of Periodicals Rev. edhn. Rs. 25/- (Out of stock)

16. Index to Seminars on North East (March 1975-April 1984) Conducted by North-East India Council for Social Science Research, Shillong. Rs. 25/-

17. ICSSR Research Abstracts Quarterly Index. Vol. I-II, 1971-1982. Rs. 10/-

18. Bibliography of Bibliographies Compiled in SSDC. Supplement 2. Rs. 25/- (Out of stock).

1983.

1. Union List of Social Science Periodicals Received in Delhi Libraries. (Out of stock). Rev. in 1985.

2. Union Catalogue of Newspapers: Delhi Libraries. Rs 25/- (Out of stock)

3. Theses in S.S.D.C.: A Bibliography. Rs. 25/- (Out of stock)

4. Bibliography of Bibliographies in SSDC. Rs 25/- (Out of stock)

5. Research Project Reports in SSDC: A Bibliography. Rs. 25/- (Out of stock)

6. Social Science Research Methodology: A Bibliography. Rs. 25/-

7. Bibliography of Bibliographies Compiled in SSDC. Rs. 25/-

8. Periodicals in SSDC: A Current List. (Out of stock) Rev. in 1985.

9. Reference Sources in SSDC: A Bibliography. Rs. 25/- (Out of stock).

1982. 1. Union List of Social Science Periodicals Received in Delhi Libraries. (Out of stock). Rev. in 1985.

NASSDOC SERIALS.

1. Acquisition Update (Monthly) Rs. 10/- per copy
2. APPINESC Newsletter (Quarterly).
3. Bibliographies on Tap (Irregular) Rs. 25/- per copy.
4. Conference Alert (Quarterly) Rs. 10/- per copy.
5. Indian Diary of Events. (Quarterly) Rs. 10/- per copy.
6. NASSDOC Dockets (Monthly).
7. Paging Periodicals (Bi-Monthly) Rs. 10/- per copy.
8. Samajik Vigyan Samachar (Monthly) (Hindi) Rs. 10/- per copy.
9. Social Science News. (Monthly) Rs. 25/- per copy.
10. Social Science Research Index. (Irregular) Rs. 25/- per copy.
11. Bibliographic Reprints. Rs. 25/- per copy.

ANNEXTURE IV

List of Current Documentation Projects

Annotated Bibliography of Research in Development Psychology.

Annotated Bibliography on Health, Nutrition and Family Planning Programmes with special reference to Tribal Setup.

Annotated Bibliography of Kannada Reference Sources.

Annotated Guide to Reference Sources in Telugu.

Encyclopaedia of Social Sciences in Hindi-Preliminary Survey.

Encyclopaedia of Social Sciences in Marathi.

Index of Articles on Agricultural Economics.

Information Requirements and Suggestions for Developing Library and Information Services for Social Scientists in India.

Union catalogue of Periodicals on Library and Information Science in University Libraries in India.

Union Catalogue of Rare Books in Social Sciences Published in 16th Century and Onwards.

Union Catalogue of 18th & 19th Century Newspapers Published or Available in the State of Maharashtra.

TWENTY

ICSSR Data Archives

INTRODUCTION

Data Archives, like libraries of printed books and documents, are organised repositories of machine-readable quantitative data. These institutions acquire, organise, document, and disseminate primary numerical data in easily processable form. The underlying assumption in preserving data with data archives is that they facilitate sharing and utilisation of existing data and thereby ensure greater return on investment in research by avoiding duplication of effort and expenditure on data collection. Three major developments have contributed to the establishment and growth of these institutions: (a) refinement in sampling theory and its application in social science research, (b) increasing use of quantitative techniques, and (c) availability of computer technology which has made the handling of complex and vast amounts of data possible.

Complex societal processes in modern times have made policy makers and researchers increasingly dependent on appropriate data. The objective of planned socio-economic change and the planning process in the post-independent India has led the policy-makers to infuse the decision-making process with appropriate data. This has resulted in direct involvement of the government in collecting fresh data on a very large scale besides what it accumulates in its routine administrative functioning. Simultaneously, individual researchers have also contributed to this effort by collecting diverse data pertaining to various aspects of socio-economic reality.

A good deal of this 'data wealth' has, however, remained under-utilised or at best partially utilised by social scientists for various reasons. A vast amount of data produced over the years by various governmental and semi-governmental agencies has not been accessible to researchers. Even the available data are in a shape that renders any meaningful analysis difficult. Most of these data are available in the form of filled-up schedules/questionnaires, hand tabulated sheets or printed documents. Proper organisation and analysis of such data entail prohibitive costs. Social scientists, therefore, suffer from serious handicaps in their efforts to utilise the existing stock of data.

OBJECTIVES

Recognising the critical role of properly organised data in improving the quality of research, the Indian Council of Social Science Research (ICSSR), established the Data Archives in its secretariat at New Delhi in 1973. ICSSR has envisaged a broader role for its Data Archives. And so, instead of establishing a huge centralised repository of data at one place, the council has decided to follow a decentralised model, in which the Data Archives is to promote and coordinate organisation of existing social science data in an easily retrievable form so that it could be analysed from several perspectives. The organisation of voluminous data is expected to be carried out with the cooperation of social scientists and user research institutions in the country. The main objectives of the Data Archives are:

i. to promote and coordinate organisation of data relevant for social science research in easily processable form;
ii. to help research scholars to have access to data gathered by governmental agencies and to act as liaison between the data gathering agencies and data users; and
iii. to develop skills and competence among researchers in computer applications in social science research and secondary analysis of data.

FUNCTIONS

These broad objectives are expected to be realised through the following functions:

1. Data repository
2. Institution-based data archives
3. Grants-in-aid for data organisation
4. Clearing-house
5. Training
6. Guidance and Consultancy Services in Data processing
7. National Register of Social Scientists
8. International collaborations
9. Computer facilities

Data repository

There are three major sources of social science data: (a) data generated by projects, funded by ICSSR; (b) data generated by individual scholars, research institutions/organisations and university departments, without the funds of ICSSR; and (c) data generated by the governmental and semi-governmental agencies.

Being part of the ICSSR, the Data Archives acquires, organises and preserves data generated by the ICSSR funded research projects and disseminates them among interested researchers for secondary analysis. On an average ICSSR finances 100 research projects a year of which about 12 per cent yield data in machine-readable form. The remaining studies are either based on non-quantitative data or do not meet the minimum criteria for acquisition: that is, these studies are either based on extremely small samples or have incomplete documentation and/or data. Also, since computer applications in social sciences are relatively new in the country, a number of even quantitative data based studies are manually tabulated. Acquiring filled-in schedules/questionnaires after the completion of the projects and then transcribing data in the machine-readable form is not feasible. Only those data sets, as are available in the machine-readable form, have re-use potential and are backed by appropriate documentation, are acquired. Efforts are being made to preserve every acquired data set on computer tapes after checking completeness of the data and its correspondence with the code book(s), etc., along with all the relevant documents required for secondary analysis.

Institution-Based Data Archives

A number of social science research institutions have generated useful survey data over the years. Most of these data are available in the form of filled-in questionnaires/schedules or are in a shape as would require investment of additional resources in order to make them usable for secondary analysis. the ICSSR proposes to utilise the existing institutional infrastructure of at least some of the major research institutions and provide additional resources wherever necessary and involve these institutions in the organisation and documentation of these data. Once the infrastructure for undertaking data archival functions has been developed in these institutions, it can also be utilised to organise government data. With this end in view, ICSSR proposes to establish a network of institution-based data repositories in important research institutions in the country. Selected institutions will be provided financial and technical support to build-up the required infrastructure. These institution-based data archives are expected to organise and maintain machine-readable data on certain specific socio-economic aspects and/or regions depending upon their research interests.

Although this programme was conceived by ICSSR since the inception of the Data Archives, it could not be implemented for lack of funds. Establishing data archives require huge investments and skilled personnel to run them, both of which are in short supply. Therefore, in the first instance, four to six research institutions are to be financially supported to develop such institution-based data archives during the seventh Plan period in a phased programme. The Data Archives will provide guidance, standards for data organisation and documentation, and coordinate their activities in order to avoid duplication of work and wastage of resources.

Grant-in-Aid for Data Organisation

The Data Archives has a programme under which scholars/institutions may approach the council for grant-in-aid for transcribing a specific data set in machine-readable form. Under this scheme scholars/institutions are provided financial assistance to cover expenses on items like coding, punching, computer time, stationery, etc., provided the data have significant re-use potential and that the scholar/institution is willing to give a copy of the organised data along with supporting documentation, viz, a copy of original questionnaire/schedule, sampling design, code book(s), etc., to the Data archives to enable other interested scholars to utilise the data for secondary analysis.

Clearing-House

It is a known fact that a large quantum of useful data collected by government organisations as well as research institutions is not publicly reported. The potential users, therefore, remain unaware about the availability of many data sets. Even when they come to know, it is extremely difficult, for most scholars, to have access to the primary data held by the government agencies. In order to resolve this problem, the Data Archives has two programmes: (a) to prepare an inventory of what kind of data exist, where and in what form, and (b) to help researchers have access to government data.

An inventory of data available with major research institutions has already been undertaken by the Data Archives. Efforts are also being made to collect relevant information about the data available with the government agencies and semi-government agencies. In addition, the Data Archives, with the cooperation of eminent social scientists and representatives of major government data producing organisations is trying to persuade government agencies to release primary data to interested research institutions through the Data Archives.

Training

A large number of social science researchers in India lack proper training in research techniques and computer applications in data-processing. This affects the organisation as well as effective utilisation of data by social scientists. Efforts are being made by universities and ICSSR to fill this gap by organising special short-term training courses in research methods. Most of these courses, however, lack emphasis on computer applications in data processing. The Data Archives, therefore, sponsors training courses with emphasis on the development of such skills and competence among social scientists. A few research institutions are being provided financial assistance to organise training courses designed to instil technical skills for data organising and analysis, and archival practices with the help of computers.

Guidance and Consultancy Services

The Data Archives has another important programme to assist interested researchers in various aspects of data processing by using computers: devising of code book(s), selection of appropriate statistical techniques for analysing a given data set, and assistance in computer programming. In addition, scholars may seek guidance in framing of research instruments for data collection and sampling designs. To enable researchers to avail themselves of these facilities nearer their normal place of work, in addition to the Data Archives, eight other research institutions provide such facilities to scholars on behalf of ICSSR. These are:

1. Centre for the Study of Developing Societies 29, Rajpur Road, Delhi-110054.
2. Sardar Patel Institute of Economic and Social Research, P.B. No. 4062, Navrangpura, Ahmedabad-380009,
3. Gokhale Institute of Politics and Economics, Pune-411004.
4. Centre for Development Studies, Aakulam Road, Ulloor, Trivandrum-695001.
5. Tata Institute of Social Sciences, Sion-Trombay Road, Deonar, Bombay-400088.
6. Centre for Social Studies South Gujarat University Campus, Udhna-Magdalla Road, Surat-395007.
7. Giri Institute of Development Studies, B-42, Nirala Nagar, Lucknow-226007.
8. A.N.Sinha Institute of Social Studies, Patna-800001.

National Register of Social Scientists

The Data Archives has brought out a *National Register of Social Scientists in India* containing comprehensive information about the academic background, research interests, publications, positions, and current addresses of over 7,500 social scientists, engaged in teaching and/or research at university departments, research institutions, and affiliated colleges. The Register is designed to help identification of scholars engaged in specific areas with a view to facilitating professional interacting and exchange of ideas among social scientists on the one hand and policy makers and scholars on the other. Simultaneously, the information has been organised on computer tapes to facilitate updating. Efforts are being made to update this information.

International Collaborations

The data archival activities in social sciences are in a stage of infancy in our country. Some of the data archives in the USA and Western Europe have made substantial progress in this field. These archives over the years have accumulated a considerable volume of social science data in easily processable form and have gained valuable experience in data archival practices. We can learn a great deal from the experience of these data archives. With this end in view,the Data Archives has become a member of the International federation of Data Organisations for Social Sciences (IFDO), an organisation trying to promote projects and procedures for enhancing exchange of data and technologies among member organisations. It has also accepted responsibility as the Asian Secretariat of the International Association of Social Science Information Services and Technology (ASSIST), a professional association of individuals engaged in acquisition, processing, and maintenance of machine-readable social science data.

The Data Archives is exploring possibilities of undertaking projects of mutual interest with IFDO-member archives. The Archives is also working out details about collaborative relations with important data archives for exchange of data and software.

Computer Facilities

The Data Archives has an in-house computer installed by the National Informatics Centre, New Delhi, as part of NICNET. These computer facilities are utilised primarily by the Data Archives for its own archival activities involving data organisation, data cleaning, and statistical processing. These facilities are also utilised for processing of data of other researchers and institutions invited under the programme on Guidance and Consultancy Services.

TWENTY ONE

Overviews: Resources

CHAPTER 1.

Bhatnagar, Usha, Indexing services in India with special reference to social sciences. *Libra* 11 1973-74 : p. 86-98.

Chopra, H.R., Social science documentation in India. *Indian Librarian* 33(4) : 1979 : p. 182-85.

Ghan, A.G., Social science documentation activities in India. *Libra* 11 : 1973-74 : p. 38-48.

Guha, B., *Documentation and Information.* 2nd edn, Calcutta, World Press, 1983 : p. 380.

Indian Council of Social Science research. Annual report. 1970

Kaula, P.N. Some facts of national policy on library and information services. *Herald of Library Science* 24(1-2): January-April 1985: p. 42-46.

Modernisation of library services and informatics for the Seventh Five Year Plan, 1985-90: Report of the Working Group of the Planning Commission 1984. 123 p. (for restricted use).

Hills, P.J., ed., *Trends in information transfer.* London, Frances Printer, 1982, p. 191.

Ranganathan, S.R., *Documentation : Genesis and development.* Delhi, Vikas, 1973, p. 310.

Schutz, H., *Function and organisation of a national documentation centre in a developing country.* Paris, Unesco, 1975, p. 218.

Vyas, S.D., Bibliographical control of social sciences in India. *ILA Bulletin* 15(1-2) : 1979 : p. 25-31.

Year's Work in Indian librarianship, 1987, by T.S. Rajagopalan Delhi, I.L.A., 1988. 234 p.

CHAPTER 2

Foldi, Tamas, Social science information and social practice. *International Forum on Information and Documentation* 8(4) : 1983 : p. 3-7.

Hogeweg-de-Haart, H.P., Characteristics of social science information. A selective review of the literature. Part I-II. *Social Science Information Studies* 3 : 1983 : p. 147-63, 4 : 1984 : p. 15-30.

Lazar, P., International information systems. *International Information Communication and Education* 2(2) : 1983 : p. 34-69.

Line, M.B., The information uses and needs of social scientists : *ASLIB Proceedings* 23(8) : 1971 : p. 412-34.

Neufeld, M. Lynne and Cornag, Martha, Secondary information systems and services. *In : Annual review of information science and technology.* Vol. 18. White Plains, N.Y., Knowledge Industry Publications, 1983. p. 151-83.

UNESCO. *Adhoc committee on social science information.* (Session 1, 1977, Nov. 14-18 : Paris). *Final report.* Paris, Unesco, 1977. 13p. (SS/77/Conf. 607/8).

Venkataramanaiah, T.V., Information seeking behaviour of Bangalore University teachers and research scholars. (Dissertation submitted to Bangalore University in part fulfilment for M. Lib. Sc. course, 1975-76).

CHAPTER 3

Bhattacharjea, S., Orientation of staff and students for better use of the libraries. *New Frontiers in Education* 8(3) 1978 : p. 15-19.

Evans, A.J., Rhodes, R.G.,and Keenan, S., *Education and training of users of scientific and technical information;* Unisist guide for teachers. Paris, Unesco, 1977.

Fjallbrant, Nancy and Stevenson, Malcolm, *User education in libraries.* London, Bingley, 1978.

Girja Kumar and Krishan Kumar, *Philosophy of user education.* Delhi, Vikas, 1983.

Harris, C., Educating the user. *Library association record.* 1977: p. 359-60.

Harris, C., Illuminative evaluation of user education programmes. *Aslib Proceedings,* 29(10): 1977: p.348-62.

Harris, Keith G.E., user education. *Libri.* 32(4) : 1982 : p. 328-36.

Iyengar, T.K.S., User orientation in University libraries. *Library Science with a Slant to Documentation* 15(4): 1978: p. 177-182.

Lubans, John, ed. *Educating the library user.* New York, R.R.Bowker, 1978.

Malley, Ian., Educating the special library user. *Aslib Proceedings.* 30(10-11) : 1978: p. 365-72.

Rajagopalan, T.S., Education and training of information users : An overview. *Library Science with a Slant to Documentation.* 15(4) : 1978 : p. 159-66.

Wilson, T.D., On user studies and information needs. *Journal of Documentation.* 37 (1): 1981: p.3-15.

Wilson, T.D., Guidelines for developing and implementing a national plan for training and education in information use. Paris UNESCO 1981.

CHAPTER 4

Chiva, I., Scholarly periodicals : Their strength and weaknesses. *International Social Science Journal* 26(3): 1974 : p. 377-92.

Dhawle, Anand S. and Ghose, Amitabha, A study of the image of Indian journals on management and social sciences in the international academic community. *Journal of Higher Education* 4(3) : Spring 1979: p. 313-26.

Girija Kumar and Jayaswal, P.K., Social Science periodicals in libraries. *Library Herald* 21(1-2) : Apr. - Sep. 1982: p. 1-27.

Gandhi, HND, Jagdishlal and Suren Agrawal, *Indian periodicals in print,* Delhi, Vidya Mandal, 1973. 2pts.

Rawat, Taj, Publishing higher educational journals. *Indian Book Industry* 27(11): 1982 : p.15-16.

Narender Kumar. Citation study as a tool for evaluation of journal collection on use : A case study. *Journal of Library Information.* 9(1) : June 1984 : p. 48-64.

Subbarao, C.V. and others, Periodical resources and balancing budgets. *ILA Bulletin* 20(3-4) : Oct-Mar. 1985: p. 135-55.

Subrahmanya, K.N., Economic publications - old and new : Why some succeed as other fold up? *Southern Economist* 24: 15 Nov. 1985: p.37-40.

CHAPTER 5

Eswara Reddy, D.B., South Asian agricultural dissertations documentation centre : A micro-filming project. 4p. (Mimeographed) Paper presented at 11th IASLIC National Seminar at Hyderabad.

Ming, Ding Choo, Access to dissertations in and on South-east asia. *Libri* 34(2) : 1984: p.88-112.

Ramaiah, L.S. and Prafulla Chandra, T.V., Research dissertations : Problems of acquisition. *Herald of Library Science* 24(3) : 1985 : p. 202-206.

CHAPTER 6

Amrik Singh, Publishing in public sector, *In : Libraries and the book trade : Papers for the All India seminar* held on February 14, 1982 at Pragati Maidan, New Delhi. ILA, 1982, p. 48-53.

Chartrand, R.L., The role of government in the information society. *Journal of Information Science* 5(4) : Dec. 1982 : p.137-42.

Krishnamurti, C.S., Acquisition of government publications. *Library Herald* 8(1-2), Apr.-July 1965 : p. 82-94.

Singh, Mohinder, *Government of India publications.* New Delhi, Budua's Press, 1982. 176p.

State governments publications in India, 1947 - 1982. New Delhi, Academic Publications, 1985. 2 v. (659p).

Schmeckebier, Laurence F. and Eastin, Roy B., *Government publications and their use.* Rev. edn. 2. Washington, D.C., Brookings Institutions, 1969. x. 502p.

CHAPTER 7

Evans, Glyn T., Delivery of service *In* : Kent, Allen, *(ed.) Resource sharing in libraries.* N.Y., Marcel Deckker, 1974 : p. 120-36.

Landwehrmeyer, R., A planned decentralised solution for national document supply : The Federal Republic of Germany. *Interlending review 9(4) :* 1981 : p. 122-27.

Line, M.B., Universal availability of publications. *Unesco Bulletin for Libraries* 31(3) : 1977 : p. 142-51.

National planning and the impact of electronic technology on document provision and supply. *Libri* 35(3) : 1985 : p. 181-90.

Nagarajan, K.S., Work flow in a document supply service. *In : Seminar on Workflow in Special Libraries, University Libraries and Government Libraries* (1966, 21-24 Nov), Delhi. (Papers). Delhi, Insdoc. 10p. (Paper S-25).

Nitecki, Danuta, Document delivery and the rise of the automated midwife. *Resource Sharing and Information Networks.* 1(3-4): 1984: p.83-101.

Reintjes, J. Francis., Application of modern technologies to inter-library resources sharing networks. *American Society for Information Science Journal* 35(1) : 1984 : p. 45-52.

Reynolds, Dennis J., Regional alternatives for inter-Library loan : Access to unreported holdings. *College and Research Libraries* 41(1): 1980 : p. 33-42.

Vervliet, H.D.L., Speaking for cindrella : Unplanned decentralised interlending. *Interlending Review 9(4)* : 1981 : p.28-30.

Vervliet, H.D.L., ed. *Resource sharing of libraries in developing countries.* N.Y., K.G.Saur. 1979. 280p. (IFLA publication, 14.)

Vickers, Stephen and Line, M.B., *Improving the availability of publications : A comparative assessment of model national systems.* Boston Spa, Wetherby IFLA International Programme for UAP, 1984.

CHAPTER 8

Agrawal, S.P. and Satya Prakash, Manpower demand : *Concepts and Methodology,* Meerut, Meenakshi, 1970 xvii, 368p.

Biscoe, E.L. and Ston, E.W., Motivation and staff development. *Journal of Library Administration 1(1)* 1980 : 55 : 71.

Braunagel, J.S., Job mobility of men and women librarians and how it affects career advancement. *American Libraries* 10 : 1979 : p. 643-47.

Elliott, Lynn., Professional staff development in academic libraries. *Journal of Librarianship* 15(4) : 1983 : p.237-53.

Mangla, P.B., Manpower development for information handling. *Journal of Library and Information Science* 6(1) : 1981 : p.29-44.

Moore, N.E., *Manpower planning in libraries.* London, Library association, 1980. 32p.

Rao, V.K.R.V., *Education and human resources development.* Bombay, Allied, 1970. 231p.

Sales Pontes, A.H. Professional development of librarians. *Indian Librarian* 36(2) : September 1981 : p. 43-55.

CHAPTER 9

Cherian P.V. Presidential address. *In* : *Seminar on Library Education, 1965*, Bombay. Report. Bombay, S.N.D.T. Women's University, 1966 p. 8.

Committee On National Policy on Library and Information system. *See* : *Indian Culture* (Department of-), *National Policy on Library and Information System* (Committee on-)

Danton J. Periam ; *Education for Librarianship*. Paris, Unesco, 1949 p. 46.

Davinson, Donald : Thoughts on a model syllabus for a two year Master's degree course. *In* : Mangla, P B *ed. Library and information science education in India*. New Delhi, Macmillan, 1981. p. 102-108.

Documentation Research and Training Centre (Bangalore) Courses in documentation and information science : Prospects and syllabur. p. 14 (cyclostyled)

Eswara Reddy, D.B : Opinion expressed at "Seminar on perspectives in education and training of LIS personnel on 22-23 Nov. 1985 at Osmania University Library, Hyderabad".

Foskett, D.J : Address at "seminar on Perspectives in education and training of LIS personnel on 22-23 Nov. 1985 at Osmania University Library, Hyderabad".

Inamdar, N.B: and Riswadkar, M.R: India. *In* : Contemporary developments in Librarianship : An international handbook, *ed.* by Miles M Jackson) London, Library Association, 1981. p. 186.

Indian Culture (Department of-), *National Policy on Library and Information System*. (Commiittee on -) National Policy on library and Information system : A presentation. New Delhi, The Committee, 1986. p. 30

Indian Planning (Commission). *Modernisation of Library Services and Informatics for the 7th Five Year Plan* (1985-90) (Working Group on -). Report. New Delhi, The Working Group, 1984. p. 123.

Indian National Scientific Documentation Centre, (New Delhi) *Information Science* (Training Course in -). Prospectus and syllabus, 1986. New Delhi, Insdoc, 1986. p. 29.

Konnur, M.B. : Transnational library relations : *The Indo-American experience.* Ph D Thesis. University of Poona, 1986. p. 216.

Kumar, P.S.G. : *Promoting the use of audiovisual aids* : Paper presented at V National Seminar of IATLIS on Use of Audiovisual Aids in Library and Information Science Teaching, Luchnow, 9-10 Nov. p. 18.

Lazar, Peter : Some considerations on the education and training of librarians and information specialists. *Annals of Library Science and Documentation* 31 (1-2) : 1984 : p. 1-12.

Mohamed, Taher and Khan, Amin Ahmed and Muhammed Burhanuddin, : Dargah libraries in India : A comparative study. *International Library Review* 18 : 1986. p. 337-45.

Neelameghan, A : Education for librarians in India. *In Encyclopedia of Library and Information Science*. Vol. 11 N.Y: Marcel Dekker, 1974. p. 323.

Ranganathan,S.R. : Education and research in library science. *Cultural Forum* (Libraries special number) 1969. p. 10.

Regional Seminar on Curriculum Development in Information Studies (Bangkok) (17-21 Sep. 1985). Final report. Paris, Unesco, PGI, 1985. p. 38. (PGI-85/NS/33).

Saraccvic, Tefko and Others. : Issues in Information science education in developing countries. *Journal of the American Society for Information Science* 36(3) : 1984: p. 192-99.

University Grants Commission. (Review Committee on 1965 Library Science in Indian Universities : Report, New Delhi, UGC. p. 2-340.

Working Groups on Modernisation of Library Services and Informatics for the 7th Five Year Plan (1985-90).
See
India. Planning Commission. Working Group on Modernisation of Library Services and Informatics for the 7th Five Year Plan (1985-90).

University Grants Commission Library and Information Science (Panelon). Recommendations. 1982 (Mimeographed).

Chapter 10

Dale, Sheila : Distance learning. London, Library Association, 1986, (Guidelines for Training in Libraries, no. 8).

Mahajan, S.G. : Distance education in Library Science. *Libra* v.20-21 : 1982 - 1984 : p.26-31.

Neela Jagannathan, : Collection development at the libraries of distance teaching universities with special reference to the Indian situation. *ILA Bulletin* 23(3) : Oct-Dec. 1987 : p. 140-48.

Sahi, S.S. and Gupta, V.K. : Open University library : A conceptual analysis. *ILA Bulletin* 21(3-4): Oct. 1985-Mar.1986: p.96-99.

Schmude, Karl G. and Luxton, Robert B. : Aquisitions for distance education : An Australian experience. *Library Acquisitions : Practice and Theory* 10:1986: p.25-31 (Collection Development and Acquisitions in a Distance Learning Environment, I)

Sherwell, John : Professional education by distance learning : Experience of the master's degree at CLW. *Library Assoication Record* 88(11) : Nov. 1986: p.544.

de Silva, Rufus : Open learning in library instruction : A case study. *Education Libraries Bulletin* 30 (2) : Summer 1987: p.15-25.

Store, R. : Library service in distance teaching : Present realities and future possibilities. *Australian Library Journal* 30(3) : 1981: p.82-86.

Taylor, James C. and White, Vernon, J. : Why distance education? *Bulletin of the Unesco Regional Office for Education in Asia and the Pacific* 26 : Dec. 1985: p.1-12.

Trask, M. and Browne, M. : External Studies in librarianship. Lindfield NSW, kuring - gai College of Advanced Education, School of Library and Information Studies, 1979. 2v.

CHAPTER 11

Atal, Yogesh. *Social Sciences : The Indian Scene*. New Delhi, Abhinav Publications, 1976 xi p. 281.

Atal, Yogesh. Social Sciences : Use for policy. *ICSSR Newsletter* 13 (2) Oc 1982-Mar. 1983, p. 1-16 refs.

Datta, Bhabatosh. Social science research : Universities and autonomous institutions. *J Higher Education* 6 (1-3) 1980-81, p. 15-24.

Indian council of Social Science Research Directory of social science research institutions in India. New Delhi, The council, 1971. p. 200.
(Research Information Series no, 4)

Indian Council of Social Science Research Financing of Social Science Research in India. Delhi, the Author, 1981, 4V.
Social Science Research Institutions in India. p. 754. vol. I.B. Directory of Social Science Research Organisations p. 256.
Vol. 2. Departments of Central and State Government

Joshi, P.C., Social science research and the institutes. *Journal of Higher Education* 8 (2) Aut 1982, p. 155-65 Bib.

Ketkar, N.M., Indian Council of Science Research and documentation. *Indian Library Association Bulletin* 7 (3) July-Sep. 1971 p. 71-75.

Naik, J.P., Role responsibilities, functions, programmes and organisation of the ICSSR, New Delhi, ICSSR, 1971. (ICSSR occasional Monograph No. 7)

Namjosh, M.V., Priorities in social science research. *New Quest* 14-Mar-Ap'1978, p. 83-93.

Sardesai, D.B., Social science data archives : Emergence of new institutions in India. *Artha Vijnana* 15 (4) Dec 1973, p. 383-90, Bib.

Shonfield, Andrew and Cherns, A.B., Social science research in India : A report, (ICSSR occasional monograph, No. 12)

Weiner, Myron, Social science research and public policy in India. *Econ. and Pol. Wkly* 14(37), Se'79, p. 1579-87; 14 (38) 22se'79, p. 1622-28.

CHAPTER 12

Eswara Reddy, D.B., National library policy for higher education and research in India. *Lucknow Librarian* 16(2) : 1984 : p. 45-52.

India. Committee on National Policy of library and Information System., *National Policy on library and information system : A Presentation.* New Delhi. The Author, 1986 : 30p.

Johry, K.N., Towards national information policy. *The Hindu,* July 30, 1985.

Judge, P.J., Policy issues and the development of information systems. *Aslib Proceedings* 23(7) : July 1971 : p. 351-61.

Neelameghan, A., Regional development information systems: Their role in developing regions. *Library science With A Slant to Documentation* 16(3) : Sept 1979 : p.91-98.

Neelameghan, A., Some issues in information transfer : A third world perspective. *IFLA Journal* 7 : 1981 : p. 8-18.

UNESCO., Information policy objectives UNISIST proposals. Paris, Unesco, 1974. 26p. (SC-74/WS/3)

National Information Systems (NATIS): *National information policy.* Paris, Unesco, 1976. 26p. (COM 76/NATIS/60)

CHAPTER 13

Marks, Arnaud, F., Some problems of networks : The case of CILO. *International Forum on Information and Documentation* 8(4) : 1983 : p. 17-22.

Meyriat, J., International and regional cooperation in social science documentation. *Unesco Journal of Information science, Librarianship and Archives Administration* 2(4) : 1980 : p. 227-33.

Palmour, Vernon E. and Nancy, K. Roderer, Library resource sharing through networks. *Annual review of Information Science and Technology* 13 : 1978 : p. 147-77.

Vickery, B.C. et al., Interactive information networks and UK Libraries. *Journal of Documentation* 40 : Mar. 1984 : p.36-49

Wood, J.L., Factors influencing the use of technical standards in a nationwide library and information service network *Library Trends* 31 : Fall 1982 : p. 343-58.

CHAPTER 14

JNU-ICSSR : Inter-Library resources Centre. New Delhi, Social Science Documentation centre, ICSSR, 1975. 21p.

Kronick, D.A., Goodbye to farewells-resource sharing and cost sharing. *Journal of Academic Librarianship* 8: 1982 : p.132-36.

Miyamoto, S. and Nakayama, K., Determination of conservation time of periodicals for optimal shelf maintenance of a library. *American Society for Information Science Journal* 32 : July 1981 : p. 268-74.

Munn, R.F., Collection developments vs. resource sharing: The dilemma of the middle-level institutions, *Journal of Academic Librarianship* 8: Jan.1983 : p. 352-53.

Stayner, R.A., economic characteristics of the library storage problem. *Library Quarterly* 53, July 1983 : p. 313-27.

CHAPTER 15-16

Bhattacharya, C., ed., New developments in library and information science in India. Bangalore. D.R.T.C., 1981. 106p.

Gowtham, M.S. and Raghavan, M., Impact of new technologies on collection development and circulation in special libraries. *Library science with a slant of documentation* 19(1) : 1982: p.21-53.

India. Planning commission. Working Group of Modernisation of Library services and Informatics for the Seventh Five Year Plan, 1985-90. *Report.* 1984. 123p.

Kararia, Kamal, Micro-computer based bibliographic information storage and retrieval system. *Journal of Library and Information Science* 6(1): 1981 : p.29-44.

Krishan Kumar, Application of computers. A challenge for change. *ILA Bulletin* 16(3-4) : 1980 : p. 122-29.

Marsterson, William, *Information technology and the role of the librarian.* London, Croom Helm, 1986. 194p.

Narayana, G.J. and Desai, H.G., Design of a computerised document handling system for a group of libraries. *Annals of Library science and Documentation* 28(1-4) : 1981 : p. 20-31.

Rajagopal, C., Photographic parameters of reprography. *Library science with a slant to documentation* 17(4) : 1980 : p. 90-94.

Ramaseshan, S., Problems in information transfer in India. *Library science with a slant to Documentation* 15(4) : 1980 : p. 204-06

UNESCO. *Computerised documentation system.* Paris, Unesco, 1978. 36p.

CHAPTER 17

Das Gupta, libraries and library system in India. *Link*: Jan.2, 1983 : p. 23-26.

Ijari, S.R., A development plan for public library system in the Karnataka State. 1983. 508p. (Thesis: Karnataka University).

Kaula, P.N. National library of India: Functions and activities, *Herald of library science* 20(3-4) : July-October 1981 : p. 190-200.

Khan, Noorul Hasan. National libraries : Definitions functions and types: *Herald of Library Science*, July-October 1981 : p. 183-190.

Mahajan, S.G., History of the public library movement in Western Maharashtra, 1805-1921. 1979, 503-51p. (Thesis: University of

Poona).

Mangla, P.B., Public library law in India. *Journal of Library and Information Science*, 8(1) : June 1983 : p. 1-24.

Mittal, R.L., Perspective development plan for public libraries in India during 7th Plan Period. *International Library Movement* 7(1) : 1985 : p. 46-60.

Neil, S.D., Books and reading and singleness of purpose. *Canadian Library Journal* 42 : April 1985 : p. 57-62.

Trehan, G.L., *Modern public library movement and services in India.* Chandigarh, Library Literature House, 1983. xvi.222p.

CHAPTER 18

Baykan, M. and Collins, S., Senior citizens : A bridge for community development. *School Library Journal* 31 : 1985 : p. 31-33.

Hannabus, Stuart, Source for information for children's book illustration. *Journal of Librarianship* 13(3) : July 1981 : p. 154-71.

Haycock, K.R., Teacher librarians - continuing to build. *Canadian Library Journal* 42 : 1985 p. 27-33.

Jackle, B.E., Books borrowing habits of urban and rural children : A survey. *Rural Libraries* 4(2): 1984 : p. 1-19.

Lindgren, Astrid, Pippi can lift a horse : The importance of children's books, *Quarterly Journal of the Library of Congress* 40(3) : Summer 1983 : p. 188-201.

Sever, Irene, A laboratory for children's librarianship : An anthropologist's view of children, books and libraries. *Libri* 36(1) : 1986: p74-83.

Das Gupta, Arjun, Role of children's libraries and librarians in India. *ILA Bulletin* 26(3-4) : July-Dec. 1980 : p. 154-61.

Fitzgibbons, Shirley, A., Reference and informations services for children and young adults : Definition, services, and issues. *Reference Librarian* No. 7-8 : Spring/Summer 1983 : p. 1-30.

CHAPTER 19

Indian Council of Social science Research. *Annual Report.* 1970.

Indian Council of Social Science Research. *ICSSR Research projects, 1969-1985.* New Delhi, ICSSR, 1986. 134p.